D0723377

FROM THE SERIES EDITOR

In the 1980s and 1990s we have witnessed a wide range of educational policy issues debated by both policy-makers and educators. The question of school choice has been among the most prominent of these issues. Moreover, it is arguably the issue for which the ratio of heat to light has been the highest; commentators from all sectors have sallied forth to tell more about choice and its impact than they could possibly know from the limited evidence that has been examined. Indeed, perhaps because so little systematic data were available, both proponents and opponents of school choice were unfettered in the construction of their claims by attention to evidence.

The present volume is a welcome corrective to the continuing debate about school choice because it presents a more complete framework for thinking about choice and a set of studies of choice practices and their effects on families, children, and school systems. By assembling a diverse set of studies that combine data from empirical investigations of choice programs and considering those studies side-by-side, the editors are able to develop a more complex and contingent perspective on the design and multiple impacts of school choice policies. Although the individual chapters sometimes assume a partisan stance, the overall effect of the volume is to construct a balanced and multiply hued portrait of the potential for school choice policies.

The volume is particularly appropriate as an addition to the *Sociology of Education Series* because it illustrates several of the strengths of the contemporary contribution of sociologists of education. It combines careful empirical analyses with a sociologically sensitive framework to develop a useful perspective on a salient issue of educational policy and practice. The chapters in this volume present studies of substantially different choice programs involving diverse populations, yet they all contribute to a more general understanding of choice phenomena. They employ different methods which together show the way for future studies of this issue.

Gary Natriello

WHO CHOOSES?
WHO LOSES?

CULTURE, INSTITUTIONS, AND THE UNEQUAL EFFECTS OF SCHOOL CHOICE

Edited by
Bruce Fuller *and* **Richard F. Elmore**
with **Gary Orfield**

Foreword by Carol H. Weiss

Teachers College, Columbia University
New York and London

Published by Teachers College Press, 1234 Amsterdam Avenue, New York, NY 10027

Library of Congress Cataloging-in-Publication Data

Who chooses? who loses? : culture, institutions, and the unequal
  effects of school choice / edited by Bruce Fuller and Richard F.
  Elmore with Gary Orfield.
      p.   cm. — (Sociology of education series)
    "This book stems from empirical papers presented at the Harvard
  School Choice and Family Seminar, which began at the School of
  Education in 1992"—P.
    Includes bibliographical references and index.
    ISBN 0-8077-3538-8 (cloth). — ISBN 0-8077-3537-X (pbk.)
    1. School choice—Social aspects—United States.   2. Educational
  equalization—United States.   3. Politics and education—United
  States.   I. Fuller, Bruce.   II. Elmore, Richard F.   III. Orfield,
  Gary.   IV. Series: Sociology of education series (New York, N.Y.)
  LB1027.9.W56   1996
  379.1'1—dc20   96-523

ISBN 0-8077-3537-X (paper)
ISBN 0-8077-3538-8 (cloth)

Printed on acid-free paper
Manufactured in the United States of America

03 02 01 00 99 98 97 96   8 7 6 5 4 3 2 1

Contents

Foreword

Carol H. Weiss

School choice is not one plan but many plans. Choice plans include magnet schools: public schools with special emphases and/or facilities that draw students from across a district, such as technology schools or music and art schools. Choice plans include charter schools, authorized by a number of state legislatures to be free of most local school district regulations; students apply for admission. There are also within-district public choice schemes that allow students to apply to any public school in the district. Some of these are "controlled" plans, in the sense that they seek to maintain racial diversity in each school within the rubric of choice. Other plans allow parents and students to choose public schools across district lines.

A further set of choice plans allows students to choose private schools as well as public schools; some of these plans limit the private schools to nonsectarian schools, but some include religious schools as well. In the most inclusive plans, "vouchers" are issued to parents to pay for the tuition at private schools (up to some dollar limit) and give them free rein on where and how they "spend" the vouchers.

School choice has been a subject of controversy since the 1950s, when the conservative economist Milton Friedman introduced the idea. But it has rarely been put into practice in any but the most restricted form, so little evidence has accrued about its consequences. The debate about school choice continues in the absence of much data on its effects on student achievement—or on anything else.

This volume assembles such data. The papers in this book present the most up-to-date empirical results yet collected. This is a real contribution to the debate. With evidence in hand, the editors take a more balanced approach to the subject than do many other authors (including some chapter authors in the book). Being able to see a range of pluses and minuses, under different conditions of operation, the editors show how evidence reduces the heat and increases the light on the discussion.

Nevertheless, as the authors note, the evidence is still slim. Only a few extensive choice programs have been adopted in this country, and only a limited number of families have taken advantage of the choice programs that exist. Results to date give clues to what happens when school choice is instituted, but perhaps the strongest finding is that the specific features of the program make a great deal of difference. The devil is in the details. It matters how the choice plan is designed. Different outcomes accompany different procedures.

In the absence of data, much of the debate on school choice has been based on rhetoric. Marvelously persuasive arguments have been made on both sides—in fact, on multiple sides. Until we gather more evidence of the type presented in this book, we are left to the vagaries of the rhetoric. Only with data on the consequences of different plans for school choice will we be able to reach sensible judgments rooted in experience.

More research is needed. That is the perpetual conclusion of researchers, and the only originality here is that it comes at the beginning of the book rather than at the end. But it is important to have the right kinds of research, to ask the right kinds of questions. One way to decide what to study is to bring to the surface the assumptions underlying school choice and to do research that tests the degree to which those assumptions are borne out in practice. This kind of research, based on a program's "theories of change," can clarify the validity of competing claims and counter-claims.

For example, pro-choice advocates argue that not only will students who choose their way out of existing schools benefit, but so will those who are left behind. One premise is that many teachers have gotten lazy in a monopolistic environment. Forced to confront competition or lose their jobs, they will buckle down and teach more effectively. Research can test the extent to which such changes in fact appear.

On the other side, critics of choice argue that voucher-supported schools would become little fiefdoms catering to the interests of their own social, ethnic, or cultural group, without concern for the larger social good. Again research could investigate whether this happens, whether such schools actually limit their enrollments to students with the same sets of beliefs or characteristics.

Research has a special place in educational debates. It provides empirical evidence about the expectations, operation, and results of educational policies, so as to inform the policy decisions that face states and localities. Research reduces uncertainty, punctures some myths, reinforces other expectations, and in so doing, it helps to make the nation's political decisions wiser.

That is important work, but research does more. Its findings trickle into the consciousness of many publics. Even school administrators or state legislators, who would not deign to pick up a research report, come to learn about the results. The findings circulate through newspaper accounts, conferences, training sessions, conversations in the elevator, allusions in magazine stories, hearings, television talk shows, lobbyists' appeals, and letters from constituents. Officials become informed and the public becomes informed. Some assumptions are strengthened, others are undermined. Research results percolate into ordinary knowledge and "common sense."

Ideas are powerful things. Research has the capacity to help weed out those that are poorly supported in the evidence and reinforce those that have an evidentiary basis. Therefore, it is important that research address itself to those ideas (and the systems based upon them) that will make a difference. That is the task that this book so nobly starts. It must be continued.

Acknowledgments

This book stems from empirical papers presented at the Harvard School Choice and Family Policy Seminar, which began at the School of Education in 1992. Without the constant support and commitment of ten individuals, neither the seminar nor this volume would ever have come to fruition. First and foremost, thanks are due to Kent McGuire and Roberta Tovey. Kent, then a program officer at the Lilly Endowment, immediately saw the utility of pulling together the most able empirical researchers working on questions related to school choice. Over a period of three years, the endowment provided two grants to finance first the seminar series, then the review and editing of the papers that appear in this volume. Roberta, over a long 18-month period, worked gently and relentlessly with authors, nudging them to refine their arguments and present their evidence more crisply. She well understood our aim of building a volume that recognized local variabilities while seeking to identify commonly observed effects of school choice programs.

Xiaoyan Liang and Helen Rodriguez worked behind the scenes to organize the seminar meetings, review earlier research, and prepare the manuscripts. Xiaoyan helped to build an annotated bibliography that enriched our Chapters 1 and 10. Her own original research extended understanding of family choice in the preschool sector. Helen worked tirelessly to refine the chapter drafts, track down authors, and keep us on schedule.

Gary Natriello, the series editor at Teachers College Press, has provided unwavering encouragement and constructive criticism from the project's inception. He saw the practical importance of this effort, particularly for policy-makers and local education leaders. Equally important, Gary nudged us to become clearer on the collective intellectual contributions of these papers, especially in how we think about cultural cohesion in local communities and its dynamic interaction with the institutional actions of politically charged school authorities. Susan Liddicoat, our editor at Teachers College Press, possesses a seemingly inexhaustible capacity to find unsubstantiated arguments, vaguely worded passages, and loose ends in logic. She and Gary took what we thought was a flawless manuscript and convinced us that it needed much more work.

Hal Rosenthal and Helen Snively joined our team during the project's final year, offering specific skills that greatly improved the book. Hal showed us how to present the numbers and the conceptual models in more engaging ways. He built all the graphics appearing in these pages. Helen assisted enormously in the final round of editing, providing fresh energy to help make the manuscript cohesive and clear.

Connie Koprowicz and Ariadne Valsamis are owed a debt of appreciation for their efforts in disseminating the principal findings resulting from the Harvard seminar. Connie, a policy analyst at the National Conference of State Legislatures, urged us to prepare a concise overview of the most policy-relevant empirical findings. This summary quickly became a best-seller. Ariadne, who works in Harvard's external relations office, has pushed us to clarify and illustrate major findings—a task that academic writers often fail to pull off effectively. Connie and Ariadne have had faith in the importance of this work. With grace (and rewording!), they have injected our key statistics and technical jargon into the public discourse, enriching the otherwise polemical debate over school choice.

Finally, our heartfelt thanks goes to the 15 scholars whose work appears in this volume. All of them have dedicated significant portions of their professional lives to better understanding how the provision of wider educational choices—for parents and children—may, or may not, improve the quality of schooling received by different kinds of youngsters. Our contributors have faced several iterations of review, criticism, and editing. We have attempted to build a volume that captures the details of local choice programs *and* that pinpoints shared effects of these initiatives on parents, children, and local schools. From their opening appearance at the Harvard seminar, through several redrafts, each author has worked very hard in the spirit of building a more coherent story from these eight evaluation studies.

Much research remains to be done. We are just beginning to understand which parents eagerly engage choice programs, how inventive schools blossom or wither, and whether (and why) student achievement rises or remains flat. This volume takes us several steps forward in placing hard evidence on the table. This serves to push off the table the proliferating piles of polemics that still dominate the school choice controversy.

Thank you all.

> Bruce Fuller
> Richard F. Elmore
> Gary Orfield
> Cambridge, Massachusetts

CHAPTER 1

Policy-Making in the Dark
Illuminating the School Choice Debate

BRUCE FULLER
RICHARD F. ELMORE
GARY ORFIELD

Many members of democratic societies, over the past two centuries, have evolved a contentious love–hate relationship with central government and the concentration of political power. Yearning for a more just society, worried about the widening effects of poverty, or searching for a more cohesive culture, Americans often ask political leaders to steer institutions with a stronger hand, to regulate citizens' behavior more forcefully, even to redistribute income and jobs to less advantaged families.

But this affection for decisive central action can be short-lived, especially when classic individualistic instincts resurface in the American psyche. On the political Right, affluent or aspiring social classes come to believe that the government is intruding too deeply into economic matters or eroding old local values and familiar ways of life. The political Left may claim that centralization undercuts local empowerment or leads to homogeneity in local institutions, such as schools, just as society is becoming culturally more pluralistic. And civic distaste may recur for the expansive bureaucracy required to carry out centralized mandates.

Inventive policy-makers, rising above this cycle of affection or disdain for strong government, eagerly search for new remedies to stubborn problems facing many local communities. Shaking off the shackles of bureaucratic assumptions, these earnest policy-crafters dash outdoors into the sunshine, joyfully announcing bold new reforms aimed at improving local schools or strengthening the family. A sprinkling of social or economic crises also helps to brew novel programmatic remedies. Indeed, a portion of these innovations have proven to be effective, altering the government's role and the character of public institutions: the New Deal's enactment of cash entitlements, notably Social Security, or the cyclical decentralizing of social services to the states or to nonprofit community agencies.

In education and family-policy circles, *family choice* is the newfound remedy, prescribed for a variety of ills, from raising the quality of local schools and boosting religious freedom to empowering inner-city parents. Contributors to this book focus on one particular variant: *school choice*. Choice experiments, spreading rapidly across the land, restrict government's traditional ability to assign children to a particular school, shifting this authority to parents. This transfer of power often is accompanied by efforts to diversify the types of schools made available to children. Versatile forms of school finance advance this power shift, such as vouchers or portable grants to schools enrolling students who opt to participate in choice schemes.

THE BROAD APPEAL OF SCHOOL CHOICE

We may think that school choice is a new idea. But inventive policymakers first discovered this broader family-choice strategy more than three decades ago. In the Kennedy and Johnson administrations, the War on Poverty aimed to outwit arcane local politicians and the welfare bureaucracy, channeling federal aid directly to ethnic-based community action agencies and to families in the form of vouchers. Limited experiments centering around the novel remedy of vouchers and tax credits quickly sprouted in education, child-care, housing, and youth employment programs.

Few policy models in the postwar era have forced as much rethinking and soul searching over the government's basic role in society, and the decision-making power granted to parents, as has family choice. The core tenets of this model challenge both the welfare state's habitual way of organizing schools and its traditional reliance on bureaucratic management. Under family-choice arrangements, the government's role is to intensify local accountability, not by building bigger administrative structures but by encouraging families to make their own decisions and to press for quality improvements. Rather than funding the organizations and professionals who offer schooling or social services, public monies flow directly to the consumer. Rather than assuming that state-chartered organizations and licensed professionals are best qualified to shape school curricula or social services, choice schemes assume that the family is highly rational, acts from clear preferences, and is able to effectively demand action from local schools and teachers.

Originally advocated in the South as a way to avoid the desegregation of public schools, school choice came to be seen by the Left as a way to empower poor and working-class families to challenge paternalistic bureaucracies. Then, in the early 1980s, the choice remedy was embraced by political conservatives who sought to improve the quality of local schools and advance the cultural and political homogeneity of particular communities (Levin, 1991). Many centrists also have come to support parental choice within the public school system, allowing parents to exit their neighborhood school in order to choose another *public* school.

An overwhelming majority of Americans support the idea of school choice, according to various polls conducted over the past decade. One recent survey found that almost one-fourth (23%) of all parents would leave their child's neighborhood school if granted the freedom to do so; much larger percentages typically favor the political right to switch schools within the public sector (Elam, Rose, & Gallup, 1991). Many Americans, too, favor public–private vouchers. By 1993 almost 6 million families were choosing to send their children to schools outside their neighborhoods. Fifteen percent of parents earning under $15,000 a year opted for a "choice school" in the public sector; the same share of families making more than $50,000 annually chose a private school (McArthur, Colopy, & Schlaline, 1995).

But many political leaders—retaining faith in public education, worried about inequitable effects, or simply fearing the wrath of teacher unions—continue to oppose giving parents the freedom to choose between public and private schools. Traditional public school interest groups oppose even public–private choice experiments aimed exclusively at low-income families, such as those operating with considerable support in poor areas of Milwaukee and San Antonio.

Ironically, the family-choice model has slowly and quietly become a sacred pillar of federal antipoverty programs. Several experiments backed by the political Left that emerged from the 1960s have matured into mainstream programs, often applauded by the Right for relying so little on bureaucracy and so much on individual-level choice. At both edges of the K–12 education sector, pro–school-choice financing schemes encourage students and parents to actively think through school options. The $6.5 billion mixed market of preschool organizations, for instance, is now supported largely by the $3 billion federal child-care tax credit program and almost $2 billion per year in parental vouchers and fees. At the higher education level, portable Pell Grants (dare we call them vouchers?) are the biggest single source of federal aid (see Chapter 9 for whether student choices have actually changed over the years). The largest antipoverty initiative in the nation is now the earned income tax credit program, providing over $18 billion annually in refundable credits to working-poor families. Poverty programs— with support that transcends the Nixon White House and the Clinton administration—commonly allocate benefits in ways that offer classically liberal authority to poor families to make their own choices among a variety of service providers. And proposals for middle-class tax credits to families with preschool-age youngsters, or those with children attending college, have returned to the policy agenda.

Yet public educators have been slow to realize the implications for this pro-choice shift in how government constructs its role and crafts its remedies. School choice acts as a lightning rod for this debate over government's optimal role. Should the State strongly shape local institutions and help make society more fair and equitable? Or should the State loosen organizational constraints on parents' choices, and tighten up on authority and resources granted to local school bureaucrats and professionals?

To set the context for this book, we ask: Why are school choice and the role of the government in education so hotly debated at this particular point in history? What are the underlying social and economic forces driving this controversy? We then describe how this book addresses the pragmatic question: What are the demonstrable effects of school choice programs?

WHY HAS SCHOOL CHOICE MOVED
TO THE CENTER OF POLICY DEBATES?

Who should choose where one's child attends school? Who should choose the forms of schooling made available to families? These questions are not new to American education. Catholic parents have long sought alternatives to secular schooling; immigrant parents and working-class progressives, since the early nineteenth century, have resisted upper-middle-class domination of school politics; wealthy parents have long shopped around for the most prestigious, effective prep schools for their children. But since the 1960s, the tandem questions of the government's proper role in shaping available forms of schooling and controlling where one's child attends school have come to be more loudly asked. Why are these issues of choice now being put forward so forcefully by parents, civic activists, local educators, and central policy-makers?

Three telling conditions have arisen or intensified since the 1960s; together, they fuel the contemporary school choice controversy.

The Civil Rights Movement

Choice first arose as a major strategy in the effort by conservatives to limit the racial desegregation of public schools. The Supreme Court's 1954 decision, *Brown* v. *Board of Education*, declared unconstitutional the school systems of 17 states and the District of Columbia, which had mandated separate schools for blacks and whites. In response, southern segregationists interpreted the Supreme Court decision as requiring nothing more than a choice for black students to transfer between two racially separate systems of schooling. This policy, euphemistically known as "freedom of choice," was the dominant southern position. A number of northern cities instituted "open enrollment," a form of choice permitting transfers to schools that had space but in many cases did not provide transportation. Typically a very small proportion of students made such transfers.

By 1966 massive tests of choice were begun under court-ordered desegregation plans in the South. In Atlanta, for example, every student was given a form on which to express school preferences. Schools were required to accept transfer requests and to provide transportation for transfer students. But even under these favorable policies, backed by strong sanctions and a committed national administration, the choice system left schools in the South overwhelmingly segregated, with no whites choosing black schools and many black families afraid to choose white schools. The U.S. Civil Rights Commission reported that freedom of choice was preserving segregation and placing the entire burden for small-scale change on black students and their families (Orfield & Ashkinaze, 1991).

Only in 1973, after the Supreme Court ruled that northern cities must also desegregate, did a new form of choice—*magnet schools*—come into the picture. Magnet schools emerged first in Cincinnati and Milwaukee, then spread to many cities in both the North and South. By minimizing mandatory requirements and creating educational incentives, these cities hoped to achieve desegregation and hold onto their rapidly fleeing middle-class white populations (Wells, 1993). Under the prompting of Senator John Glenn (D-Ohio), whose state was faced with desegregation litigation in the 1970s, federal support for magnet schools was added to Congress's desegregation assistance program. Ironically, white parents have proven to be more likely than ethnic-minority parents to choose magnets within the framework of a mandatory desegregation plan. (Chapter 8 details the current extent and known effects of magnet schools nationwide.)

By the late 1980s, political conservatives had successfully detached the broadening debate over choice from the more painful desegregation issue. Yet at the local level choice was still deeply intertwined with the persisting question of how to reduce race-based inequity. Hundreds of communities were still under desegregation orders or maintained plans, and many were shifting to choice-driven models. Cambridge, Massachusetts, for instance, pioneered *controlled choice*, requiring all parents to rank their school preferences; school authorities honored these preferences to the greatest extent possible within desegregation guidelines. Parent information centers were created. All schools in the city developed clearer identities and curricular strengths. Local school authorities exercised leadership in pursuing the public interest in desegregation while maximizing responsiveness to parents' own preferences.

The Fading American Dream

Profound change in a quite different arena is further spurring support for radical school reform: the reduced upward mobility felt by millions of Americans since the mid-1970s. For two centuries political leaders and educators have promised that more spending for public schools and higher school achievement would boost upward mobility and spark economic growth. Indeed, during much of the past century, the American middle class grew steadily as school achievement rose. But since the 1973 oil crisis, real income for many families has leveled off. Between 1979 and 1987, for example, the median real earnings of young, male high-school graduates fell by 12%. The share of young high school graduates who earned over $20,000 annually was almost 60% in the late 1970s but fell to 46% by 1987. As Levy and Murnane (1992) have shown, the American job structure is becoming "hollowed-out" in the middle: Minimum-wage jobs are growing rapidly in the service sector, as are highly paid technical occupations in the professions and in high-technology manufacturing. But semiskilled manufacturing and service sector jobs are drying up, many of them moving overseas, where labor costs are lower.

With upward mobility becoming more elusive, many parents are redoubling their pressure on the public schools. Close behind are employers, especially in fast-growing service industries, who are having difficulty finding young workers with basic literacy and communication skills. Ironically, the wage returns for basic cognitive skills are rising, while the capacity of public schools and families to impart these proficiencies remains static at best (Murnane, Willett, & Levy, 1995). As political pressure on schools builds and prior reform strategies fail to yield observable gains in achievement, the appeal of more radical remedies, such as school choice, continues to grow.

The Impact of Cultural Pluralism

The growing ethnic diversity of American society drives attempts to offer variable forms of schooling to differing communities and parents. Contentious debates over education, of course, involve not only who gains access to material benefits but also deeply held values about how one's children should be raised and socialized, through what language, and according to which cultural rules and norms. This source of contention is not new to urban schools. But since the 1960s, urban and suburban communities have become vastly more diverse ethnically. For example, by 1994 Latinos comprised 15% of all public school students; in 1960, they made up just 3% of national enrollments. Urban school districts are often dominated by "minority" families. The Los Angeles school district is now two-thirds Latino and 18% African-American. In California, soon after the year 2000, children of white origin will comprise the *minority* of all students. No ethnic group is made up of homogeneous families that hold identical expectations for child socialization or uniform commitments to schooling. But growing numbers of Latino, black, and Asian families are, without doubt, pressing a more diverse set of expectations and goals on public schools, compared to the narrower white middle-class agenda that held widespread credibility just a generation ago. In turn, "white ethnics" and religious communities are seeking alternatives to schools they see as dominated by secular-humanist values.

Demands placed on the public schools are even more intense when ethnic diversity coincides with pluralistic forms of family structure. Just 51% of all children (33 million) live in conventional families with two natural parents. Another 15 million children live in single-parent households. Among black children, 49% live with just one parent; among Latino youths, 31%. Single-parent households, in general, have much lower incomes. These parents (mainly mothers) have less time to read to their children, supervise homework, or interact with school staff (Astone & McLanahan, 1991; Fuller, Eggers-Piérola, Holloway, Rambaud, & Liang, in press; Schneider & Coleman, 1993).

These demographic patterns are intensifying in ways that are exogenous to the public school institution. In-migration of families from Latin America, the Caribbean, and southeast Asia has risen since the early 1970s. The erosion of conventional black family structures and the implosion of inner-city labor markets are beyond the control of public educators. Yet the implications of these demographic and economic shifts are enormous for public schools. The family structure, when brittle and breaking, is often less supportive of children's learning, yet lower levels of achievement are attributed to alleged weaknesses of the local school. An eroding tax base, felt in many urban areas, makes it more difficult to respond to new and diverse demands. Families and employers grow more frustrated over graduates' low levels of literacy and basic skills. Civic and ethnic groups predictably begin to mobilize around more radical school reform strategies—such as school choice.

Mobilizing Political Will

The three social and economic conditions discussed above have thoroughly shaken how we think about society, mobility, and the motivations of culturally diverse communities—sustaining the nation's resilient interest in educational change. But what structure should educational reform take? The political process by which varied interest groups come to craft credible reform strategies also fuels the school choice debate. Central controls, of course, are rarely popular in the decentralized political structure of the United States. Until the 1960s, however, big and uniform social institutions—schools, universities, health care and welfare systems—were viewed as the best way to organize democratic and equitable forms of social support. The common school was to educate all children toward universal cognitive and moral goals. Welfare systems would efficiently distribute cash benefits and humanely aid impoverished mothers and their young children.

But the heyday of grand institutions came to a crashing end in the 1960s, primarily attacked by social critics and the political Left. The civil rights movement, the rise of black pride, and similar rediscovery of ethnic commitments (and their now-confident political expression in civil society) challenged the largely white, upper-middle-class bases of many social institutions, including public schools and universities. Other large institutions—from hospitals to basic government services—came to be seen as out of touch with local people, as alienating and impersonal. In the early 1980s, and again in the mid-1990s, the political Right surged back, struggling to uphold the cultural agenda and fading universals that once characterized Anglo-American society. At the same time, the Right argued that the social welfare bureaucracy, which had grown rapidly since the 1960s, had become bloated, costly, and, most damning, *ineffective*. Billions of taxpayer dollars were being spent on compensatory education, opportunity programs within universities, and welfare benefits to families. But was poverty going down? Were the test scores of poor children going up?

The new policy medicine of family choice thus emerges with great force. If antipoverty remedies lodged in sluggish institutions are not working, why not simply allocate cash benefits to *the family*—allowing parents to choose their school, child-care provider, or form of subsidized housing? And even if this policy strategy is not more effective, it certainly is more popular, more "democratic." Family-choice remedies shed two crucial political liabilities: They do not require hiring more government workers, and they set aside the assumption that universal remedies fit diverse ethnic neighborhoods and families. The first helps diffuse opposition to the expansion of antipoverty initiatives. The second appeals to social democrats on the Left who believe that central government should forcefully redistribute income but allow pluralistic communities and families to pursue their own preferences. This latter force will only increase in urban and suburban areas of the United States, as they become more diverse culturally and more strongly organized along ethnic lines.

Family-choice remedies are sold, in part, as being rooted in the decentralized magic of markets. For example, if families are empowered (with vouchers or tax credits) to act from their particular preferences and definitions of high quality, the array of schools and service providers will diversify and become more accountable. What is fascinating—surfacing in several chapters of this book—is that the local political economy of ethnic neighborhoods at times complements neoclassical economic thinking. When benefits (redistributed by central political agencies) are targeted to low-income families, many parents *do* actively choose a school that they believe better fits their educational agenda than does the neighborhood school.

Community action strategies—building public remedies from the ethnic neighborhood's distinct leadership structure and culture—came to be strongly endorsed by architects of the War on Poverty. Domestic advisors to presidents Kennedy and Johnson argued that antipoverty programs would only work if local school and social welfare bureaucracies could be bypassed, lessening their authority relative to the new power being awarded to poor and working-class families (Katz, 1989). This strategy was brought to life by school voucher experiments, such as the now-infamous Alum Rock program serving working-class communities on the edge of San Jose, California. Advocated by the first federal Office of Economic Opportunity (OEO), the project held only modest effects on parents' rate of exit from their neighborhood school and on real organizational reform of alternative schools (Jencks, 1970). But Alum Rock represented the first volley from contemporary progressives, who argued that direct empowerment of communities via liberalized (yet guided) market conditions would spark school improvements and broader gains for poor families.

These origins of school choice were distinguished by two important elements, which were largely shed as conservative political leaders took up the charge. First, the OEO experiments with vouchers were embedded within a larger community-organizing strategy. Vouchers were not the only tool made available to families that lacked political voice and solidarity. The intent of the Kennedy White House was to move resources into agencies crafted by local activists. These fledgling organizations would create alternative social services, including new schools, to serve local families. Vouchers would help finance innovative education and social services. (This is largely what is happening with the contemporary voucher experiments in Milwaukee and San Antonio.) Second, under the initial OEO experiments with choice, vouchers and cash transfers were targeted for low-income and working-class families. The aim was not to privatize the entire school system, which would surely exacerbate inequities in school quality and per-pupil spending, but to help equalize the purchasing power and involvement of poor families.

The tandem goals of community-level organizing and targeted vouchers remain very much alive in the current financing of preschools and child-care centers. Original community action agencies still run many Head Start centers. And while state and federal preschool funding now flows both to service providers and directly to parents via vouchers, both funding streams are targeted on impoverished and working-poor families (Fuller & Holloway, in press).

Sustaining a political focus on these two key elements within the public school arena, however, has proven difficult, in part due to democratic government's preoccupation with balancing civil authority between institutions (acting on behalf of the defined public interest) versus awarding power to the individual family. The welfare state's concern with assimilating individuals into the secular nation-state increasingly conflicts with the pluralistic agendas of many local communities and families, be they middle-class white ethnics, Latinos, African-Americans, or immigrant Koreans.

Contemporary family-choice remedies have undoubtedly succeeded in mobilizing wider political support for antipoverty programs.

While support for institutional or bureaucratic remedies has collapsed in many policy circles, political will behind tax programs and vouchers for educational and social services has climbed dramatically over the past decade, even when targeted on the working poor or families living below the poverty line. But political mobilization is only the first step. The next is to determine whether family-choice and school choice remedies are *more effective* in bringing about their promised benefits, from lessening poverty to boosting children's school achievement. This is the question that motivates this book.

WHAT ARE THE EFFECTS OF SCHOOL CHOICE PROGRAMS? GRAND CLAIMS, MODEST EVIDENCE

The debate over school choice is rich in rhetoric but dismally poor when it comes to hard evidence. Activists of all shapes and sizes, arriving at the doorsteps of legislatures or school boards with the choice remedy firmly in hand, advance strong claims about the magical benefits that allegedly will flow to children, parents, and schools. Opponents parry with equally impassioned claims about the damage that choice schemes will do to public schools. Yet despite the breathtaking emotion and steady rise of choice programs across the country, little is known about the actual effects of these experiments. And scholars have been slow to study the dynamics of mixed educational markets and choice remedies.

The simple aim of this book is to close the gap between grand rhetorical claims and scarce empirical findings. The new evidence reported in this volume simply begins to test the claims made by choice advocates and opponents. As these research studies are completed, we begin to see patterns in how school choice programs operate and the effects these programs have on families and school organizations. For example, better-educated parents who already attend most closely to their children's schooling and performance are significantly more likely to participate in choice programs, whether we look at inner-city Milwaukee or suburban Minnesota. Delineating these kinds of patterns is the first step toward providing empirically grounded advice to policy-makers, local educators, and parents.

Claims of School Choice Proponents

Proponents of choice argue that eliminating the school bureaucracy's power to assign children to particular schools will make parents effective market actors who actively compare the qualities of alternative schools and push for greater accountability at the neighborhood level. This claim raises two important empirical questions: Are certain types of parents more likely to exercise choice and exit their neighborhood school (Issue 1)? If so, and if parents' tendency to exercise choice varies according to their affluence or ethnicity, will school choice reinforce social-class inequality (Issue 2)?

Choice proponents also argue that, by unleashing market dynamics and incentives, schools will be held more accountable than at present, and school principals, presently entangled in bureaucratic rules and hog-tied by teacher unions, will be able to reward strong teachers and prune their schools of weak teachers. To determine whether this claim is true, we need to focus empirical research on a third question: Do choice programs and liberalized market conditions spark the creation of more effective forms of schooling (Issue 3)?

Finally, choice advocates claim that parental satisfaction and involvement with their child's schooling will rise. They assume that if parents are more satisfied, they will more eagerly attend to their children's schooling and socialization. This brings us down to the bottom-line question: Will student achievement rise as a result of stronger accountability, more discriminating and involved parents, and the rise of novel forms of schooling (Issue 4)?

Recognizing the evidential poverty surrounding the school choice debate, we began in 1992 to invite empirical papers from research teams around the country that spoke to these four empirical issues. The Harvard Seminar on School Choice and Family Policy, with generous support from the Lilly Endowment, hosted presentations by most of this book's contributors. We commissioned additional papers to include findings from other research groups. Together, the chapters selected represent the most recent empirical findings on school choice programs—speaking to which parents actually exercise choice and whether inequities emerge, innovative schools sprout, and children learn more.

Emerging Evidence: A Story of Cultural and Political Logics

Readers of this book may search for patterns among the many empirical findings reported. Crisp and clean answers are difficult to pinpoint. Our final chapter delineates a few patterns observed thus far, and we link evidence presented in the chapters to earlier research on school choice. One fundamental conclusion from this emerging research is that the effects of choice programs are highly dependent on local conditions: the organizational structure of the particular choice initiative, the community situation facing parents, and parents' range of resources and educational commitments. Keeping this crucial proviso in mind, certain patterns are discernible across different communities and choice programs; two basic conceptual frameworks have emerged over the course of this project that help to explain these patterns.

The Cultural Logic of Families. Activists and academics, of course, are engulfed in their own ideas about how society and government *should* operate. Some implicitly link social progress to breaking down the ethnic, sectarian, and social-class boundaries that divide local communities. These schisms also may undermine the government's own legitimacy and effectiveness. Indeed, defining a clear role for central and local policy-makers becomes more slippery as the American polity becomes more pluralistic culturally and politically. Other activists and analysts—including proponents of school choice—assume that the post-Depression age of great public ideas that once unified civil society is over. The government has simply gone too far in pushing equity and the redistribution of income and jobs, in homogenizing the basic structure and content of public schooling, and in creating school institutions that protect the interests of teachers and managers but seem unresponsive to children's needs and parents' particular ways of raising their children.

This polarization around the choice issue is unfolding largely within empirical darkness. Many policy wonks and commentators know very little about the *cultural logics* employed by different types of families as parents attempt to make sense of, and benefit from, public schools. Gross generalizations, for instance, are made about parents in low-income communities: Either they are incapable of making wise choices for their children and need a lot of guidance from professional educators, or choice programs will instantly "empower" them, resulting in positive pressure on the local schools. But as several chapters in this book illustrate, low-income families are quite diverse in their commitment to their children's schooling, in the time they can afford to aid their child at home, and in their market behavior—that is, how they search out school alternatives and participate in choice programs.

It may be surprising to read that when choice schemes are established, many inner-city parents choose *not* to participate, continuing to send their daughter or son to the neighborhood school even when they suspect it is of lower quality than alternative schools newly made available. Why? Parents report, both in surveys and during in-depth interviews, that they are attracted to the familiarity and proximity of the local school and that they want their children to feel comfortable. These are the same things that white middle-class parents seek in a "nice neighborhood": cultural familiarity, a sense that fellow parents share their values, beliefs, and customs. This is the first cultural logic that appears to drive the impassive reaction of some parents to school choice experiments.

But few local cultures simply reproduce themselves over time without some penetration by outside social forces. Indeed, many parents jump at the chance to exit their neighborhood school and enter an alternative school that appears to be of higher quality. When St. Louis schools, for instance, began to allow inner-city children to attend predominantly white suburban schools, over 13,000, mostly black, families chose to participate, despite the anxiety and costs they incurred (see Chapter 2, this volume). The phenomenal growth of magnet school enrollments provides further evidence of many parents' willingness to exercise choice to find a higher-quality school (see Chapter 8, this volume).

Thus we cannot see inner-city or middle-class family cultures as uniform or unchanging. Parents formulate their educational agendas in diverse ways; they are shaped not only by indigenous norms and values but also by outside incentives and influences. In Milwaukee, the vibrant inner-city voucher program was begun by ethnic activists on the Left who sought higher-quality schools (implicitly linked to the goal of assimilation) *and* schools that would focus directly on African-American or Latino topics within the curriculum (a particularistic, community-centered goal). Historically, the modern state has seen ethnic localisms as provincial or backward, threatening to nation-building. But many parents in pluralistic America seem to want both assimilation and particularistic forms of socialization. The complexity of local cultures and the multiple ideals that shape different parents' educational preferences comprise the second facet of cultural logic explored in this book. (For empirical work on how educational preferences may vary among groups between and within social classes, see Fuller et al., in press; Matute-Bianchi, 1986; Ogbu, 1978; Wells, Chapter 2, this volume.)

The cultural logics employed by low-income families are becoming more differentiated, due largely to the distinct successes of the civil rights movement and Great Society reforms. For example, Elijah Anderson's (1990) long-term study of poor Philadelphia families details how many blacks, aided by affirmative action programs, have joined the middle class and fled the ghetto. These parents move into neighboring communities that have safer streets and higher-quality schools. Left behind are families that typically have less education and fewer job options. *Nouveau* middle-class black parents essentially vote with their feet; parents remaining within impoverished city blocks more frequently invoke the conventional script of sending their child to the local school, no questions asked. The cultural logics of low-income parents related to school choice are somewhat pliable, but only when the broader opportunity structure opens in recognizable ways. In the absence of real improvement in job opportunities or educational openings, the scripted behavior of many low-income and even middle-class parents will be more difficult to alter.

The Political Rationality of School Institutions. The original political logic of schooling in North America was quite simple: Local communities built a one-room schoolhouse, hired a teacher, and used available readers. Within this standard pedagogical technology, variable community norms about religion, virtue, and literacy did at times penetrate into the classroom. Central government was nowhere to be found in the administration of local schools until the Progressive era, beginning in the late nineteenth century. As late as 1890, the average state department of education had just two employees (Meyer, Tyack, Nagel, & Gordon, 1979). But as American society became more urban and culturally pluralistic (through recurring waves of European immigration and northward migration of blacks from the South), the school's political rationality became more complex, depending on local priorities.

First, urban school districts sprouted, growing into classic bureaucracies, often explicitly following the tenets of factory-like and allegedly more efficient firms (Tyack, 1974). This allowed urban authorities to expand the number of schools and the scale of public schooling. Administrative progressives at the turn of the twentieth century argued that bureaucracy would offer more uniform types of school organization and pedagogy, expressing faith that standardization would ensure orderly expansion of schooling and buffer the diversity of demands being placed on urban schools. Even in the absence of strong government involvement, at either the state or federal level, the organizational form and content of public schooling became remarkably similar as professional organizations formed and the legitimacy of bureaucratic administration rose (Meyer, Scott, Strang, & Creighton, 1988).

Second, moving the clock forward to the 1960s, bureaucratic school administration proved quite successful in responding to democratic pressures to serve nonmainstream students in novel, rather than uniform, ways. Programs were begun to aid desegregation in the South, to boost achievement of low-income children, to help Spanish-speaking children assimilate more rapidly, and to address the complex needs of disabled children. In each case, school districts—still largely under local political control yet often responding in standardized ways to specific mandates—added staff to implement these categorical programs emanating from Washington and state capitals. Thus local school bureaucracies became larger and more complex, responding to democratic pressures from various interest groups. These more differentiated urban interests began to argue that their children were diverse and different, requiring the panoply of programs that have been enacted since the Great Society, from bilingual to vocational to special education programs (Cohen & Spillane, 1992; Fuller & Izu, 1986; Rowan, 1990). Yet the classroom institution remained largely unchanged and remarkably similar across diverse communities (Goodlad, 1984).

This contradiction entraps many school districts and drives their cautious political logic. On the one hand, school leaders and their bureaucratic forms of management earnestly try to respond to a variety of democratic pressures and vocal interests, advanced by parents, civic and ethnic activists, teacher unions, and employers critical of the public schools. Pivotal to the argument put forward by school choice advocates is that over time the locus of educational decision-making has become the faceless, unapproachable district office downtown. This is where school authorities are centrally trying to mediate contradictory pressures. No longer can the local school principal or head teacher sit with parents and town leaders, talk through concerns held by the local community, and act on these problems (Chubb & Moe, 1990). This is undoubtedly true in a good number of local areas.

At the same time, deep-seated organizational scripts, not only surface-level administrative practices, reinforce the status quo and the infamous uniformity found in American schools and classrooms. Indeed, schools are resilient, often impenetrable *institutions*: Actors behave within age-old social roles, and basic structural elements persist (during 50-minute periods kids are expected to sit and absorb knowledge solely within the walls of classrooms, reading textbooks that must have universal acceptability, since they are designed by national publishers). The classroom's technology remains simple and highly routine. Advocates of choice programs threaten to shake up these institutional routines and rituals.

Choice programs also rattle the established micropolitics surrounding school districts, comprised of interdependent administrators, teacher unions, and civic activists. To begin with, choice schemes threaten to alter budget allocations between traditional neighborhood schools and alternative schools. As Jeffrey Henig shows in his study of Montgomery County's magnet school program (Chapter 5, this volume), these resource shifts may be limited and kept very quiet so as not to rile parents and interest groups that remain tied to neighborhood schools. The starting point for charter schools is simply to discard education laws and regulations that teacher unions have spent generations setting in place to enhance their members' interests. And powerful progressive interests—watching over bilingual and special education programs—are nervous about uncontrolled choice programs that render the implementation of categorical programs more difficult. In sum, a large part of school administrators' political logic is to move reform ever so slowly, so as not to threaten the institution's legitimacy or to risk opposition from vocal interest groups.

The political logic around choice also involves a broader debate over the importance of public ideas and the desirability of a national culture. Government's fundamental legitimacy and the credibility of policymakers rest on popular faith in political goals that are national or regional in scope. These involve unifying ideals, such as making society more fair and equitable, advancing traditional "family values," or assuring economic growth and upward mobility. What is most threatening to the central government about choice remedies is that they place *local* social-class and ethnic commitments on an equal par with national civic ideals. School choice implies, for instance, that if young white professionals want to have schools serving their particular educational interests, they should have a right to a share of public resources to pursue their private interests. Of course, the liberal democratic state has long struggled with this contradiction between government for the common good and government for the pursuit of individual interests. Which way should the government move? Which interests of what particular social groups should receive priority? And how is the government's own legitimacy (including the credibility of school authorities) best advanced in the long run?

ORGANIZATION OF THE BOOK

Contributors to this book provide detailed portraits of how, when a new choice scheme is put in place, both the cultural logic of families and the political calculus of school authorities act to enhance or constrain the actual range of school options created. The chapters in Part I focus on the cultural bounds within which parents and children operate. How do parents perceive the quality of their neighborhood schools? Which parents choose to participate in choice schemes? How do these families differ in social class and ethnicity from those who do not actively choose? How do parents *and* children experience their move to an alternative school?

In Part II, contributors address how school organizations have responded to more liberal market conditions. Do innovative forms of schooling arise? How do school authorities encourage low-income and working-class families to participate? What effects result from different school choice programs, especially in terms of parental satisfaction and—the bottom line— children's achievement?

In the conclusion, we distill the major lessons that emerge from this new body of evidence. Principally authored by Richard Elmore, this chapter also discusses additional empirical research being conducted on the effects of school choice. Two earlier projects have synthesized early empirical work: the Carnegie Foundation's 1992 study of school choice (*School Choice: A Special Report*), and papers debated at a conference hosted by the Economic Policy Institute and resulting in an edited book, *School Choice: Examining the Evidence* (Rasell & Rothstein, 1993; see also an initial review, Raywid, 1985). Our conclusion incorporates several empirical studies that have come out since these reviews (for a complete literature review, see Liang & Fuller, 1994). We attempt to delineate major patterns that are observed across this growing body of evidence and put forward tentative policy advice.

THE LIMITS OF EMPIRICAL EVIDENCE

Many political leaders and local activists are anxious to know more about the local effects of school choice programs. Proponents hope to observe novel, robust schools rising within newly liberalized market conditions. Opponents eagerly hope to read of no or slight effects on parental satisfaction and student achievement. But until recently choice programs have been small in number and modest in size. Larger programs and richer empirical evidence are coming from overseas, most notably from England and Scotland (Willms & Echols, 1993). We can learn one major lesson from the chapters in this book: Local economic and cultural conditions, as well as the structure of a particular choice scheme, make an enormous difference in its effects. We should be extremely careful not to generalize findings from one setting to another. Within the United States, it will take time before we have sufficient evidence to judge the efficacy of the national school choice experiment.

Readers also must be aware of the technical limits of the extant empirical work. First, almost no longitudinal data exist on how student learning changes over time and as a result of participating in a neighborhood versus a choice school. This volume includes the most soundly constructed longitudinal evaluation in the United States: John Witte's work in Milwaukee (Chapter 6). Sophisticated quantitative analysis can do a lot of things. But without longitudinal data, it is impossible to unambiguously attribute learning gains to program participation. Second, most studies to date assess family background and educational parental practices only in a limited way. Parents of differing social classes and ethnic groups vary enormously in how they encourage their children to do well in school. Patterns of school choice certainly vary with these parenting practices. If we fail to remove the effects of these parenting practices, we can incorrectly attribute gains in achievement only to schools. This has occurred in the school-effects literature in general and is already spilling over into school choice research (Fuller & Clarke, 1994; Lockheed & Jimenez, Chapter 7, this volume). Third, researchers are still not digging into the crucial issue of *why* private or non-neighborhood schools at times boost parental satisfaction and student achievement. Does the civic "right" to choose your child's school result in a feeling of efficacy and invite involvement? Do selected schools really differ in their ability to incorporate parents' preferences and participation? How do the organizational features of choice schools differ from the typical neighborhood school? And is the contingent *fit* between parental practices and the school's attributes, not simply the school's characteristics, the key? A small number of scholars are just beginning to dig into these basic issues (most notably, the 1993 Bryk, Lee, and Holland study of Catholic schools).

In short, this empirical work should be read carefully and critically. Government's commitment to family choice and to empowering local communities is here to stay. We are just beginning to study the real effects of this appealing policy remedy. We still have much to learn about its benefits, unanticipated outcomes, and negative effects on different children, parents, and schools.

REFERENCES

Anderson, E. (1990). *Street wise: Race, class, and change in an urban community.* Chicago: University of Chicago Press.

Astone, N., & McLanahan, S. (1991). Family structure, parental practices, and high school completion. *American Sociological Review, 56,* 309–320.

Bryk, A., Lee, V., & Holland, P. (1993). *Catholic schools and the common good.* Cambridge, MA: Harvard University Press.

Carnegie Foundation for the Advancement of Teaching. (1992). *School choice: A special report.* Princeton, NJ: Author.

Chubb, J., & Moe, T. (1990). *Politics, markets, and America's schools.* Washington, DC: Brookings Institution.

Cohen, D., & Spillane, J. (1992). Policy and practice: Relations between governance and instruction. In G. Grant (Ed.), *Review of research in education* (Vol. 13; pp. 3–49). Washington, DC: American Educational Research Association.

Elam, S., Rose, L., & Gallup, A. (1991). The 23rd annual Gallup Poll of the public's attitudes toward the public schools. *Phi Delta Kappan, 73,* 41–56.

Fuller, B., & Clarke, P. (1994). Raising school effects while ignoring culture? *Review of Educational Research, 64*(1), 119–157.

Fuller, B., Eggers-Piérola, C., Holloway, S., Rambaud, M., & Liang, X. (in press). Rich culture, poor markets. *Teachers College Record.*

Fuller, B., & Holloway, S. (in press). When the state innovates: Institutions and interests create the preschool sector. In A. Pallas (Ed.), *Sociology of education and socialization.* Greenwich, CT: JAI Press.

Fuller, B., & Izu, J. (1986). What shapes the organizational beliefs of teachers? *American Journal of Education, 94,* 501–535.

Goodlad, J. (1984). *A place called school.* New York: McGraw-Hill.

Jencks, C. (1970, July 4). Giving parents money to pay for schooling: Education vouchers. *The New Republic,* pp. 19–21.

Katz, M. (1989). *The undeserving poor.* New York: Basic Books.

Levin, H. (1991). The economics of educational choice. *Economics of Education Review, 10,* 137–158.

Levy, F., & Murnane, R. (1992). U.S. earnings levels and earnings inequality: A review of recent trends and proposed explanations. *Journal of Economic Literature, 30,* 1333–1381.

Liang, X., & Fuller, B. (1994). *School choice and family policy: annotated bibliography.* Unpublished manuscript, Harvard University, Graduate School of Education, Cambridge, MA.

Matute-Bianchi, M. (1986). Ethnic identities and patterns of school success and failure among Mexican-descent and Japanese-American students. *American Journal of Education, 95*(1), 233–255.

McArthur, E., Colopy, K., & Schlaline, B. (1995). *Use of school choice* (Education Policy Issues Bulletin #95–742). Washington, DC: National Center for Educational Statistics.

Meyer, J., Scott, W. R., Strang, D., & Creighton, A. (1988). Bureaucratization without centralization: Changes in the organizational system of American public education, 1940–1980. In L. Zucker (Ed.), *Institutional patterns and organizations* (pp. 139–167). Cambridge, MA: Ballinger.

Meyer, J., Tyack, D., Nagel, J., & Gordon, A. (1979). Public education and nation-building in America. *American Journal of Sociology, 85,* 591–613.

Murnane, R., Willett, J., & Levy, F. (1995). The growing importance of cognitive skills in wage determination. *The Review of Economics and Statistics, 77,* 251–266.

Ogbu, J. (1978). *Minority education and caste: The American system in cross-cultural perspective.* New York: Academic Press.

Orfield, G., & Ashkinaze, C. (1991). *The closing door: Conservative policy and black opportunity.* Chicago: University of Chicago Press.

Rasell, E., & Rothstein, R. (Eds.). (1993). *School choice: Examining the evidence.* Washington, DC: Economic Policy Institute.

Raywid, M. (1985). Family choice arrangements in public schools: A review of the literature. *Review of Educational Research, 55,* 435–468.

Rowan, B. (1990). Commitment and control: Alternative strategies for the organizational design of schools. In C. Cazden (Ed.), *Review of research in education* (Vol. 16; pp. 353–389). Washington, DC: American Educational Research Association.

Schneider, B., & Coleman, J. (1993). *Parents, their children, and schools.* Boulder, CO: Westview.

Tyack, D. (1974). *The one best system.* Cambridge, MA: Harvard University Press.

Wells, A. (1993). *Time to choose: America at the crossroads of school choice policy.* New York: Hill & Wang.

Willms, D., & Echols, F. (1993). The Scottish experience of parental choice. In E. Rasell & R. Rothstein (Eds.), *School choice: Examining the evidence* (pp. 49–86). Washington, DC: Economic Policy Institute.

PART I

The Cultural Bounds of School Choice

The availability and exercise of choice is constrained by the cultural boundaries and institutional settings within which families live. Parents and youths are not blank slates, as proponents of idealized markets would have it. They have plentiful experience in their particular communities and often in their neighborhood schools. Government and educators may present a new range of institutional options. But families come to the table with diverse and particular preferences, distinct interpretations of their available school choices.

Part I details how cultural and institutional forces shape parents' attitudes toward their neighborhood schools and new options that become available. Strong factors play a role in parents' and youths' responses to new school options: family ethnicity, social-class position, and the perceived quality of their familiar neighborhood schools. This story begins in Chapter 2, where Amy Stuart Wells reports on how inner-city black youths in St. Louis respond to the metropolitan school choice program. Spurred by desegregation orders and a large investment in magnet schools, thousands of African-American children and youths leave their neighborhood schools, bound for urban magnets and white suburban schools that ring the city. But many African-American adolescents, largely independent of their parents' own preferences, opt not to participate in this metropolitan choice scheme. Others retreat to their neighborhood school and environs after riding buses to inner-city or suburban schools. These youths are the focus of Wells's qualitative study. She finds that while "objective measures" of school quality do play a role, choices can be more powerfully shaped by feelings of familiarity, ethnic solidarity, and school proximity. Many young white families settle in leafy suburbs in order to find neighborhood schools that provide familiar social values and teachers who seem similar to themselves. Is it any surprise that other ethnic groups employ the same cultural logic?

23

Chapter 3 takes us to San Antonio to examine which Hispanic parents choose to participate in a public school choice program. Low-income, most often Catholic, parents apply to magnet schools that offer a bicultural curriculum with considerable instruction in Spanish. A privately funded effort supporting tuition for families selecting parochial schools is also available. Both choice programs are extremely popular among Hispanic parents seeking a cross-cultural educational program, as well as safe and orderly schools. But Valerie Martinez and colleagues find that the public choice program exacerbates inequality. While the San Antonio neighborhoods served are comprised of poor and working-class families, it is the better-educated and more active parents who more frequently exercise their choice. We see how ethnic values drive demand for innovative schools—but parents' class position often determines which parents most effectively express choice.

Chapter 4 turns to the case of Detroit, where Valerie Lee and colleagues studied how inner-city and suburban families perceive the quality of their neighborhood schools and their support for school choice. They find that black inner-city families by far have the most negative perceptions of their neighborhood schools; they are especially concerned about basic issues of safety and teacher quality. These families express the strongest support for more school options. Parents living in predominantly white suburbs surrounding downtown Detroit do not share this negative view of their local schools; they feel much less urgency over school choice. One's present options and experiences—bounded by local institutional and social conditions—influence the desirability of greater choice.

We should emphasize that the cultural preferences of families are not immutable. Institutional conditions and actions interact with earlier beliefs about the form and quality of schools. And the political rationality of civic leaders and public school authorities constrains the range of school options available, whether advanced by voucher, magnet, or charter school organizations. Part II will address how institutional dimensions of public and private schooling are evolving under choice programs—and the essentially political process defining the range of school options that become available to families and children.

CHAPTER 2

African-American Students' View of School Choice

AMY STUART WELLS

Proponents and opponents alike offer simplistic views of families' responses to newly enacted choice programs. Proponents generally assume that all parents and students will respond to such programs in a similar goal-oriented and self-interested fashion, systematically seeking the highest-quality schools. Opponents of such school choice plans, on the other hand, often overemphasize the extent to which low-income families of color will passively withdraw from competition within the educational free market.

Both sides tend to underestimate the role of human agency—the freedom of individuals to act independently—in creating a wide array of reactions to such massive deregulation. The result is little discussion of the powerful ways in which the immediate cultural context of individual actors guides decision-making. This chapter focuses on how parents' and youths' social norms and ethnic identity constrain the range of school choices that are credible in their own eyes.

THE INFLUENCE OF CULTURE AND HUMAN AGENCY

This lack of attention to agency and culture in debates concerning educational choice is all the more surprising given recent research findings. In sociology of education, for instance, resistance theorists, including Willis (1977) and Everhart (1983), have shown that students from lower-class families are not passively shuffled through the educational system and consigned to the lowest-paying jobs as structural Marxists (Bowles & Gintis, 1976) would lead us to believe. Rather, according to these sociologists, lower-class students are active agents in reproducing their social-class position, resisting the dominant culture's achievement ideology that characterizes school life.

Apple (1985) argues that researchers and theorists must challenge beliefs about the passivity of students in social reproduction. "This assumption tends to overlook the fact that students . . . are creatively acting in ways that often contradict these expected norms and dispositions which pervade the school and the work place" (p. 95). Apple and others have shown that though students act out their opposition in inherently contradictory and relatively disorganized ways, these practices will continue to exist. "To ignore them is to ignore the fact that in any real situation there will be elements of resistance, of struggle and contradiction" (p. 93).

Critical theorists, building on neo-Marxist theories of cultural domination and resistance, have demonstrated the role that students can play in the educational system. Fine's (1991) research, for instance, illustrates the "complicated, contradictory consciousness" (p. 107) operating within the minds and lives of poor and minority adolescents. She found that students who succeed academically and graduate from high school "seem to deny, repress or dismiss the stories of failure, and persist undaunted in their personal crusade against the odds" (p. 134). Meanwhile, the students who failed in school and eventually dropped out were more critical of social and economic circumstances. These dropouts also retained strong connections to their community, kin, peers, and ethnic identity, resisting the dominant culture's emphasis on individualism and the achievement ideology—that those who work hard in school will get ahead.

Similarly, Ogbu's research has illustrated what he calls paradoxical behavior among African-American students: On one hand, black parents and black communities emphasize education for getting ahead in life, but on the other, black parents and students are very aware of the "job ceiling" in the labor market that prevents many blacks from getting high-paying jobs despite their degrees. These conflicting messages lead many black students to adopt an oppositional culture, rejecting the traditional achievement ideology and labeling black students' commitment to school achievement as "acting white." For these students, black culture becomes a symbol of identity and a basis of self-worth that stands in opposition to the dominant culture (Fordham, 1988; Ogbu, 1988; Stevenson & Ellsworth, 1993).

Along with this increased emphasis on human agency and cultural resistance, the last 15 years have seen the growing influence of Pierre Bourdieu's notions of *cultural capital* and *habitus*. According to Bourdieu, *cultural capital* is a system of implicit and deeply internalized values passed down by generations and influenced by social class, ethnicity, and parents' education. For example, the kinds of books that parents read to their children or the types of entertainment they expose them to—film, theater, music, museums—provide students with different bases of knowledge upon which they draw when trying to construct meaning from school experience. Educators tend to perceive the cultural capital of those who control the economic, social, and political resources as the natural and only proper sort; thus they favor students who possess the cultural forms held by dominant groups (Harker, 1984).

Bourdieu (1977) argues that degrees of economic and cultural capital are not perfectly correlated. For example, university teachers generally have far more cultural than economic capital, while members of the capitalist class generally have more economic than cultural capital. Bourdieu's theory thus shifts emphasis from more deterministic structural models of social reproduction based on class conflict in the economic realm and introduces a cultural dimension of stratification that can apply to ethnic-group conflict as well. Furthermore, Bourdieu highlights the role of agency as he describes the various ways students who lack the dominant group's cultural capital interact with the educational system. Some try to bluff their way through, picking up bits and pieces of the valued cultural capital along the way; others simply give up when they realize that they lack the cultural capital that schools reward (Bourdieu & Passeron, 1979).

This variability in how individual students make sense of the world and the opportunities presented to them is perhaps best illustrated by Bourdieu's concept of *habitus*, or the way in which a culture is embodied in the individual (Harker, 1984). Bourdieu (1971) defines *habitus* as a system of lasting dispositions, which integrate past experiences into "a matrix of perceptions, appreciations, and actions" (p. 183). Furthermore, while these dispositions are usually generated by objective conditions, they tend to persist even after alteration of those conditions (Bourdieu & Passeron, 1977, p. 161). For example, some African-Americans view themselves as inferior to whites years after the abolition of slavery and legal segregation. More simply put, *habitus* is how one's view of the world is influenced by the traditional distribution of power and status in society.

According to Bourdieu and others who have employed the concept, members of different cultural groups can share a *group habitus*, or set of dispositions that shape conduct and opinion. Bourdieu's work has focused on strictly class-based habitus, which reflects the more classist French society. But when the concept is applied to the study of schooling in the United States, researchers such as MacLeod (1987) have employed the concept of habitus as it relates to racial and ethnic identity. Group habitus is then redefined and incorporated within a family habitus and finally within the habitus of the individual. A person's social class, race, and religion thus strongly affect his or her habitus, but family influences and encounters with the world make each person's habitus unique (see DiMaggio, 1979; Robbins, 1991).

How does this new theoretical framework inform the contemporary school choice debate? The concepts of resistance, opposition, cultural capital, and habitus all suggest that the complex ways in which schools and students interact and redefine students' experiences in the educational system are not predictable or deterministic. Allowing for human agency explains why individual students or parents, despite demographic similarities, react to the same set of circumstances and opportunities quite differently. In order to accurately predict the impact of school choice policies, policy-makers need to pay more attention to this body of research and theory. In doing so they will better understand why changing the structure of the educational system may not empower all parents and students to compete for seats in high-quality schools. This framework also illuminates why similar families choose not to participate in this competition as they resist the dominant culture it symbolizes or they perceive their chances of winning to be slim. Others may choose to participate eagerly in a school choice plan, seeking upward mobility through access to higher-status schools.

Contributing to the small body of research addressing some of these issues pertaining to family choice, I interviewed 71 African-Americans—both youths and their parents—who live in inner-city St. Louis and who possess urban and suburban school options (see also Wells & Crain, 1996). My study demonstrates that the school choice process for these students is neither predictable nor uniform; wide variations within ethnic and social-class groups exist. Students' and parents' views are filtered through a habitus that is partly informed by a shared racial-group perspective and partly shaped by family and individual experiences.

SCHOOL CHOICE IN ST. LOUIS: THE CHOOSERS AND NONCHOOSERS

Since 1983 African-American students who reside in the city of St. Louis have had the option of participating in an interdistrict transfer program—an urban–suburban desegregation plan that allows black youths to attend 120 predominantly white county schools instead of all-black neighborhood schools. St. Louis County contains all of the suburbs participating in the desegregation plan. Families receive brochures and other information on the transfer program and the 16 participating suburban school districts. The program is publicized through radio, newspaper, and television public service announcements. African-American students who want to transfer to a county school simply fill out an application form and send it to the state-funded agency that administers the transfer process.

Currently, about 13,500 black students participate in the voluntary city-to-county transfer program. Under a federal district court order, the suburban districts are not allowed to turn away prospective transfer students on the basis of prior school achievement. Because this is choice-centered and voluntary desegregation, black students are not compelled to participate. From many black families' perspective, the transfer plan is regulated school choice skewed in their favor to assure the greatest number of options. Although the St. Louis transfer program is not a deregulated voucher plan in which parents are given public funds to spend at private schools, it does provide thousands of students choices and researchers an opportunity to test assumptions concerning how these choices are made. In fact, I would argue that black students in the city of St. Louis have more real choice under this desegregation plan than they would under a voucher plan that might not provide free transportation, cover the expenses for every receiving school, or require predominantly white schools to increase their black enrollment.

I interviewed three groups of black high school students and their parents for this study. The *city* group consisted of those who chose to remain in all-black city high schools. The *transfer* group included those who transferred to suburban schools and were still enrolled in these schools at the time of the interview. The *return* group was comprised of those who had transferred to a county school but had since returned to all-black city schools or had dropped out of school. Samples of students from each of these three categories were drawn from three predominantly black city neighborhoods identified as *middle-income, working-class,* and *low-income,* based on Census Bureau descriptions of the residents' education, employment, and income. Individual students were selected from each neighborhood based on the proximity of their homes to the all-black neighborhood high school. Thus all the students in the sample live within walking distance of an all-black city school. All students were enrolled in tenth grade when they were selected. They were interviewed during either their sophomore or junior year.

The final sample consisted of 17 boys and 20 girls, all between the ages of 15 and 19, and 34 parents (or grandparents if they were essentially the guardians). This chapter focuses primarily on the student interviews, drawing on the parent responses only to illustrate parent–child relationships (see Wells, 1993, for details on parent interviews). In the discussion below, the names of all the students have been changed.

Although this study was designed to understand the meaning each family made of its school choice, some general description of the students and their parents helps to set the scene. The distinctions between families of the three student groups—city, transfer, and return—were more pronounced than those between the families located in the three different neighborhoods—middle-income, working-class, and low-income. The city and return students in this sample were, as a group, further behind in school than the transfer students (Table 2.1). City students in this sample had more siblings, and their parents had fewer years of education. More city and return students' parents were unemployed at the time of the interview, and not one of the city students' parents held a job that took him or her across the city–county color line.

This small sample suggests that city students who stay behind in the urban schools and return students who end up back in urban schools (or out of school altogether) tend to be more disadvantaged in terms of parental education and employment than the transfer students who choose to enroll in predominantly white suburban schools. Furthermore, a quantitative evaluation of the St. Louis desegregation plan (Lissitz, 1992) found, in a comparison of 2,350 African-American tenth graders who remained in all-black, nonintegrated city schools and 864 students who transferred to county schools, that the parents of the transfer students had completed more years of education. For instance, 29% of the mothers of the transfer students as opposed to 21% of the mothers of students attending nonintegrated city schools had at least

Table 2.1: Demographic Differences Between City, Transfer, and Return Students

Student Characteristics	City Students ($n = 12$)	Transfer Students ($n = 12$)	Return Students ($n = 13$)
Behind in school	7	1	7
Average years behind	2	1	1
Average number of siblings	4.8	2.5	2.2
Parents with high school degrees	5	9	9
Parents unemployed	4	1	5
Parents work in the county	0	5	5

some years of college. Also, the students in the nonintegrated city schools tended to be, on average, four months older than the transfer students in their same grade. There were no differences, however, between the transfer and city students in the percentage who qualified for free or reduced-price lunches (58%).

Other research supports the notion that nonchoosers are more disadvantaged in terms of parents' education and social class than choosers in most educational choice programs (see Wells, 1991, for a review). But the main point of this research was to get past simplistic generalizations and make sense of the complex school choice process from the perspective of the people making the decisions. In the students' explanations of how and why they chose the schools they did lies the impact of culture and human agency.

Our interviews illustrate that for these African-American students, three overlapping and intertwined factors strongly affected their school choices:

1. The degree of parental involvement in the initial school choice
2. Students' acceptance or rejection of the achievement ideology, and their perception of what it takes to get ahead in the world
3. Students' and parents' racial attitudes—their fear or distrust of whites and the degree to which they accept the dominant view of white superiority

All three factors were heavily influenced by both students' and parents' habitus as it related to their understanding of the kind of cultural capital needed to succeed in a predominantly white suburban school.

PARENT INVOLVEMENT AND
THE ACHIEVEMENT IDEOLOGY

The first two factors—parent involvement and the achievement ideology—were closely linked because students tended to adopt their parents' ideology with regard to achievement; there also appears to have been a link between the parents' ideology and their involvement. Researchers have demonstrated a positive correlation between the degree of parent involvement in education and parent socioeconomic status (SES) (see Epstein, 1987; Lareau, 1989), but there are exceptions. In St. Louis many low-income, poorly educated parents are very involved in their children's education and in turn in the school choice process. Thus it is important to look more carefully at the human agency side of the equation. How do individual students' and parents' perceptions of where they fit into the larger social structure affect their interpretation of the achievement ideology, and how does that interpretation play a role in their school choices?

With few exceptions, overall parent involvement in the students' education and the degree to which parents directed and controlled their children's educational decisions varied greatly between the city students who remained in all-black neighborhood schools and the transfer students who chose to attend predominantly white suburban schools. City parents, in almost every case, absolved themselves of the school choice responsibility, leaving the decision entirely to their adolescent children. Transfer parents, on the other hand, pushed their children onto buses heading for the suburbs. Parents of the return students were frequently involved in the initial choice of a suburban school but less involved in helping their children cope in the new setting; they eventually had little say in their children's final decision to leave the suburban school. Furthermore, black students from St. Louis can choose to transfer to a suburban school at any grade, and I found that transfer students were more likely than return students to transfer at an early age. For instance, only two return students, as opposed to six transfer students, had attended a suburban elementary school. Meanwhile, seven return students, compared to only one transfer student, did not transfer until high school. This pattern also suggests different levels of parental involvement in the choice process.

Achievement ideology was closely linked to parents' involvement. Parents who were more involved in their children's choices tended to accept the dominant achievement ideology, an acceptance they generally passed to their children. Transfer students thus tended to believe that school status and the right cultural capital would help them succeed. City students, on the other hand, adopted a "learn anywhere" ideology that downplayed the significance of attending higher-quality schools. The achievement ideology of return students was more varied. Some accepted the dominant achievement ideology but felt that they could not live comfortably with it; others rejected the ideology outright.

City Students: Comfort and Learn-Anywhere Ideology

Eight out of the twelve city parents (or grandparents) said that the youth alone made the decision to remain in a city school. Half of these parents said that they did not even discuss this decision with their child. Only one parent in the sample, a teacher in the city school system who maintains a strong black separatist attitude, said she had actually decided which school her son would attend. These city parents in general appeared particularly withdrawn and alienated from the educational system. They spoke as if they could be of no help to their children regarding educational decisions.

Left to their own devices, city students opted for the nearby and the familiar: the all-black neighborhood school. Interviews revealed that what city students were really choosing was the sense of kinship and shared culture represented by their all-black school. Because their parents did not insist that they ride a bus to the suburbs, city students remained in schools in which they felt more comfortable.

When asked what they like most about their city high schools, nine of the twelve city students gave responses that had nothing to do with learning, the quality of the school, or their goals. Familiarity with students or teachers, tradition and pride associated with sports or extracurricular activities, or closeness to home dominated the responses. Venicia said what she liked most about her neighborhood high school was being on the pompom squad. What Leo liked most was that he knew everybody, and Chandra said there was nothing she liked about her city high school except that it was close to home. Salina, who is 19 years old and still in the tenth grade, said what she enjoyed most about her city school were the pep rallies, the choir, and the glee club.

Erin, a friendly young woman who talked a great deal about the importance of being well liked by her peers, said her favorite aspect of her local city high school was "I know a lot of people up there . . . and I don't feel lost." Erin's life, like that of many high school students, seemed to revolve around the social events at her school. She noted that she was not excited about a special internship program she was selected to participate in during junior year because it would take her away from the school and her friends for half of each school day. Luckily, she said, the program would allow her to miss work for school events such as "Colors Day," when all the seniors dress up and "you vote for the best couple, class clown, best dressed, athletes, and stuff like that."

Only three city students gave answers related to school achievement: Angie said the teachers at her neighborhood school help her learn, and Gwenn said the teachers at her school "want to see us make it." Paulette said what she liked best about her high school was that it was close to home and that she knew some of her teachers, but she added that these teachers would "really be on me about my work. You need teachers like that that care about what you do."

Yet even those youths who were achievement-oriented mentioned a sense of belonging to the school, a degree of attachment to the teachers and students in the city schools, and a sense that their cultural ways would be recognized and valued in an all-black institution. Virtually all of the city students' responses concerning what they liked about their high schools incorporated this sense of shared culture. The traditions of their all-black schools—for instance, the songs the choir sang or the more rhythmic, less stiff style of cheerleading—reflected the history and culture of the students in ways that these activities at predominantly white suburban schools did not. These and other city student responses are consistent with a phenomenon found in other studies of school choice situations: that cultural familiarity or shared values frequently dominate over factors of school quality per se (Henig, 1990; Holloway & Fuller, 1992; Maddaus, 1990).

When asked if they ever considered attending a county school and, if so, why they did not transfer, the city students responded in ways that once again suggest the importance of the cultural unity they experienced at an all-black school, as well as their lack of information about the transfer program. Venicia said, "I wanted to go, but I didn't. I don't know why . . . I didn't want to leave the pom squad . . . I didn't want to go that far." Keenya also said that she wanted to go, but her father told her that information on the transfer program came too late.

Only two respondents—Leo and Paulette—defended their choice to remain in a city school by insisting that the quality of the education in their school was comparable to that of a county school. According to Paulette, "some say the work is harder in the county school; I don't think so." Leo said he never considered going to a county school: "The education is the same here . . . I think the county schools are intentionally taking city students to tear them down—keep people confused, keep them under control."

Four of the city students' responses to questions concerning transfers to county schools were laden with insecurity and fear of the unknown: Chandra not wanting to meet new people, Manny not wanting to go "way out," Salina worrying about not understanding what is not taught, and Erin wanting to stay where "I know a lot of people." None of these students discussed his or her decision in terms of the quality of the school attended or the quality of the school not attended. Once again, the comfort of the familiar was a deciding factor in the school choices.

With little parent involvement in their school choices and little emphasis on factors of school quality in discussing their choice, most of the city students have adopted a "learn-anywhere" achievement ideology. "It doesn't matter who might be teaching," said Paulette. According to Erin, there is no difference between the city and the county schools: "If you're going to learn something, you do your best anywhere you go."

Similarly, Venicia downplayed any differences between city and county schools: "It doesn't really matter where you go . . . if you want to learn—you got the ability, you will."

In short, the evidence suggests that when parents left the choice to their youngsters, these youngsters followed the path of least resistance to a familiar, nearby school where they fit in and felt comfortable. In an attempt to rationalize this choice in the face of popular opinion that suburban schools are better than city schools, the city students have adopted an achievement ideology that minimizes the importance of school quality. This is not a portrait of self-maximizing families who carefully evaluated their options and their long-term goals and decided that a city school would better serve their needs than a county school. Offering these students the choice of higher-status schools did not free them from a habitus of fear and insecurity in a world that places them at the bottom of the social structure.

Transfer Students: Parent Involvement and Sacrifice

Where city parents were withdrawn and seemingly resigned to fate, transfer parents tended to be much more aggressive and bent on making the lives of their children better than their own. In contrast to the responses from eight city parents who said the school choice process was left entirely up to their children, only one of the twelve transfer parents said she had left the school choice up to her daughter. Meanwhile, six of the eleven transfer parents said that they had made the decision for their children to attend a county school themselves, and three said that the decision had been made jointly with their children (Wells, 1993). This explains in part why eleven of the twelve transfer students began attending suburban schools at the elementary or middle level.

Because of their parents' more active involvement, transfer students had far less control over the school choice process than the city students, and they appeared to have very different parent–child relationships. Transfer parents were assertive, demanding, and not easily intimidated. And their children, with one exception, seemed to enjoy this high level of parent involvement and accept their parents' attitudes about city versus county schools.

Of the three groups of students and parents interviewed, the transfer parents and their children best fit the vision of school choosers that seems to drive proposals for greater choice in education. They were more goal-oriented and focused on school quality as an important variable in the school choice process, although they admitted to having little first-hand knowledge of the quality of particular schools. The parents were highly involved in their children's education, and the students, for the most part, respected their parents' decisions. These were the "rational choosers"—intent on making the most of themselves in a highly instrumental and goal-oriented fashion.

Transfer parents and their children seemed less concerned about which suburban school they attended, so long as it was out in the county. In this sense these parents and students are not the ideal educational consumers they appear to be. Transfer parents and students lacked information about the 16 county districts and about particular schools, suggesting they were not making the best choice but rather making the best choice possible given the limited amount of information available (see Simon, 1987).

Factors such as perceived status or popularity of a school—the designer label—played a major role in the choices these families made. "I heard a lot of people talking about Westridge, wanting to go to Westridge," said one transfer student. "I'd always wanted to go to Westridge, I just like the name," said another. Despite the vast differences between the various county school districts in terms of resources, class sizes, teacher qualifications, and so forth, the transfer parents and students indicated that the major choice was between a city school and a suburban school—any county school.

None of the parents or students had ever visited the county schools they chose. Despite their lack of specific information on the county schools, transfer students were highly motivated to attend predominantly white schools many miles from their own home. In the way they spoke to a white interviewer, in the way they carried themselves, and in the way they explained why they got up at 5:00 A.M. to get to their suburban schools every day, the transfer students were far more confident and goal-oriented than their counterparts in the city schools. They were, for the most part, steeped in an achievement ideology that stresses the importance of going to the "best" school in order to get ahead in life. Unlike the city students who argued that schools don't make a difference, that it is up to the individual to achieve, the transfer students perceived a more complex opportunity structure—one in which school status and perceived academic quality would make a difference in their lives.

When asked what they liked most about their suburban high schools, five of the twelve transfer students cited factors that would help them attain long-term goals: "classes that will help you with college," "good teachers and good counselors," and "they give you the freedom to be grown up, young adults." Three of the transfer students cited their involvement in a variety of extracurricular activities, including the computer club. The remaining three students cited more social factors: "a lot of people know who I am" and "meeting other transfer students from different parts of the city." Yet even these less academic factors differ to some degree from those cited by the city students. The transfer students were not talking about the comfort or familiarity associated with attending a predominantly white suburban school.

In fact, the transfer students' responses to questions concerning what they liked least about their county high schools revealed that they are willing to put up with a great deal of discomfort—including racial prejudice, a lack of respect for their cultural capital, and long bus rides. Most of them believed this sacrifice would pay off in the long run. For instance, when Morris—"Mo"—was asked what he liked least about his county high school, he said, "I have to try to be two people instead of just being myself. I have to act one way in school and another way in my neighborhood." Tammy commented that black students were not as involved in certain high-status activities—particularly those for girls, such as cheerleading and pompoms. "We feel like we are visitors and not part of the school," she said. In fact, Tammy, more than any of the other transfer students, was keenly aware of the subtle and not-so-subtle racism that transfer students confront in their predominantly white schools. She said the labeling of black students as voluntary transfer students, or VTS, is degrading and makes them feel like they don't belong:

> We *hate* that. I mean, they will call a meeting then on the loud speaker and they will always go "voluntary transfer students please come to the gym," and really what they are saying is all the black students come here. . . . I mean, even though we're coming out there and it's supposed to be our school too . . . whenever blacks and whites get into it, the first thing they [white students] say is this is *our* school, you're coming out to *our* school.

Two other transfer students noted that some of the teachers in their county schools were prejudiced, while a third said that some of the teachers would not help you if you got the wrong answer. Val noted that what he liked least were the racial comments such as "whites stereotyping blacks as street people."

When asked, "In what ways would you rather have gone to the city school in your neighborhood?" transfer students talked about additional sacrifices they had made in transferring to a school 20 or more miles from their home: Cathy said she would have had more time to do her homework and study. Tammy, Arlene, and Urma stated that they would have been more "comfortable"—they would have fit in better and known more people—in their neighborhood schools.

Several of the transfer students acknowledged throughout their interviews that the coursework in the suburban schools was more difficult than that in the city schools. The students in county schools "learn a little bit faster," and the county schools appeared to have more resources. Students saw their discomfort as the price they must pay for the opportunity to attend "better," more challenging schools. And because of an achievement ideology that tells them they will be able to cash in on these opportunities in the long run—that schools indeed make a difference in their lives and chances for future success—nearly all of the transfer students, with the notable exception of Tammy, believed in what their parents had decided for them. Yet even Tammy, the one transfer student with a strong critique of the white schools, understood why her mother believed that the transfer program would pay off in the long run:

> She'll tell you that when you fill out an application [for a job], when you put Washington [the city school] down or you put Plymouth [the county school] down, it's a better chance that they will pick a Plymouth student . . . because it like means a good opportunity.

Return Students: Resisting the Achievement Ideology

Unlike the distinct circumstances and attitudes of the city and transfer families, the sample of return families provides a more diffuse blend of experiences and perspectives. A few of the parents in this group were assertive and demanding, similar to the transfer parents. Others were withdrawn and alienated, as were many of the city parents. Similarly, the return students varied widely from bold and outspoken to meek and soft-spoken. These students were also more complicated in terms of the school choice process, because they actually made two choices: first to transfer to a suburban school, and second to return to their neighborhood school or drop out altogether. What is more interesting about the return students is that their habitus (how they view themselves in relation to the rest of the world) had everything to do with why they left their suburban school.

Where the city students were safely tied to their familiar neighborhood schools and the transfer students were pushed toward what their parents perceived as better schools, the return students appeared to be caught between their need for comfort and positive reinforcement and the realization that the white schools represent something they once wanted but were unable to attain. With less support from their parents, return students had more trouble tolerating the stresses of attending a largely white suburban school. Some of these students were intimidated by the dominant culture and withdrew from competition; others rejected the white culture outright.

Return students' answers to why they quit the transfer program fit into three distinct categories:

1. Four return students said that they were "put out" or "pushed out" of their suburban schools as a result of disciplinary actions by white administrators. Rarely were these students expelled from their county schools. More frequently they received longer and longer suspensions—a 10-day suspension followed by a 30-day suspension followed by a 90-day suspension—until they missed so much school work that it was no longer possible to catch up. This is what they mean by being "put out" or "pushed out" of a white school. All four of the students who had this experience saw it as the result of racial bias on the part of the white administrators in the suburban schools. These students were generally bolder than the other return students; like Tammy, they were the resisters. Although these resisters had originally been sent to the county schools by strong parents, they were not willing to put up with the suburban schools' disciplinary codes or the perceived attitudes of the white educators who enforced them.

2. Five return students said that they left the county schools for comfort or convenience reasons, from not liking the bus ride to finding the white county students unfriendly. Four of these students cited cultural factors that had to do with perceived prejudice in the county schools. These students, with one exception, tended to be the quieter return students, the ones who did not cause a lot of trouble, but who wanted to return to a school environment in which they felt more comfortable. They resembled the city students who liked their neighborhood high schools because they were close to home and full of people they knew. Their parents, meanwhile, like many of the city parents, were less involved in their educational decisions.

3. Three return students said they left the white schools for academic reasons; one said she was skipping class too much in the county school, and the other two said that they came back to the admittedly less difficult city schools so they could improve their grades. The latter two were clearly going through a "cooling-off" process during which they came to internalize their lower social status and lack of cultural capital, removing themselves from a competitive school

environment. The parents of two of these students had pushed their children to go to the county school in the first place, and all three said they wished their children had stayed there. But the parents seemed unable to provide the kind of support, guidance, and strong dose of achievement ideology that transfer parents gave their children. The remaining return student did not provide a consistent explanation.

Given these various reasons why return students leave the suburban schools, a more focused picture emerges as to who these students are and how their achievement ideology differs from city and transfer students. Details of interviews with three return students help to provide such a picture. Gail typifies those students who returned for reasons of comfort or academics. Robert typifies the resistance of those return students who were "put out" of their suburban school, while Charles shares characteristics of both Robert and Gail.

Gail, a shy 19-year-old with a 2-year-old son, was pregnant with her second child when she was interviewed. She said she withdrew from the suburban school and returned to the all-black high school in her low-income neighborhood so that she could earn better grades. Although she considered the city school to be inferior to the county school she had attended, she said she disliked the county school

[because] you know how they break down the work for you, they don't really explain it to you. Some teachers they explain and others let you go on your own. . . . I didn't do so good—walked out with a 1-point grade average and I went back to public [city] school, and [got] my grades back up to normal. I'm a B student but I was between a C and a D [in the county], and I didn't like that. I knew I was better than that. I knew I could function better than that. . . . It's just that you have to be real . . . your mind had to be real wise to be out there [in the county school].

At the time of the interview, Gail still had a year of coursework to complete before graduating from her neighborhood high school, which she described as "ain't so hot, but it'll do. It's trouble, I go there now and . . . it's trouble . . . you're around a lot of blacks, and they're just fighting."

Robert, from the same low-income neighborhood as Gail, first went to a white suburban school in the fourth grade and reported that he was very popular in each of the county schools he attended. He was the quarterback on the freshman football team at his suburban high school and had made it onto the basketball team when he and his friends started getting into trouble. According to Robert, "the principals were prejudiced to two people in the school—me and my best friend. Every time something happened, they came and got us. They don't like us. I feel like they didn't want us in their school."

He said he and his friend were accused of stealing a leather jacket out of a locker—an accusation he denied. And finally, he was "put out" for fighting with a white student. Robert enrolled in the high school in his neighborhood, where he made straight F's and was eventually asked to leave. In less than a year, Robert had gone from being a "popular" football quarterback with a C average to a very angry high school dropout. His two best friends were also "out of school." His first child was due in a few months.

Robert recalled that once he felt he had been treated unfairly by the administrators in the suburban school he began to act out and resist the educational system as a whole. His final comment on the transfer program: "They need to change their attitude. Principals' attitudes gonna get them into trouble. Just a whole lot of brothers like to punch them clean in the face."

Charles, an outspoken student from a middle-class family, represents a cross between Gail and Robert. He quit the transfer program to enroll in his neighborhood high school, in part because he found the work too difficult in the county school and in part because he was resisting the culture of the mostly white environment—an environment that devalued the cultural capital he brought with him from his all-black neighborhood. In talking about the curriculum and the level of the work, he noted:

> I thought I could hang tough with it. You know, going to bed early and getting up and . . . but I didn't expect all those science projects and reading all this history. Work on top of work, on top of work. . . . In the city they give you more lectures, and they talk to you like . . . you just got so many chapters. . . . In the county, they go too fast.

He then shifted to issues of cultural domination and his critique of what the county schools were trying to do to the black students: "They brainwash you to go out there—that they teach you more. Then you get there. Oh, you're integrated. You're not yourself no more. Your voice changes like you are a little nerd or something. I felt like I was not myself anymore." He added that he had not had any discipline problems in the county school because "I was totally brainwashed. You think you're smart. I went with the system and I thought, 'I go to a county school.' You just think you are better than everybody else. Then you find out you are not."

Although a greater number of transfer than return students cited prejudice as what they liked least about their county high school—five versus four—the transfer students were steeped in an achievement ideology their parents had ingrained in them. This, I believe, helped them tolerate the racial prejudice they encountered, viewing it as a sacrifice that would pay off in the long run. The parents of the return students seemed to have one set of beliefs concerning racial issues in the suburban schools while the students themselves were living another reality. For instance, return parents had very few complaints concerning the county schools. All thirteen return parents agreed that the suburban schools were "better" than the city schools; in fact, they were less critical of the suburban schools than the transfer parents. This is somewhat surprising considering that transfer parents still had children enrolled in these schools and return parents had children who had left these schools—mostly because of perceived prejudice. Similarly, the transfer students said their parents were more likely to talk to them about prejudice and what to expect from whites in the county, whereas only a few of the return students said their parents had talked to them about these topics. With little or no discussion between the parents and students, the return students' decisions to leave the county schools won out in the long run. Transfer students, mostly because of their parents, were more likely to internalize a reward structure that led them to value academic achievement over comfort or a strong oppositional attitude.

RACIAL ATTITUDES AND SCHOOL CHOICE

City, transfer, and return students were all aware of the general status of blacks in American society. For some, this had been internalized and manifested in their fear of competing with white students and in their criticisms of all-black schools. In this way they shared a group habitus. But this common understanding of how blacks are viewed by the rest of society played itself out differently among and within the three groups of students.

City Students: Safely Segregated

The extent to which racial attitudes and fear of competing with whites affected the city students' perceptions of the transfer program and suburban schools is encapsulated in the concern of one city student, Salina, who was afraid of not understanding what is *not* taught in the suburban schools. Her comment suggests that Salina, like the lower-class French students Bourdieu and Passeron (1979) studied, sensed that she lacked the kind of cultural capital rewarded in suburban schools. Her school choice (or choice not to choose), like that of most of the city students, was informed by her sense that she would not be able to keep up with white students. Leo's assertion that the county schools were just taking city students to "tear them down" and "keep people under control" demonstrates his views on white dominance in American society. In fact, Leo's critique of black–white relations—a black separatist ideology he shares with his mother—colored every angle of his perspective on the transfer program. When asked what he thought of black students who go to county schools, he replied that the transfer students were "confused" and that "they let themselves be programmed by people."

Most of the city students, however, said black students who want to go to county schools are "doing the right thing" by transferring. "I have no disagreement with kids who go to the county. They should have the freedom to go wherever they want to," said Salina. Other responses to the question of whether transfer students were doing the right thing contained hints of defensiveness: "If they think they can handle it, they should go," said Venicia. "They're just trying to show off. They are not better," said Chandra.

When asked the more general questions of "What are the benefits of going to an all-black school?" and "What are the benefits of going to an integrated school?" the responses of city students revealed that while they may feel far more comfortable in an all-black school, society has taught them that these all-black schools lack the cultural capital associated with attending whiter, wealthier schools. Thus, seven of the city students responded to questions of the benefits of an all-black school with a criticism of either black schools or blacks in general.

According to Venicia, "There isn't any benefit—any benefit at all; it's just an all-black school." Likewise, Casey said he really could not think of any benefits. Troy noted that there was "nothing" good about all-black schools—"there's lots of fights over silly stuff." Gwenn said, "When us black people get together, we don't know how to act. We try to appear more than ourselves when we're with our own kind." According to Chandra, in all-black schools, "The teachers care, but the students just don't want to learn—they be carrying on and partying too much."

Two of the city students' responses on the benefits of an integrated school showed a sense of racial inferiority and insecurity. Salina, for instance, said the benefit of going to an integrated school is that "whites are more mature; black students play in the halls, skip class." Angie stated that she would like to go to a "mixed" school but "I don't know how they would react to me."

Guided by a view of race that leads them to believe that black students are more unruly and less mature than white students, city students talk of being more hesitant and even fearful of interaction with the more mature and well-behaved white students. Clearly these beliefs have affected their school choices.

Transfer Students: White Is Right

As noted above, not one of the transfer parents or youths actually visited a county district before listing the three top choices on the transfer application. In fact, in their interviews the transfer parents and students did not mention the degree to which one county school district might better serve their particular educational needs. While this finding does not say much about the effectiveness of the educational marketplace, it does suggest that school preferences are frequently defined more by the race and social class of the students within them than by the academic offerings in a particular school. Transfer parents and students appear to have automatically assumed that any of the predominantly white suburban schools were better than any of the all-black city schools. Unlike city students, however, transfer students believed they could compete in that white world.

In terms of black–white interactions, transfer students tended to be much less fearful of whites and less likely to suggest that they themselves felt inferior to whites than their counterparts who attended city schools. But this does not mean that transfer students possessed a greater sense of black pride or that they held a higher opinion of blacks in general. In fact, like the city students, many of the transfer students found fault with the behavior of other blacks—either those in the city schools or their fellow black transfer students. In fact, some of these upwardly mobile transfer students suggested that one reason they attended predominantly white schools was to acquire the white cultural capital so valued in our society.

When asked about the benefits of an integrated school, Cathy said "white kids can offer you more." She then told how a white girl had let a close friend use her car when she went off to college: "If it was a black person, they would probably let the car sit there." Cathy explained that she did not want to go to an all-black school because black people are always trying to prove a point by saying something that they know they could have kept to themselves, and blacks stereotype each other because of the way they look or dress.

Seven of the twelve transfer students responded negatively to the question concerning the "benefits" of going to an all-black school by citing the problems they would encounter. Typical answers included, "more trouble," "gangs fighting," and "I would not learn as much." Only three of the transfer students actually cited potential benefits of going to an all-black school: Tammy said she would be more comfortable; Tina said, "It wouldn't be so boring," and Arlene stated that she would "be able to learn more about black people and black history."

When asked about the benefits of attending an integrated school, eight of the twelve transfer students gave extremely positive answers. Five of these eight stated that they could meet people of different races and backgrounds. According to Val, "I get to know people, friends who will get into the business world." Dawain said that there was less peer pressure to get into trouble in an integrated school, and Tina cited academic factors—that the teachers "teach more" in integrated schools. Three of the transfer students said they could not think of any benefits or that they had never really thought about it. Only Tammy gave a negative response:

> In some things they [the integrated schools] are much better than a city school—learning techniques are better. But I mean what's the purpose? For whites and blacks to get along? White students keep it separate, 'cause in the beginning they had control over everything.

It is not surprising that students who choose integrated over segregated schools are less fearful of interaction with whites and see more academic and social benefits in attending a predominantly white school than do black students who remain in all-black schools, but it does imply a sorting process between choosers and nonchoosers that is related to racial attitudes and students' willingness to interact with people of other races. The choosers seek to separate themselves from members of their own race who signify the lower status of their group.

Return Students: Cooling Off

The racial attitudes of the return students, like every aspect of this diverse group, are difficult to define. Some put down members of their own race and wanted to separate themselves from all-black schools. Still, return students as a group tended to report more fear of whites—

or at least fear of competition with whites—than transfer students. Their anxiety about competing with white students was more sophisticated than that of the city students, since they had first-hand experience.

Keenya, a shy but perceptive young woman, said she went to her county school with high expectations because of "all the good things" she had heard about the school—"how people are friendly." But she was immediately surprised by the coldness of the white students: "If you asked them where was the classroom, they acted like they did not want to tell you." She also described subtle ways in which the teachers made her feel more uncomfortable in the suburban school:

> So basically, when the teacher was teaching and they would make an example about something . . . like they would say something like that was out in the county, and I wouldn't know what they were talking about. But the white students would, because they are out there . . . you know like a shopping mall or something, and I wouldn't know what they were talking about.

Keenya recalled other classroom situations in which she felt uncomfortable, like the time her English teacher showed a film that "was like putting blacks down," or when she gave a speech in her public speaking class.

> I was the only black, and . . . you had to get up and speak in front of the class. And I got so I felt real uncomfortable because of my speech. All the white kids you know just stared at me. And when like the speech was over you try to be nice and applause for somebody—they would not applause for me.

Feeling that the white students rejected her and people of her color was reason enough for Keenya to remove herself from the higher-status school despite the objections of her mother, who was skeptical about the poor treatment of black students in county schools.

Still, return students' fear, distrust, and even resistance toward whites does not lead them to adopt a strong pro-black stance. Only four of the thirteen students said they could think of a possible benefit of attending an all-black school, and of these, three spoke of the familiarity of the people who went to the school: "I know most of the people up there" or "people are more outgoing, I feel more comfortable." Only Charles cited a benefit of an all-black school that dealt with black culture: "You're around your own culture, your own people, you can keep up with things and the trends in your neighborhood."

Six of the return students made derogatory comments when asked about the benefits of an all-black school. For example, Barrett, who was not allowed to continue at his suburban high school, said, "I hate black schools. . . . I don't hate them, just don't like being with same people—acting out and getting written up by teachers." Donald, who was "put out" of the county school for fighting, said, "None [no benefits to an all-black school] . . . it's a downfall. Classes with black students and white teachers—don't want to learn." And Robert, also "put out" of his county school, saw "nothing challenging" about all-black schools. "I'm not saying that black people are dumb, but most don't know shit. They all want to go sell drugs all their life."

This deprecation of other African-Americans by three students who were basically thrown out of their county schools indicates that their anger and resistance toward the white educators and students in the county had not been translated into an appreciation of those they left behind when they made the initial choice to attend a county school. These and other comments suggest that the all-black city schools and the students within them serve to remind return students of their own failure to attain higher social status by succeeding in the mostly white county schools.

The racial attitudes of the return students imply that, like the transfer students, they prefer mostly white schools to mostly black ones. And like the transfer students, much of what they perceived to be better about suburban schools had to do with the higher status of the students and their cultural capital. The return students' first school choice—to transfer to a county school—was at least partly affected by their racial attitudes. Paradoxically, their negative experiences in the predominantly white schools appear to have done little to change these views.

IMPLICATIONS FOR SCHOOL CHOICE POLICIES

Policy-makers must understand that students and parents do not act monolithically, responding to changes in the structure of the educational system in a predetermined, goal-oriented fashion. These variable responses to structural changes will cut across ethnic and class boundaries, although students from white and higher-SES families will no doubt be in a position to take greater advantage of the educational market. After all, they will have the most resources and the fewest reasons to resist the dominant school culture. And while both race and class affect students' habitus, and therefore the way they perceive school choice opportunities, not all low-income minority students and parents will react to choice options in the same way. Some will actively seek out schools that they believe will help them attain higher status; others who fear competition or failure in a higher-status school and those who have lost faith in the educational system will most likely choose not to choose.

What will happen to these children in an educational free market predicated on the existence of both winners and losers? Who will advocate for them? Who will respond to their sense of injustice or their need for the security and cultural familiarity of a neighborhood school? These are important policy questions. In a truly deregulated system there is no guarantee and no safety net for these students.

Research on the relationship between culture and human agency and how students and parents mediate this relationship through their habitus reveals how little we know about how individuals react to structural changes. To the extent that we can craft school choice policies that are inclusive rather than exclusive, policies that make sure every student and parent must choose a school, we will minimize the potential negative effect of choice programs on inner-city youths like Salina, Venicia, and Robert.

Acknowledgment. This chapter presents data from a study of the St. Louis metropolitan desegregation plan. The study was funded by the Spencer Foundation; Robert L. Crain, professor at Teachers College, Columbia University, was the principal investigator.

REFERENCES

Apple, M. (1985). *Education and power*. Boston: Ark Paperbacks.

Bourdieu, P. (1971). Intellectual field and creative project. In M. K. D. Young (Ed.), *Knowledge and control: New directions for the sociology of education* (pp. 161–188). London: Collier Macmillan.

Bourdieu, P. (1977). Cultural reproduction and social reproduction. In J. Karabel & A. H. Halsey (Eds.), *Power and ideology in education* (pp. 487–510). New York: Oxford University Press.

Bourdieu, P., & Passeron, J. C. (1977). *Reproduction in education, society, and culture* (R. Nice, Trans.). London and Beverly Hills: Sage.

Bourdieu, P., & Passeron, J. C. (1979). *The inheritors: French students and their relations to culture* (R. Nice, Trans.). Chicago: University of Chicago Press.

Bowles, S., & Gintis, H. (1976). *Schooling in capitalist America*. New York: Basic Books.

DiMaggio, P. (1979). Review essay: On Pierre Bourdieu. *American Journal of Sociology, 84*(6), 1460–1474.

Epstein, J. L. (1987). Parent involvement: What research says to administrators. *Education and Urban Society, 19*(2), 119–136.

Everhart, R. B. (1983). *Reading, writing, and resistance.* Boston: Routledge & Kegan Paul.

Fine, M. (1991). *Framing dropouts.* Albany: State University of New York Press.

Fordham, S. (1988). Racelessness as a factor in black students' school success: Pragmatic strategy or Pyrrhic victory? *Harvard Educational Review, 58*(1), 54–84.

Harker, R. R. (1984). On reproduction, habitus and education. *British Journal of Sociology, 5*(2), 117–127.

Henig, J. R. (1990). Choice in public schools: An analysis of transfer requests among magnet schools. *Social Science Quarterly, 71*(1), 69–82.

Holloway, S. D., & Fuller, B. (1992). The great child-care experiment: What are the lessons for school improvement? *Educational Researcher, 21*(7), 12–19.

Lareau, A. (1989). *Home advantage.* New York: Falmer.

Lissitz, R. W. (1992). *Assessment of student performance and attitude: St. Louis metropolitan area court ordered desegregation effort.* St. Louis, MO: Voluntary Interdistrict Coordinating Council.

MacLeod, J. (1987). *Ain't no making it.* Boulder, CO: Westview.

Maddaus, J. (1990). Parental choice of schools: What parents think and do. In C. B. Cazden (Ed.), *Review of research in education* (pp. 267–296). Washington DC: American Educational Research Association.

Ogbu, J. (1988). Class stratification, racial stratification, and schooling. In L. Weis (Ed.), *Class, race, and gender in American education* (pp. 163–182). Albany: State University of New York Press.

Robbins, D. (1991). *The work of Pierre Bourdieu.* Boulder, CO: Westview.

Simon, H. (1987). Rationality in psychology and economics. In R. M. Hogarth & M. W. Reeder (Eds.), *Rational choice: The contrast between economics and psychology* (pp. 25–40). Chicago: University of Chicago Press.

Stevenson, R. B., & Ellsworth, J. (1993). Dropouts and the silencing of critical voices. In L. Weis & M. Fine (Eds.), *Beyond silenced voices: Class, race, and gender in United States schools* (pp. 259–272). Albany: State University of New York Press.

Wells, A. S. (1991). Choice in education: Examining the evidence on equity. *Teachers College Record, 93*(1), 156–173.

Wells, A. S. (1993). The sociology of school choice: Why some win and others lose in the educational marketplace. In E. Rasell & R. Rothstein (Eds.), *School choice: Examining the evidence* (pp. 29–48). Washington, DC: Economic Policy Institute.

Wells, A. S., & Crain, R. L. (1996). *Stepping over the color line: African-American students in white suburban schools.* New Haven, CT: Yale University Press.

Willis, P. (1977). *Learning to labor.* New York: Columbia University Press.

CHAPTER 3

Public School Choice in San Antonio
Who Chooses and with What Effects?

VALERIE MARTINEZ
KENNETH GODWIN
FRANK R. KEMERER

In 1983, the San Antonio Independent School District (SAISD) initiated a school choice program to improve the education of Latino students. *Multilingual thematic schools* were created to prepare selected students for study and employment in international settings by providing intensive instruction in foreign language and culture. The founder and first director of the program, Alonso Perales, believed that a schooling experience rich in the language, culture, and values of Latino students would promote higher achievement among low-income students. The multilingual program thus could serve as a prototype for schools throughout the country that serve primarily Mexican-American students.

The multilingual program evolved from a separate academy into an enrichment program in three neighborhood schools. Our study focuses on two middle schools (grades 6–8) that house the multilingual program at the middle school level. Both are located in inner-city neighborhoods. About half of each school's enrollment consists of multilingual-program students from throughout the district; students who are not in the program come from local attendance zones. One of the schools is 95% Latino, and the other, located about 35 minutes away on the other side of town, is actually 55% African-American.

We examine the numerous factors that motivate parents to choose an alternative school, including the importance of cultural and ethnic values. We then report evaluation findings regarding short-term effects on parent satisfaction and student achievement. To determine the specific effectiveness of the SAISD choice program, we asked three questions: (1) Which families choose to participate in the choice program and why do they leave their neighborhood schools? (2) What impact does the multilingual program have on student achievement? (3) What impact does the program have on parental satisfaction? The results we present are based on data collected during the first two years of a three-year study.

ISSUES CENTRAL TO THE SCHOOL CHOICE DEBATE

Choice proponents claim that schools which better match students' talents, interests, and family background will raise achievement and family satisfaction while reducing student attrition. Yet initial evidence suggests that school choice may harm already disadvantaged students. The Carnegie Foundation's 1992 report on school choice concluded that most low-income parents do not select schools on the basis of academic quality per se. In contrast, initial studies of magnet school programs show that better-educated parents frequently do take into account quality indicators linked to particular schools. These selection patterns bias enrollment in magnet schools toward upper socioeconomic status (SES) students (Archbald, 1988; Moore & Davenport, 1990; Nault & Uchitelle, 1982). When choice is statewide, early research shows that better-educated parents take advantage of this option to a significantly greater degree than less educated parents (Rubenstein, Hamar, & Adelman, 1992; Willms & Echols, 1992).

By taking the best students out of attendance-zone schools, magnet and thematic choice schools might reduce educational benefits for those students left behind. If the best students leave a school, the "pull-up" effect that good students have on other students decreases. In addition, if the most interested and involved parents enroll their children in choice schools, attendance-zone schools may have less political leverage at budget time due to lack of parental support.

A second set of empirical questions centers around evaluation methodology: Can researchers attribute differences between the amount learned at choice versus neighborhood schools to the school programs, or do unmeasured variables account for differences in learning? Failure to control for prior family characteristics has been a major weakness in the evaluation of many choice programs. Research shows that the number of children in the household, the mother's employment status, the parents' religious preferences and values, the structure of the family, and the family's participation in welfare programs significantly influence educational performance (Hanushek, 1992; Haveman, Wolfe, & Spaulding, 1991).

Even when researchers adjust for such characteristics, they may not take into account the critical variable of having parents who choose to participate in school choice programs. If two children have similar socioeconomic characteristics, cognitive abilities, and past academic performance, the entrance of only one of the two children into a school choice program indicates that the two families possess different values about education. Is the subsequent difference in their performance a function of differences between family values or differences between the schools? This problem of selection bias plagues evaluations that compare students in choice programs with students whose parents did not choose to send them to such programs. The research reported below at least partially overcomes selection bias by comparing students who actually enrolled in the choice program with similar students who attempted to enroll but could not because of space limitations.

PUBLIC SCHOOL CHOICE IN SAN ANTONIO

SAISD enrolls just over 60,000 students. Latinos comprise 81%, African-Americans 12%, and Anglos 7%. Approximately 80% of the district's students qualify for free or reduced-price meals. In addition to the two middle schools we investigated, one high school offers the thematic school program. All three schools also enroll regular students from their respective neighborhoods. Multilingual-program students receive district transportation to and from the schools. Students apply in the fifth grade and are selected on the basis of test scores, grades, and teacher and parent recommendations. Students enroll in the sixth grade and make a commitment to continue in the program through high school. The program admits no new students after the sixth grade.

The multilingual program admitted a total of 675 students into the sixth grade in 1992–93. Another 307 applicants, most of whom qualified academically, could not enroll because of space restrictions. In this chapter we refer to all those who applied to the program as *choosing* and those who did not as *nonchoosing*. Among the former, we refer to all those whom the program enrolled as *enrollees* and those who applied but were not admitted as *nonadmits*. The district does not have a formal waiting list, since officials do not want to foster unrealistic expectations among parents. Many parents, however, continue to pressure school officials to admit their children, and they occasionally succeed when vacancies materialize before school opens in the fall. Though oversubscribed, the multilingual program remains the district's only intradistrict choice option. Note that this may well be a source of selection bias when we empirically compare these parents with so-called nonchoosers.

Since its inception, the program has emphasized integrating language study with other courses. For example, students in eighth-grade U.S. history researched and identified political and economic relationships between the United States and the country whose language they were studying (Perales, n.d., p. 8). Today, multilingual-program students have a choice of Spanish, French, German, Japanese, Latin, and Russian. Students study their chosen language one period a day in the sixth grade and two periods a day in later grades. The extended study time in the seventh grade enables teachers to include cultural components in the instructional program. Extracurricular activities provide further language enrichment, and students frequently participate in regional and statewide language competitions. Teachers of both regular and multilingual sixth-grade students began a team-teaching program in 1993 to integrate cultural concepts and materials in all academic subjects. The integration of cultural components throughout school life gives researchers the opportunity to evaluate the extent to which immersion in their own culture enhances Latino students' performance. A drawback of the program is that this immersion context does not exist for African-Americans, as there is no instruction in any African language or culture.

During its early years, the program operated as a school within a school, with a separate faculty. In 1988, political infighting and charges of elitism and "skimming" led to the program's conversion from a separatist academy to a thematic program. Now multilingual-program students take all classes except foreign language with regular students. As a practical matter, however, a number of multilingual students remain separated from regular students through honors and enriched classes. Our interviews with district administrators revealed that teachers and administrators at attendance-zone schools still worry that by removing talented students the program harms neighborhood schools.

SAISD officials recognized the skimming issue and addressed it in detail in a recent study. The study attempted to determine whether the overall aggregate test scores at all schools would change significantly if multilingual-program students were returned to their neighborhood schools (Cadena & Walling, 1994). The SAISD report found that because only a few multilingual program students come from any one attendance-zone school, overall school performance at only one of fifteen SAISD middle schools would be significantly affected by their return. For the purposes of our study, it was assumed that their return would not affect the test scores of other students in the school.

The SAISD report asserts that because the percentage of students who leave an attendance-zone school is small, skimming does not harm the remaining students; it does, however, also observe that taking a few students from many schools and placing them in the two multilingual schools creates a critical mass of high-performing students. SAISD and multilingual school administrators believe that the presence of so many high-performing students at thematic schools not only benefits the multilingual students but also has a "pull-up" effect on students in these schools who are not part of the program. Students "benefit from the enriched settings for instruction and social interaction (with talented children), and also from the expectations of students, parents, and school staff concerning outcomes of schooling appropriate to these students" (Cadena & Walling, 1994, p. 10).

ASSESSING CLAIMS ABOUT SCHOOL CHOICE

Past research suggests the following hypotheses about which families choose to participate in choice programs, what impact these programs will have on student achievement, and what impact these programs will have on parental satisfaction:

- Who participates?

    Families of higher SES
    Families that stress the importance of education, religion, and cultural values
    Children with higher levels of academic performance
    Parents who are less satisfied with their child's attendance-zone school
    Parents who are more involved in their child's educational activities

- What is the impact on student achievement?

    Children admitted to choice programs will have larger gains in test scores than children who applied but were not admitted.
    Children from choosing families will have larger gains in test scores than children from nonchoosing families.
    Children immersed in their own culture through thematic choice

programs will show larger gains in test scores than children whose choice programs do not relate directly to their own culture.

• What is the impact on parental satisfaction?

Parents who enroll their child in a choice program will be more satisfied with their child's school.

Parents who attempt to enroll their child in a choice program and are unsuccessful will be less satisfied with their child's school.

Parents who enroll their child in a choice program will become more involved in their child's school.

Parents who attempt to enroll their child in a choice program and are unsuccessful will become less involved.

To assess these claims we mailed questionnaires to two groups of *choosing* families in the fall of 1992: those whose children enrolled in the multilingual schools, and those whose children applied to these schools but could not enroll due to limited enrollment space. We made available English and Spanish versions of the questionnaires. In addition to the above groups, we surveyed by telephone a stratified random sample of *nonchoosing* families who did not attempt to participate in the choice program. The telephone survey sample of 3,470 students was stratified by grade levels. The combined data set of the three groups contains 1,758 cases or families: 1,325 families who did not attempt to participate in the choice program, 336 families who applied and enrolled in the program, and 97 families who applied and were not admitted. A year later, in 1993, we conducted a follow-up survey of these same families to obtain comparative information.

Response rates were 48% for enrollee families, 53% for nonadmit families, and 39% for nonchoosing families. Although the reported response rates may seem low, they are higher than average for mail surveys to comparable groups (see Marín & Marín, 1991). Nonetheless, to identify possible sample bias, we compared survey respondents with the applicant population, as provided by SAISD, on key demographic variables and found only two significant differences: Latinos and employed women are underrepresented among choosing respondents. A demographic comparison of nonchoosing respondents with the 1992 U.S. census data for the city of San Antonio indicates no significant sample bias.

The survey requested standard socioeconomic and demographic information as well as opinions regarding children's past educational experiences, the extent of parental involvement with children's education, and the relative value placed on education. (In this chapter, we use the terms *parent* and *parental* inclusively to refer to any adult, relative, or guardian who is legally responsible for the child.) The questionnaires sent to choosing families also requested information about how families learned of the program and the factors they considered in deciding to participate. SAISD provided achievement percentiles, grade levels, and normal curve equivalents (NCE) on the Norm-Referenced Assessment Program for Texas (NAPT) for all students included in the family surveys.

Our analysis of this data as it relates to the three central questions is presented below. For the most part, our results support the hypotheses posited about which families choose and about the impact on student achievement and parental satisfaction.

WHICH FAMILIES CHOOSE AND WHY?

To determine whether choosing families differ from nonchoosing families, we examined socioeconomic and demographic characteristics of the children and their parents, including factors that might create stress on the household, such as unemployment, and the child's education, including such indicators as parents' satisfaction with the attendance-zone school and measures of the child's academic performance. (See Table 3.1 for list of variables and their measures.) Because the SAISD choice program enrolls only sixth graders, we confine our analysis to children in the sixth grade who took the math and reading portions of the NAPT in both 1992 and 1993.

The analyses described below show that the driving forces in becoming a choosing family are the mother's education, high parental educational expectations, and the student's past academic performance. Our analyses of which families choose a public thematic school as an alternative to neighborhood schools support the hypotheses concerning higher SES, academic performance, and parental involvement.

Bivariate Analysis

The first part of our analysis provides statistics that describe the characteristics of each group. Table 3.2 provides a simple overview of the proportional differences among the surveyed groups on some family characteristics, including student test scores. We then used the standard statistical test (*t*-test) to determine whether the observed differences (1)

Table 3.1: Definitions of Variables

Variables	Operationalization
Gender of child	Dummy = 0 if male, 1 if female
Female (male) education	1 = < 9th grade, 2 = some high school, 3 = high school graduate, 4 = some college, 5 = college graduate
Female (male) employment	Dummy = 0 if not employed full-time, 1 if employed full-time
Family income	1 = 0–2,999, 2 = 3,000–4,999, 3 = 5,000–7,499, 4 = 7,500–9,999, 5 = 10,000–14,999, 6 = 15,000–19,999, 7 = 20,000–24,999, 8 = 25,000–34,999
Receiving assistance	Dummy = 0 if not receiving AFCD or Medicaid, 1 if receiving AFCD or Medicaid
Number of children	Continuous variable, 1–8
Two-parent family	Dummy = 0 if not married, 1 if married
Poor	Dummy = 0 if family income less than $10,000
Education expectation for child	1 = some high school, 2 = high school graduate, 3 = vocational school, 4 = attend college, 5 = graduate or professional school
Latino	Dummy = 0 if non-Latino, 1 if Latino
White	Dummy = 0 if nonwhite, 1 if white
Chooser	Dummy = 0 if nonchoosing family, 1 if choosing family
Child's 1992 standardized test scores	NCE for reading + NCE for math (range = 2–198)
Goods vs. education index	Importance of enough money + good place to live + good job. Reliability of scale: alpha = .67
Help at home index	Times per week parent helps with homework + reading + math + writing. Reliability of scale: alpha = .83.
School satisfaction index	Parental satisfaction with school discipline + amount child learned + school location + overall school atmosphere (1 = very dissatisfied, 2 =dissatisfied, 3 = satisfied, 4 = very satisfied)
Contact index	Times last year parent visited child's classroom + worked as volunteer + participated in fundraising + helped in classroom. Reliability of scale: alpha = .72.
School activity index	Parent attended parent-teacher conferences + joined PTA + attended PTA meetings + participated in PTA activities. Reliability of scale: alpha = .85.

between choosing and nonchoosing families and (2) between enrolled and nonadmitted families were statistically significant (see Table 3.3).

Socioeconomic and Demographic Characteristics. One of the criticisms of choice programs is that better-educated, more affluent families are more likely to participate. Our data support this expectation. Both sets of choosing parents—those whose children were enrolled and those whose children were not admitted—are more than twice as likely as nonchoosing parents to have attended college. In addition, enrollees are more than twice as likely as either nonadmits or nonchoosers to have

Table 3.2: Characteristics of Families

Characteristics of Families	Nonchoosers ($n = 517$)	Enrolled Choosers ($n = 319$)	Nonadmitted Choosers ($n = 94$)
Socioeconomic and demographic characteristics (%)			
Parents with some college	12	32	30
Parents with less than 9th grade	34	13	14
Annual family income $35,000 or more	8	18	7
Annual family income less than $10,000	34	20	41
Female parent unemployed	34	22	34
Receiving federal income assistance	30	12	32
Two-parent family	63	68	48
Fewer than three children	26	43	36
Ethnicity (%)			
White	4	6	5
Latino	82	75	82
African-American	13	15	12
Other racial/ethnic minority	1	4	1
Student gender: Female students (%)	32	67	58
Mean age of students	14	12	11
Students' test scores (reported as NCE)			
Math scores	27	56	48
Reading scores	27	57	46
Total scores	54	113	94

Note: Sample sizes vary based on response rates to specific questions.

annual family incomes above $35,000. Only 12% of those students accepted into the multilingual program come from families on federal assistance, compared with 32% of those who apply but are not admitted. The data in Table 3.2 suggest that the SAISD's multilingual admissions process, which requires students and parents to complete comprehensive application forms, may work against students from families with extremely low incomes, even when they qualify academically for the program. More work is required to determine which elements of the application process screen out less assertive parents.

Choosing families also tend to have fewer children. The percentage of enrollees and nonadmits from families with fewer than three children are 43% and 36%, respectively. In contrast, only 26% of nonchoosing families have fewer than three children. This may indicate that firstborns with siblings and children without siblings do better in school. Finally, the most striking difference between choosing and nonchoosing families is the preponderance of female students seeking (and gaining) admittance into the program.

Table 3.3: Differences Between Choosing and Nonchoosing Families

Variables	Nonchoosers/ Choosers[a]	Nonadmitted Choosers/ Enrolled Choosers[b]
Family demographic characteristics		
Female parent education	10.74	n.s.
Male parent education	9.32	n.s.
Family income	3.03	5.45
Female parent employment	4.53	n.s.
Male parent employment	n.s.	3.84
Receiving assistance	-4.80	-3.68
Two-parent family	n.s.	2.96
Number of children	-6.96	n.s.
Family values		
Importance of religion	4.89	2.20
Importance of ethnic traditions	2.22	1.95
Religious attendance	n.s.	n.s.
Goods versus education index	5.58	n.s.
Education expectation	18.13	2.59
Child's education		
Child's test score	25.30	4.58
Parents' satisfaction with previous school		
School discipline	8.86	n.s.
Amount learned	12.08	n.s.
Overall school grade	4.51	2.38
Satisfaction index	8.91	n.s.
Parental invovement in education		
Help at home index	7.74	-6.50
School contact index	-2.39	-4.84
School activity index	5.03	-3.33

[a] t–ratios indicating statistically significant differences (if > 2.00) between nonchoosers and choosers

[b] t–ratios for nonadmitted versus enrolled choosers.

Note: n.s. indicates lack of statistical significance, p is not $< .05$

Family Values. Our analysis indicates that the level of parents' educational expectations for their children significantly correlates with whether or not parents will be choosers (see Table 3.3). In addition, those families that actively choose express stronger feelings toward ethnic traditions and toward religion, most often Catholicism. Active choosers believe that discretionary income is better spent on aiding their children's education rather than on purchasing more household goods.

Child's Education. The clearest bivariate differences among nonchoosers, enrollees, and nonadmits are scores on standardized tests. Students enrolling in the multilingual program have an average NCE score of 56 for math, compared to 48 for the nonadmits and only 27 for the nonchoosers (refer to Table 3.2). These differences are highly significant statistically, as shown in Table 3.3.

Dissatisfaction with attendance-zone schools might push families toward alternatives; certainly this is the case for parents who choose private schools (Martinez, Kemerer, & Godwin, 1993; Witte & Rigdon, 1992). This is not true for SAISD public school choosers. They are substantially more satisfied with their child's neighborhood school than nonchoosing families (refer to Table 3.3). Choosers are also more involved in their child's education through homework assistance, contact with schools, and participation in school activities. Surprisingly, parents of nonadmits are more involved than parents of enrollees.

Multivariate Analysis

We next turn to multivariate analytical methods to study the relative importance of each family and student characteristic in explaining who chooses, how students' test scores change over time, and how parental satisfaction changes over time. Because students cannot apply for the multilingual program until grade 5, we limited our analysis of nonchoosing families to those with students in grades 5 and above. We also excluded any families with missing information, such as missing student test scores. To determine the characteristics that best predict who chooses, we used probit analysis, a regression technique for dependent variables that have a limited range of values. If the parents attempted to enroll their child in the multilingual program, their score as a choosing family is 1. Otherwise, the score is zero.

We initially placed in the probit model all the factors that prior research indicated might affect choice and that we found statistically significant in our first, bivariate analysis. These simplified models are presented. In the best-fitting model, five of these are statistically significant in distinguishing between choosers and nonchoosers: the child's gender, the mother's education, the parents' educational expectations, the child's standardized achievement test scores in reading and math, and the level of parental involvement in educational activities at home (see Table 3.4). Overall, this probit model correctly predicted 84% of the cases. The full models are available from the authors, but they do not reveal any additional substantive effects.

We used path analysis to better understand how the significant variables relate to each other and to the parents' choice of the multilingual program. Although path analysis is based on ordinary least squares regression and, for that reason, the final paths to being a chooser are

Table 3.4: Effect of Selected Variables on the Probability of Families Choosing and Being Accepted to the Multilingual Program (Probit Estimates)

	Choosing	Accepted
Variables (Probit Coefficient)		
Female student	.66*	.34*
Mother's education	.17*	n.s.
Educational expectation for child	.37*	.17***
Child's 1992 standardized test scores	.04*	.02*
Parental help at home index	.07**	n.s.
Family income	n.s.	.79*
Number of families	615	353
Cases of choosing/accepted families	353	301
Correctly predicted	84%	86%
Dhrymes pseudo R^2	.5	.14

Note: "Choosing" includes families of multilingual enrollees and nonadmits plus nonchoosing families with children in grades 5–8; "Accepted" includes only families of multilingual enrollees and nonadmits. Does not include children in grades 1–4.

* Variable is statistically significant at the $p < .001$ level (one-tail).

** Variable is statistically significant at the $p < .01$ level (one-tail).

*** Variable is statistically significant at the $p < .05$ level (one-tail).

slightly biased, we believe that the paths shown are quite reliable. The t-ratios and the Dhrymes pseudo R^2 in the probit analysis are almost exactly the same as those in the path analysis.

Figure 3.1 shows the results of this analysis. The number reported beside the arrow pointing from test scores to public school choice (.49) indicates that test scores have the strongest impact on whether parents choose the multilingual program. This is no surprise given that superior academic performance is a requirement for application to the program. More important, however, two variables stand out because of their centrality to all other variables in the model: mother's education and educational expectations. Mother's education not only has a direct impact on choice; it also indirectly affects choice through parents' participation in the child's education at home, educational expectations, and the child's test scores. In addition to the direct effect that high parental expectations have on choice, they indirectly affect choice through parents' participation in the child's education at home and test scores. Being a female student has a direct effect as well as an indirect effect through educational expectations. Being Latino has a negative impact on choice through its substantial effect on mother's education.

Of all the family and student characteristics we initially analyzed, only four significantly influence the likelihood of acceptance into the SAISD multilingual program: gender of child, parents' educational ex-

Figure 3.1: Path Diagram of the Decision to Choose a Public Multilingual School

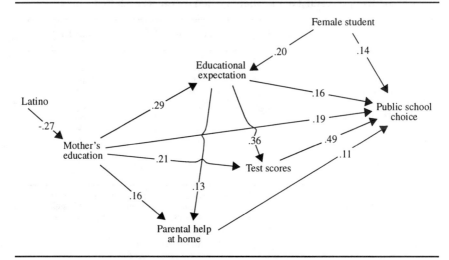

pectations, standardized test scores, and family income (Table 3.4). In addition, a path analysis (not shown) found that the mother's education has important indirect effects on program admittance through its impact on test scores and educational expectations.

In summary, our analysis of who chooses and who is accepted into a public thematic school as an alternative to neighborhood schools supports hypotheses concerning higher socioeconomic status, academic performance, and parental involvement. The results do not support the expectations that traditional religious values and parental dissatisfaction with the previous school would lead to greater participation in choice programs.

DOES THE CHOICE PROGRAM AFFECT ACHIEVEMENT?

We hypothesized that both being in a thematic school and being from a choosing family would have positive impacts on academic performance. The results of our data analysis support these hypotheses. To determine whether or not the multilingual program had an impact on student learning in math and reading over one year, we compared the change in enrollees' NCE math and reading scores with those of non-admits and those of students from nonchoosing families. It is important to note that the primary purpose of the multilingual program is to teach students foreign-language skills and cultural awareness, not to increase their math and reading achievement levels. In later stages of our study, we will seek to determine how effective the program is in these areas. However, as noted earlier, the multilingual program is now well integrated into the regular curriculum. Given the academic qualifications of the multilingual students and the general emphasis on curricular rigor at the multilingual schools, we believe there is merit in comparing the impact of the multilingual schools versus nonmultilingual schools on student reading and math achievement. These comparisons will also help us learn more about the role the act of choosing plays in increasing student achievement. The presence of the group of nonadmitted students allows us to separate the effects of being from a choosing family from the effects of attending a choice school. A *t*-test comparing the enrollees with the nonadmits shows that math and reading NCE scores increased for enrollees but declined for nonadmitted students. The difference in these average gains and losses was statistically significant.

Can we attribute this difference to the multilingual program, or are other factors operating? To answer this question, we factored in the influence of other variables: family background, student past performance, values, and parents' educational expectations. Despite the inclusion of all of these factors, the multivariate analysis shows that participation in the multilingual program has a statistically significant positive impact on both math and reading performance.

In addition to participation in the program, two other factors also predict changes in math and reading scores: prior test scores and parental expectations (see Table 3.5). The effect of prior test scores, is, as expected, negative. This reflects the regression-toward-the-mean effect that typically occurs in any study of change.[1]

The effects of parental expectations are positive and clearly significant, but not as important as participating in the multilingual program. To ensure that the statistical significance of the multilingual-program effect is not due to its correlation to high family expectations for the child, we removed the program variable from the regression equation. Its removal reduced the variance explained to 4% for math and 9% for reading.

Although the total variation in changes in math and reading scores that we can explain is modest—16% and 11%, respectively—we believe these findings are substantively very significant. The measurement error in test scores is high from one year to the next, and standardized test scores are notoriously inefficient measures of change when the period examined is only one year. In such a situation, unless the impact of a

Table 3.5: Reduced Regression of Change in Math and Reading
Scores on Background Variables of Choosing Students

Variables	Math		Reading	
	Beta	*t*-value	Beta	*t*-value
Prior test score	-.297*	-5.64	-.381*	-7.35
Parents' expectation for education	.124**	2.35	.137**	2.69
Participation in multilingual program	.199**	3.78	.205*	3.93
Constant		3.243		3.823
N		335		338
R²		.156		.111

* Variable is statistically significant at the *p* < .01 level (one-tail).
** Variable is statistically significant at the *p* < .001 level (one-tail).

program is particularly powerful, it is unlikely to have a statistically significant effect, even if the program actually is quite influential (King, Keohane, & Verba, 1994).

Do choice programs have a negative effect on students who apply but are turned down? No. We compared the 1992 and 1993 NCE scores of the nonadmits who remained in neighborhood schools with the students from nonchoosing families. Math and reading scores dropped for both groups, but after controlling for regression to the mean, being from a choosing family emerges as a positive influence on test scores even if the child does not enroll in a choice school.

DOES CHOICE AFFECT PARENTAL
SATISFACTION AND INVOLVEMENT?

As a part of our fall 1992 survey, we asked parents to evaluate aspects of the neighborhood school in which their child was enrolled during the previous school year. The results showed that choosing parents were significantly more satisfied with their children's schools, more active in school functions, and more involved in their children's homework and other educational activities than nonchoosing parents (reported earlier in Martinez et al., 1993). Choosing parents had fewer contacts with the school than nonchoosing parents, possibly reflecting fewer academic problems with their children. When we compared enrollees with nonadmits, we found little difference in satisfaction level. Parents of nonadmitted students, however, reported significantly more involvement in school functions, contact with teachers and administrators, and participation in their children's educational activities than parents of enrollees.

Did the satisfaction and involvement levels of parents change following admission of some, but not others, into the middle school multilingual program? Our follow-up survey a year later (fall 1993) showed that the satisfaction levels of nonchoosing parents and their participation in school activities remained the same. The number of contacts with the school declined significantly, probably indicating lower levels of contact between parents and teachers when students leave elementary school and enter middle school.

Parents of nonadmitted children, as we hypothesized, had lower levels of satisfaction. Although the overall satisfaction level, contacts with teachers and administrators, and participation in school events such as PTA meetings all declined significantly for both groups of choosing families (see Table 3.6), after controlling for regression to the mean, we found that while satisfaction of nonadmits had declined significantly, that of enrollees had not. To determine if the drop in satisfaction among choosing parents simply reflected a regression to the mean, we regressed change in satisfaction scores from 1992 to 1993 onto the satisfaction score from 1992 and dummy variables for being the parent of an enrolled student and for being a nonadmitted student. We also included the background variables used in analyzing the fall 1992 satisfaction levels. The reduced equation indicates that parents of children who applied and were not admitted experienced significantly greater declines in school satisfaction. These declines were over and above the effect of regression toward the mean. The decline in satisfaction among parents of enrollees, however, appears to be an artifact created by regression to the mean.

Table 3.6: Change in Average Parental Satisfaction, Contact with School, and Participation in School Activities

Groups	Satisfaction Index 1992	1993	Contact Index 1992	1993	Activity Index 1992	1993
Nonchoosers	2.15	2.09	3.13	2.06	1.70	1.83
t-value for change	.29		3.56**		-.74	
Enrolled choosers	3.27	2.00	2.66	2.28	1.86	1.72
t-value for change	3.71*		2.58**		2.50**	
Nonadmitted choosers	3.21	2.11	4.09	3.68	2.06	1.72
t-value for change	3.02*		1.58		2.68*	

* Variable is statistically significant at the $p < .01$ level (one-tail).

** Variable is statistically significant at the $p < .001$ level (one-tail).

CONCLUSIONS

The San Antonio multilingual program was designed to provide an intensive learning experience in language and culture for Latino parents desiring such a program for their children. Given the ethnic makeup of SAISD, they remain the primary beneficiaries of the program.

Because the multilingual program can accommodate only a limited number of students, admission is selective. Thus it should come as no surprise that the single most important predictor of who will be admitted to the program is student test score performance. Our analysis also reveals that parental education—especially the education of the mother—in combination with parental aspirations for their children's education plays a major role in identifying choosing parents. The importance of the mother's education and parents' educational expectations for their child are critical variables that policy-makers must consider when designing choice programs. If they do not, choice programs are likely to lead to stratification of school enrollment by SES.

Noteworthy, too, is that the female child is the primary beneficiary of the choice program. Female students are more likely to be in the top 20% of their class and thus more likely to qualify for the program. Female students also may be more interested in language and learning than their male counterparts and thus more likely to apply for admission. Interviews with choosing and nonchoosing families will enrich our understanding of what motivates parents and students in making educational decisions.

While designed for language enrichment, the multilingual program enhances student math and reading performance: Within one year of beginning the program, students were learning more than students not in the program. At the same time, our findings demonstrate that just being from a choosing family has a positive effect on student math and reading achievement—even if the child does not enroll in the choice program.

How well the multilingual program performs in promoting language achievement awaits further study. The original idea for the multilingual program was to immerse Latino students in the Spanish language and Latino culture. As discussed above, the founder and first director of the multilingual program envisioned schools that would encourage Latinos to learn and excel by integrating their own cultural history into the entire curriculum and by providing them extensive training in Spanish. When perceptions of elitism and political infighting threatened continuation of the immersion concept, the current multilingual program became the compromise solution.

Despite the compromise, it may be possible to test the effectiveness of the original idea by comparing the performance of those Latinos who chose Spanish and whose other courses stress the Latino culture with the performance of other students in the multilingual program. Latinos who choose Spanish can be compared both with Latinos who choose other language options and with non-Latino students. As sixth-grade students in the multilingual program have only one period a day for language study and the immersion into the cultural elements expands in the seventh grade, tests of the success of cultural immersion must wait until students have completed at least the seventh grade.

With only one year of change reflected in the data and with the absence of test scores reflecting foreign-language achievement, our conclusions regarding the academic impacts of the multilingual program must be tentative. If, however, at the end of the three-year evaluation project the underlying pattern of these results remains unchanged, then SAISD administrators and school board members must consider the impact of the program on those who are not admitted. While the multilingual program improves the performance of enrolled students, it contributes to a lack of satisfaction and involvement in school activities by parents whose children could not gain admittance. This reduction in satisfaction and involvement by parents of nonadmitted children is not offset by similar increases in support by parents of enrolled children.

The first phase of this study has demonstrated that the relationship between school choice and impacts on students is more complex than many assume. Both coming from a choosing family and going to a choice school have significant positive impacts on academic performance. During the next phase of the research, we will expand our study to look more intensively at the characteristics of the multilingual schools in comparison with attendance-zone schools and private schools participating in a privately funded voucher program in San Antonio. Through this investigation we hope to learn the ways school characteristics are linked to student outcomes.

NOTE

1. Regression toward the mean occurs in numerous areas from test scores to baseball batting averages. To understand how it works, imagine that two students, John and Jane, take a test. Assume that both students' true ability places them at the 50th percentile. However, on this particular day, John is sick and he is unlucky in his guesses. Jane, in contrast, feels great, concentrates hard, and is also very lucky. On this day, John might receive a score of 40 while

Jane might receive a 60 in her guesses. Given that their true abilities are 50, we would predict that if they took a similar test on a different day, John's score would move upward toward 50 and Jane's score would move downward toward 50. A similar phenomenon occurs in baseball. A hitter who has been very lucky in May, has several "bloop" hits, and has been "in the zone" for the entire month might be hitting over .400. However, we know that he is unlikely to stay lucky or in the zone for the entire season. Therefore, we can predict that his batting average will fall toward the average for all players.

Because the mean score is, by definition, the average score for a group, people who were lucky on a given test day are more likely to be found with scores above the mean while people who were unlucky on that day have a higher probability of scoring below the mean. Thus, on average, the scores of people who tested above the mean on the first test will drop. For similar reasons, the scores of people who tested below the mean on the first test will rise.

REFERENCES

Archbald, D. (1988). *Magnet schools, voluntary desegregation and public choice theory: Limits and possibilities in a big city school system.* Unpublished Ph.D. dissertation, University of Wisconsin–Madison.

Cadena, J., & Walling, S. (1994). *The performance of multilingual students on the Texas assessment of academic skills* (Report No. 16). San Antonio, TX: San Antonio Independent School District.

Carnegie Foundation for the Advancement of Teaching. (1992). *School choice: A special report.* Princeton, NJ: Carnegie Foundation.

Hanushek, E. (1992). The trade-off between child quantity and quality. *Journal of Political Economy, 100,* 84–117.

Haveman, R., Wolfe, B., & Spaulding, J. (1991). Childhood events and circumstances influencing high school completion. *Demography, 28,* 133–157.

King, G., Keohane, R., & Verba, S. (1994). *Scientific inference in qualitative research.* Princeton, NJ: Princeton University Press.

Marín, G., & Marín, B. V. (1991). *Research with Hispanic populations.* Newbury Park, CA: Sage.

Martinez, V., Kemerer, F., & Godwin, K. (1993, May). *Who chooses and why? Baseline demographic report, San Antonio School Choice Project.* Denton: University of North Texas, Center for the Study of Education Reform. (ERIC Document Reproduction Service No. EA 025 031).

Moore, D., & Davenport, S. (1990). School choice: The new school sorting machine. In W. Boyd & H. Walberg (Eds.), *Choice in education: Potential and problems* (pp. 187–224). Berkeley, CA: McCutchan.

Nault, R., & Uchitelle, S. (1982). School choice in the public sector: A case study of parental decision making. In M. E. Manley-Casimir (Ed.), *Family choice in schooling: Issues and dilemmas* (pp. 85–90). Lexington, MA: Lexington Books.

Perales, A. (n.d.). *Characteristics of a multilingual school as an "effective school" model for Mexican American students: Research implications* (Education Paper No. 9). San Antonio, TX: San Antonio Independent School District.

Rubenstein, M., Hamar, R., & Adelman, N. (1992). *Minnesota's open enrollment option* (U.S. Department of Education Contract No. 89089001). Washington, DC: Policy Studies Associates.

Willms, J. D., & Echols, F. (1992). Alert and inert clients: The Scottish experience of parental choice of schools. *Economics of Education Review, 11,* 339–350.

Witte, J., & Rigdon, M. (1992, September). *Private school choice: The Milwaukee low-income voucher experiment.* Paper presented at the annual meeting of the American Political Science Association, Chicago.

CHAPTER 4

Equity and Choice in Detroit

VALERIE E. LEE
ROBERT G. CRONINGER
JULIA B. SMITH

The central intent of choice is to increase opportunities for all children to receive a high-quality education. In theory, this would improve the educational opportunities offered to disadvantaged families. But an equally important consideration is whether choice will decrease or increase social stratification. The question is not easily answered. We have few evaluations of choice programs in settings with large low-income and minority populations (see Chapters 3 and 6, this volume). An even smaller number of evaluations investigate the effects of choice over time, and none that we know of consider the aggregate effects of choice, that is, the long-term effects on all public schools in a given geographic area. Nonetheless, choice has been offered as a solution to the educational inadequacies that plague urban schools, so it is important to consider just what effects choice might have in these settings.

We argue that the benefits of choice can be seen from two policy perspectives: public and private. If we emphasize the private effects of choice, that is, the increased educational opportunities that could be made available to *individual* poor and minority families, choice could be empowering. It could provide urban families with educational possibilities that they did not have before, possibilities that resemble the opportunities available to affluent families in surrounding school districts. If we emphasize the public effects of choice, that is, the *aggregate* effects, the benefits are far less clear. There is reason to believe that choice would accentuate inequities between schools, exacerbating the problems that characterize urban education. These two perspectives highlight important and conflicting considerations about choice as an educational policy option. Unfortunately, the public-interest perspective is often absent from debates about the merits of choice.

This chapter reveals how parents' support for wider school choices stems from their immediate local experience with neighborhood schools. This is linked to sharp differences in the perceived quality of inner-city and suburban schools. We also consider the possible stratifying effects of school choice in the Detroit area, posing three empirical questions about choice:

1. Who is in favor of choice and who is opposed to it?
2. What qualities do parents consider most important when choosing schools for children?
3. Who is most likely to exercise choice, and what effect might student transfers have on schools with large enrollments of minority and low-income families?

We review research relevant to these questions. Then, reporting our new empirical findings, we address each question within the context of the Detroit metropolitan area. In concluding, we return to a consideration of the private versus public benefits of choice for families and urban communities.

PREVIOUS RESEARCH ON SCHOOL CHOICE

Who Wants Choice? Who Doesn't?

Many who favor school choice are motivated by a desire to leave an undesirable school. We might therefore anticipate that disadvantaged families, who typically have access to less effective schools, favor choice. Using evidence from existing survey data, Plank, Schiller, Schneider, and Coleman (1993) concluded that low-income and minority families would take advantage of expanded choices if made available. In an investigation of the effects of a tuition tax deduction plan on choice behavior in Minnesota, Darling-Hammond and Kirby (1985, 1988) found that low-income parents were more likely to consider alternatives to their local public schools. Similarly, Strate and Wilson (1991) found on average that low-income families in Detroit favor school choice policies.

Suburban school and private school administrators, as well as the families they serve, however, may oppose choice. Suburban school administrators and families may not want to make the changes in school programs required to accommodate students from diverse social and educational backgrounds, particularly if they think changes will undermine the quality of their local schools. Private school administrators and families may also be reluctant to enroll choice students if doing so entails compliance with state regulations in such areas as teaching certification, curriculum content, or students' rights. In their Minnesota study, Darling-Hammond and Kirby (1985, 1988) reported that upper-income parents had less reason to consider alternatives because of their access to better schools. Strate and Wilson (1991) also found that suburban families hold less favorable attitudes about choice policies generally.

What Qualities Do Parents Consider Important in Choosing Schools?

In Chapter 2, Wells reported on a recent study of low-income minority parents participating in St. Louis's metropolitan desegregation plan. The evidence suggests that in selecting between the 160 suburban schools available to their children, very few parents considered the specific educational offerings of individual schools. Rather they relied on anecdotal information and the perceived social status of the school. Actually, most parents believed that suburban schools were better than those in the city, so in their minds there was little risk of making a bad choice (see also Wells, 1993). Willms and Echols (1993) discovered similar beliefs among the families in Scotland who decided to send their children to schools outside their neighborhood. Lower-status families believed that if they sent their children to schools that served higher-status families, they would do better academically.

Families rely on anecdotal information or seemingly superficial assessments of school quality because to do otherwise requires gathering substantial amounts of information, much of which is not easily obtained from schools. These information needs increase dramatically as the choices provided by schools become more complex and varied (e.g., choices between programs with different academic emphases, instructional philosophies, or discipline policies). Elmore (1990) has argued that even in the health care field, where greater effort is made to inform families about the choices available to them, the task of making an informed decision can be extremely difficult, if not overwhelming.

When the schools available to families are equally effective, the choices that parents make will have few educational consequences. But if schools are unequal, that is, if they present families with important and meaningful differences in educational opportunities, then uninformed decisions may not turn out to be beneficial. They may even be harmful. This may be especially problematic for poor and minority families who must consider not only a school's overall effectiveness but its effectiveness with children who come from backgrounds like their own. Bryk, Lee, and Holland (1993) demonstrate that schools with the highest average achievement levels are not necessarily those in which low-income and minority students do best. The risks of uninformed decisions are probably greatest for those who, at least in theory, have the most to gain from exercising choice.

Will School Choice Increase Social Stratification?

Exemplifying the argument supporting the special benefits of choice for disadvantaged families, Coons and Sugarman (1978) suggest that the absence of choice in public education works against the ideals of equal educational opportunity. "The poorer the family," they write, "the less its ability to furnish home remedies for educational ailments . . . the more difficult it is to escape an underfinanced or mismanaged public school system by changing residences . . . the less its ability to induce the public system to provide the alternative classroom or program that it prefers" (p. 26). Boaz (1991) argues that choice would break the monopoly that public schools exercise over the educational needs of poor and minority families, making them more effective consumers of educational services.

Other studies are less sanguine about the participation of disadvantaged families in choice programs and the beneficial effects they would have on school districts that enroll large populations of poor and minority children. Wells (1993) found that disadvantaged minority families who participated in the St. Louis plan came from relatively more educated families headed by adults who were more assertive about their children's education. Willms and Echols (1993) similarly concluded that parents in Scotland who exercised choice had more education and more prestigious occupations than those who sent their children to neighborhood schools. They also found that parents chose schools that only marginally benefited their children in terms of examination performance, once differences in average family background between chosen and neighborhood schools were considered.

Some research also questions the effects of school choice on achieving a more equitable distribution of educational opportunities and resources. A recent study of magnet schools (Schmidt, 1994) concluded that in general they do not significantly encourage districtwide efforts to reduce racial isolation, improve racial balance, or stem "white flight." Another study of magnet programs in large cities (Moore & Davenport, 1989) concluded that choice only served to further differentiate school quality, permitting some schools to get better while many others got worse. Fine (1991) and Kozol (1991) reach similar conclusions about within-district choice in urban school districts. Such programs tend to further stratify the educational experiences of inner-city children, creating two sets of schools: those serving the poorest families and those serving less poor families.

CHOICE IN THE DETROIT METROPOLITAN AREA

School choice is a much debated topic in both the state of Michigan and the city of Detroit. The Republican governor, John Engler, was reelected in 1994 on a pro-choice platform, and he continues to call for new efforts to promote choice, including charter schools and the privatization of school services. The governor pushed for the passage of a number of statewide choice programs in his first term, though his success was limited. A statewide open enrollment plan, which included provisions for transportation and parent information, was delayed by an inability to reach an agreement about state aid for transportation, estimated at $20 million annually (Carnegie Foundation, 1992). An attempt to include the plan without the transportation provision as part of Michigan's school finance reform package also failed. The governor did manage a small victory, however, in that the new financing plan approved by voters permits state funding of charter schools.

Support for choice is strong at the local level in Detroit. A group of Detroit school board members was elected on a strong pro-choice platform in 1988. Top Detroit school administrators (including a former superintendent, Deborah McGriff, now with the Edison Project) have reflected the city's advocacy for choice. In response to the defeat of the governor's 1991 plan, which would have required within-district choice for all parents and the piloting of cross-district options in six counties, an editorial argued, "Parents and taxpayers should pressure their boards of education to hold salary increases hostage until parents are given an opportunity to hold educators directly accountable for their actions through schools of choice" ("The House vs. Choice," 1991, p. 8a).

The history of social stratification in schooling is particularly troubling in the Detroit metropolitan area. White flight began in the 1950s and accelerated with the construction of interstate highways, the availability of federally subsidized loans for suburban housing, and the 1967 race riots. Although a federal district court ordered the desegregation of Detroit's public schools by forming a metropolitan wide school system with 53 suburban school districts, the plan was overturned by the Supreme Court, which ruled that suburban districts could not be compelled to participate without proof that governmental actions had caused "an interdistrict segregatory effect" (*Milliken* v. *Bradley I*, 1974). Nonetheless, a subsequent decision, which was affirmed by the Supreme Court (*Milliken* v. *Bradley II*, 1977), required the district and state to fund extensive improvements in Detroit's educational programs to rectify the effects of racial segregation. Although the district and state were found to be in compliance in 1988, the court-ordered remedies had little effect on either white flight or the gross inequalities that characterize urban and suburban school districts in the area.

By 1980, the Detroit metropolitan area was one of the most segregated in the country (Detroit Strategic Planning Project, 1987; Farley & Frey, 1994).[1] Enrollment in the Detroit schools in 1988 was 89% African-American. Unfortunately, not only is Detroit among the most segregated cities in the country, but its children are also among the poorest. Using data from the 1990 census, the Children's Defense Fund (1992) reported that of the nation's 100 largest cities, Detroit ranked first in the proportion of children living in poverty. Nearly half (46%) of all children 18 years old or younger who live in Detroit are poor. Compared to 1980, when 31% of Detroit's children lived in poverty, this is an increase of almost 50%.

Combined with striking increases in segregation and childhood poverty over the years, the quality of Detroit public schools has deteriorated dramatically. Differences in academic achievement between Detroit and surrounding communities—measured by graduation rates or test scores—are substantial. Some of the disparity is attributable to differences in school financing. Indeed, concern over the extreme inequities in educational resources between districts in the state was a major factor prompting a change in Michigan's school finance strategy, which until recently relied heavily on local property taxes. Differences in state-equalized value-per-student stood at nearly 10 to 1 between the most and least affluent communities, with differences between Detroit and surrounding suburban districts exemplifying some of the more extreme cases. Although recent legislation eliminates property taxes as a basis for school funding, it is too early to tell how this legislation will affect ongoing finance inequities (Christoff, 1994).

RESEARCH CONTEXT

We used data from a 1991 survey to explore the possible effects of enhancing school choice for families in the Detroit metropolitan area. Since the area does not have an existing choice program, we can only speculate about the possible effects of school choice on the stratification of educational opportunities. Nonetheless, as we intend to demonstrate, our speculations do not have to be uninformed. We use these data to further clarify the three questions we posed earlier:

1. *Who wants choice? Who doesn't?* Does support for school choice vary by race, social class, and school district? Do families of the same race and social class living in different school districts feel the same way about choice? Or does their support for choice depend on the characteristics of their district and their beliefs about local school quality?
2. *What school qualities do residents believe are most important in selecting schools for children?* Do families that favor choice value different qualities than families that oppose choice? Is there a connection between the qualities that families desire and the actual or perceived characteristics of their local schools?
3. *Who is likely to exercise choice, and what might be the effects of choice on school districts with large proportions of disadvantaged students?* What do our findings and the previous attempts to pass cross-district choice plans in the state suggest about the limitations of choice in the Detroit metropolitan area? How might these limitations influence the participation of disadvantaged families in choice plans?

STUDY SAMPLE

The sample for this study is drawn from the 1991 Detroit Area Study (DAS), which consists of 1,042 households in three counties immediately surrounding Detroit (Macomb, Oakland, and Wayne counties). Macomb County includes rural and industrial areas, with a low- to middle-class conservative population. Oakland County, one of the wealthiest in the country, is composed primarily of affluent suburbs and a few high-tech industries. Detroit is located in Wayne County, which is heavily industrialized, with several mostly white working-class suburbs immediately outside of the city. Of the 49 different communities in the sample, 12 are in Macomb County, 18 in Oakland County, and 19 in Wayne County.

The DAS collects data from household heads on important current and enduring social issues. Topics for these annual surveys are conceived of by University of Michigan faculty in social science departments. The 1991 DAS was conducted by Howard Schuman. The school component, which we developed and conducted, comprised about 10 minutes of the 60-minute interview time.

The characteristics of the sampled households closely resemble the characteristics of households in the Detroit metropolitan area. About three-quarters (76.7%) of the respondents are white, about a fifth (19.7%) are African-American, with only a small fraction (3.6%) from other ethnic groups (mostly Hispanic or Arabic). Respondents range in age from 18 to 91; the majority are in their 30s and 40s. Only about half the households are comprised of currently married couples. While 74.3% of the respondents have children, only about one-third (33.8%) have school-age children. The majority of respondents live in Detroit (21.1%). Although our sample is middle-class on average (mean income of $39,747 and education of 12 years or more), considerable proportions of households can be characterized as lower or upper class.

We asked respondents whether they favored, opposed, or had no opinion about choice plans that would allow parents to send their children to any school in the state—public or private. Specifically, respondents were posed the following question:

> Many states, including Michigan, are considering funding different types of choice programs for schools. These programs would allow parents to choose any school—public or private—for their children to attend from kindergarten through high school. Would you favor or oppose these types of choice programs, or haven't you thought much about it?

Of the 1,042 respondents, about 50% said that they favored choice, 18% said that they opposed it, and 32% said that they had no opinion. Respondents who had school-age children were more likely to have an opinion about choice than not, and respondents with higher levels of family income and more education were also more likely to take a position on choice. We decided that dropping the respondents with no opinion about choice would clarify our analysis, allowing us to focus on the more meaningful (and substantial) comparison in our sample: those favoring and opposing choice. Our final sample with complete data included 710 respondents residing in 45 public school districts in the tricounty area. The large majority of this reduced sample (72.5%) favors choice.

Significant differences were observed in personal attributes and district characteristics between those who favored choice and those who opposed it. The values for respondents without opinions generally fell between these extremes. While dropping the respondents without an opinion required a substantial reduction in our sample, we also use a statistical technique in our analysis (hierarchical linear modeling) that adjusts for the reliability of estimates based on small sample sizes (Bryk & Raudenbush, 1992). We are confident that the results we report are not biased by restricting our sample to respondents with opinions about choice.

FINDINGS

Who Wants Choice? Who Doesn't?

Previous research suggests that positions on choice will vary by family characteristics and the quality of local schools. To test this hypothesis, we identified two sets of measures: those that characterized respondents and those that characterized their school districts. Family characteristics included respondents' social class (a composite value for household income and education stemming from a principal components analysis) and whether or not respondents had school-age children, belonged to a minority group (mostly African-Americans), or had ever lived in inner-city Detroit. We also considered respondents' beliefs about the quality of their local schools, measured as the grade they would give the public schools in their community. We asked respondents the following question:

> Students are given grades for their work, often A as the highest grade, B, C, D, and F for fail. Suppose the public schools in your community were graded in the same way. What grade would you give to your public schools: A, B, C, D, or F?

We converted their answers into a numeric scale that ranged from 0 to 4. Survey respondents also were asked about qualitative attributes valued in their schools, data that we detail below.

We included indicators of each school district's financial resources (taxable property per student), social composition (the proportion of students receiving a free lunch), and academic achievement (the average percentage of students achieving "mastery" on Michigan's norm-referenced tests and the percentage of high school students who graduate annually).

Table 4.1: Family and District Characteristics Within and Outside Detroit

Family Characteristics	Within Detroit ($n = 152$)	Outside Detroit ($n = 558$)
Favoring choice (%)	86.18*	68.82
Belief about school quality (0–4)	1.91	2.67**
Minority (%)	86.39**	8.26
Social class	-0.50	0.23**
Years education	12.47	13.43**
Family income (in thousands)	$23.63	$46.24**
With school-age children (%)	46.71	39.78
Former Detroit residents (%)	—	49.28

District Characteristics	Detroit School District ($n = 1$)	Tri-county Districts Outside Detroit ($n = 44$)
Property value per students (SEV in thousands)	$27.00	$107.50
Students on free lunch (%)	53.76**	8.40
Average student mastery MEAP tests (%)	63.83	82.20
High school students graduating per year (%)	15.34	24.50
Resources composite	-2.78	0.06*
Minority enrollment (%)	91.55**	8.63

* $p < .01$; ** $p < .001$

Note: We tested mean differences for family characteristics with two-tailed t-tests; we tested differences for district characteristics with confidence intervals based on the distribution of districts outside Detroit.

Observed Family and District Differences. Means on all variables are displayed in Table 4.1, separately for tricounty respondents who do and do not reside in the city of Detroit. The top panel displays comparisons of family or respondent-level measures. Significantly, more Detroit residents favor school choice than non-Detroiters, 86.2% and 68.8%, respectively. These positions are inversely related to the grade respondents give to their local school districts, Detroiters giving grades to their public schools that are substantially lower than those given by residents outside of Detroit (76% of a standard deviation). We followed the standard described by Rosenthal and Rosnow (1984, p. 360). Effects larger than one-half a standard deviation (SD) are large, effects between .3 and .5 SD are moderate, effects between .1 and .3 SD are small, and effects below .1 SD are trivial.

As would be expected, given the history of segregation and poverty in the area, demographic differences between the two groups of respondents are striking. While Detroit residents are overwhelmingly minority (86.4%), almost all those outside the city are white (only 8.3% are mi-

nority). Social-class differences (.73 standard deviation) also are substantial. Social class is measured by an index which combines family
income and parents' educational levels.

Group means for school district resources or district-level measures
are displayed in the lower panel of Table 4.1. One measure of financial
resources—the state-equalized value of taxable property per student
(SEV)—is nearly four times as large for surrounding districts compared
to Detroit. The social composition of student enrollment in Detroit also
is extremely different from the social composition in surrounding districts, with the proportion of students poor enough to qualify for free
lunches and minority enrollment much higher in Detroit. Academic
characteristics vary considerably, with Detroit public schools showing
lower average mastery on state tests and considerably lower annual
graduation rates relative to the tri-county average. This rate is simply
the percentage of all students enrolled in high school who graduate
in June. The Michigan Educational Assessment Program (MEAP) tests
fourth, seventh, and tenth graders in reading and math. The tests are
objective-referenced and grade-specific. MEAP defines "mastery" as
meeting 75% of the objectives on a test. The average percentage of
students "mastering" state objectives is the sum of the percentage
meeting this criterion in reading and math divided by 6 (three grade
levels, two tests).

Mean difference on the composite measure of school resources is
very large, with Detroit almost 3 standard deviations below the average
for other school districts in the metropolitan area. We define the notion
of school district resources quite broadly. While there is a certain
amount of subjectivity, perhaps even class bias, in any measure used to
tap the desirability of schools (Wells & Crain, 1992), the school resources that we use in our study are strongly correlated with the grades
that advantaged *and* disadvantaged families gave to their local school
districts. We combined these attributes (listed in the bottom panel of
Table 4.1) into a single measure of district resources using factor weights
from a principal components analysis. The eigen-value was 2.7, captur-
ing 67% of the total variance in the four measures. Cronbach's alpha for
the composite was .83.

Table 4.1 confirms what other studies of choice have found: Poor
and minority families in school districts with a weak resource base favor
school choice as an educational policy. Children of Detroit residents,
compared to those living in other districts in the area, do less well on
state tests and are less likely to graduate from high school in four years.
Detroit residents recognize this, as they rate the quality of their public
schools considerably lower than residents outside of the city. Given the

Table 4.2: HLM Estimates of Effects of Family and
District Characteristics on Attitudes Toward School Choice

Characteristic	Model 1 Family Characteristics Only	Model 2 Family Characteristics and District Resources	Model 3 Family Characteristics, District Resources, & Detroit
Family (*n* = 710)			
Proportion favoring choice (base) [a]	0.67***	0.67***	0.67***
Social class	-0.05*	-0.05*	-0.05*
Minority status	0.18***	0.13*	0.14*
School-age children	0.01	0.02	0.02
Belief about school quality (grade)	-0.03	-0.03	-0.03
District (*n* = 45)			
Resources composite		-0.04**	-0.05*
Detroit school district			-0.04

* $p < .05$; ** $p < .01$; *** $p < .001$

[a] Position on choice coded: favor = 1, opposed = 0, no opinion = missing.

more positive opinions about choice held by residents within the city, these results suggest that Detroiters may see choice as a vehicle for accessing better schools outside of the city.

Adjusted Family and District Effects. Table 4.2 presents the results of a multivariate analysis of how family and district characteristics influence parents' positions on choice. Given the multilevel nature of our research questions (i.e., the effect of district resources on individual respondents' opinions), we used hierarchical linear modeling (HLM). What is most important to note is that HLM allows us to examine the effects of school district characteristics on opinions about choice while adjusting for differences in the characteristics of families residing in school districts. HLM thus provides a valid test of the proposition that opinions about choice are based on the quality of local schools.

Model 1 estimates effects for family-level characteristics. Included in these effects are respondents' social class, an indicator of whether the respondent belongs to a racial or ethnic minority (primarily African-American), whether the respondent has school-age children, and respondents' beliefs about the quality of the local school district. Model 2 adds estimated effects for differences in district resources, and Model 3 considers whether or not living in the Detroit school district has a unique effect on respondents' position on choice. The outcome, of course, is the probability that respondents favor choice rather than oppose it. It is expressed here as a function of not only family characteristics but the attributes of the districts in which respondents live.

Our findings strongly support previous studies of school choice. While nearly three-quarters of the respondents in our study favor choice, poor and minority families are more likely to do so, regardless of where they live. In all three models that we tested, social class is negatively associated with respondents' position on choice (coefficient = −.05); minority status is positively associated with favoring choice (coefficients = .18, .13, and .14). Beliefs about school quality are marginally significant in Model 1, but when we take the composite school measure into account, the effect is nonsignificant (though the size of the coefficient does not change). These findings indicate that family characteristics have an independent effect on opinions about choice.

Our findings also indicate that actual characteristics of school districts influence positions on choice (coefficients = −.04 and −.05). Families in districts characterized by low property wealth, high proportions of poor students, low mastery rates on the state tests, and low graduation rates are more likely to favor choice; families in districts characterized by more positive values on these measures are more likely to oppose choice. These district-level influences are independent of family-level relationships, indicating that attributes of local schools also shape family opinions about choice. The nonsignificance of the coefficient for Detroit in Model 3 indicates that these effects are not unique to Detroit but are shared more broadly in the metropolitan area.

What Qualities Do Parents Consider Important in Choosing Schools?

What type of schools might parents select if given more options? Proponents of choice assume that parents would select schools that provide the best educational experiences available. By creating a demand for greater academic achievement, choice could promote school improvement. If this market argument were valid, we would expect the parents in our sample, especially those who favor choice, to place the greatest emphasis on the academic qualities of schools.

Our study permits a limited test of this proposition. Respondents rated the relative importance of seven school qualities that they would consider when deciding where to send a child to school. We averaged the answers for each quality, higher scores indicating more important rankings (see Table 4.3). Detroit-area residents rate two nonacademic qualities of schools the highest: school safety (a mean rating of 5.11) and whether schools support their moral and ethical values (4.80). They rate

**Table 4.3: Respondent Rating of Qualities They
Consider Important in Choosing a Child's School**

School Quality Statements[a]	Mean Rating $(n = 704)$[b]
The school is safe (Safety)	5.11
The school supports moral and ethical values I want my children to learn (My values)	4.80
The school requires students to take a lot of classes in basic subjects, like math, English, and science (Many requirements)[c]	4.79
The school offers a wide variety of courses (Variety of courses)	4.36
School district is strict (Strict discipline)	3.68
The school is close to parents' home or workplace (Close proximity)	3.23
The children's parents have educational and occupational backgrounds similar to mine (Similar to me)	2.15

[a] We asked respondents to answer the following questions: "People consider a number of different things when they choose a school for their children. Even if you do not have school-age children, please tell me the three qualities on the list that you would consider most important in choosing a child's school. Which quality would you consider to be the least important?" The qualities are worded exactly as we presented them to respondents during the interview.

[b] Respondents ranked their important qualities most important, second most important, and third most important. We used this information to calculate mean scores, coding their answers as follows: 7 = most important quality; 6 = second most important quality; 5 = third most important quality; 3 = qualities not selected; and 1 = least important quality.

[c] The original wording for this item was "The school has a good academic reputation." Field testing indicated that respondents associated this aspect of schools most clearly with course requirements.

academic qualities—strong academic course requirements (which we consider a proxy for academic reputation) and a varied set of course offerings—toward the top of the list (ratings of 4.79 and 4.36, respectively). Strict school discipline (3.68) and proximity to parents' home or workplace (3.23) are considered less important. The social composition of schools, that is, the educational and occupational backgrounds of other parents, is rated least important.

Table 4.4 compares ratings for respondents who favor choice and those who oppose it (columns 2 and 3), as well as respondents who live in Detroit and those who reside in surrounding school districts (columns 4 and 5). Given the differences in position on choice, as well as the differences in actual school experiences on which those positions are based, we might expect some variation in how respondents rank these qualities. The overall rankings of school qualities for these groups, however, are strikingly similar. Nonetheless, there are important exceptions. Those who oppose choice rank academic requirements significantly higher than those who favor choice (5.01 vs. 4.70). Residents of

Table 4.4: Mean Ratings of School Qualities for Respondents Who Favor and Oppose Choice and Respondents Residing In and Outside Detroit

School quality	Opinion on Choice		Residence	
	Favor ($n = 512$)	Oppose ($n = 192$)	In Detroit ($n = 512$)	Outside Detroit ($n = 192$)
Safety	5.15	5.00	5.36*	5.04
My values	4.85	4.66	4.63	4.84
Many requirements	4.70	5.01*	4.56	4.85
Variety of courses	4.29	4.54	4.09	4.43*
Strict discipline	3.73	3.55	4.04**	3.58
Close proximity	3.25	3.15	3.26	3.25
Similar to me	2.11	2.24	2.16	2.15

* $p < .05$; ** $p < .001$

Note: We tested mean group differences with two-tailed tests.

Detroit also place a somewhat higher value on school safety (5.36 vs. 5.04) and strict discipline (4.04 vs. 3.58) than residents in surrounding school districts. Residents outside of Detroit also rank course variety somewhat higher than those in the city.

Our results do not support the contention that advocacy of choice is motivated solely by a desire for schools with higher academic standards or more comprehensive curricula. Recent media reports highlight the prevalence of guns in schools, as well as the dangers of attending inner-city schools, so it is not surprising that Detroit-area residents put safety at the top of the list. Concern about student behavior probably also accounts for the relatively stronger emphasis placed on safety and school discipline by Detroit residents.

Our results vary somewhat from other reports of how parents choose the schools that their children attend. Social status of parents and proximity, for example, are qualities described as especially important in other studies; however, Detroit-area respondents describe these considerations as relatively unimportant. This discrepancy may reflect problems that parents have in translating their values into action. Attributes, such as school safety or moral values, can be difficult to determine. Other school qualities or proxies that are associated with these attributes may actually drive decisions. Qualities such as location or social status, for example, may be seen as highly informative, irrespective of their intrinsic value to parents.

Who Might Participate and What Might Be the Effects of Choice?

The benefits of choice for low-income and minority families depend on three factors: who chooses to exercise choice, the nature of the choices actually available to families, and the effects of choice on schools that serve large numbers of disadvantaged families. Although our results do not address these questions directly, they provide insights into probable answers, particularly when seen in the context of results from other choice studies and recent political events in Michigan.

We have shown that support for choice is strong in the Detroit area, and even stronger among low-income and minority families. A substantial proportion of low-income and minority families, therefore, might use choice as a way to gain access to schools with more educational resources. Recall, however, that nearly one-third of the respondents (32%) who had no opinion about choice had significantly less education and less family income than those who favor choice. If we assume that families with no opinion are less likely to exercise choice than families who favor it, the particular disadvantaged families most likely to exercise choice are those with relatively more education and higher family incomes. This is consistent with the findings of other studies about families who participate in choice programs: They have more education, higher family income, and stronger beliefs about the value of education. If choice were offered in the Detroit area, we would expect less advantaged families to participate, but we would also expect those that do to be more educated and have greater financial resources than those that remain in their neighborhood schools.

The benefits of choice for poor and minority families would also depend on the extent to which policies are designed to facilitate access to and information about schools (Elmore, 1990). The Carnegie Foundation (1992) makes a similar point; it argues that choice, if implemented fairly and effectively, requires substantial financial support. Not only must school districts develop new strategies for informing parents about the services they provide, they must also develop programs for supporting the involvement of families who may reside in different communities. There is no indication that this kind of support would be available to families in Michigan if choice became a reality. On the contrary, plans to pilot cross-district choice have been repeatedly delayed by the state legislature's failure to allocate financial aid for transportation. The absence of tangible support to facilitate disadvantaged families' choices would undoubtedly limit the number who could actually use choice to access better schools for their children.

The benefits of choice to disadvantaged families also depend on the quality of choices provided to them. Less advantaged families may want to exercise choice, but if schools refuse to receive them, or if schools with only marginally better resources are available, the benefits of choice would be questionable. Our results suggest that the most desirable school districts, as measured by our composite of school resources, might oppose opening their borders to outside students. Strate and Wilson (1991), who also surveyed residents in the Detroit metropolitan area, find less support for cross-district than within-district plans. Local community leaders also have expressed concerns that statewide open enrollment would interfere with local control of schools. The governor's statewide choice proposal included a provision that would allow school boards to withdraw from participating in the plan, effectively closing their borders to families from other communities (Michigan House Bill No. 5121, Section 1147A, 1993).

While debates on the merits of choice emphasize opposition from public school bureaucracies, our findings, as well as political events surrounding choice in Michigan, suggest that school districts and *residents* in more prosperous communities oppose choice. We believe that there would have been greater polarization of attitudes about choice had we narrowed the survey item to statewide open enrollment or cross-district plans. Our estimates of the effects of family and school district characteristics most likely represent the lower limits of these relationships for more controversial choice policies, such as cross-district choice.

If opponents pressure policy-makers to limit the access of low-income and minority families, as they have in Michigan, then the benefits of choice to less advantaged families may be more illusory than actual.

Suppose, however, that an active and viable choice plan was adopted in the Detroit metropolitan area, one that provided meaningful opportunities for poor families to improve the education provided to their children. What might be the effects of such a plan on the educational experience of the poor and minority children who did not participate and were thus left behind in their local schools? Our findings suggest that the children most likely to transfer to other districts would be from families headed by adults with relatively more education and higher family incomes. If these families left in large numbers, the consequences for children who remained would undoubtedly be negative. Without additional external support for inner-city schools to improve their programs, and thus compete more effectively for students and families, choice would simply exacerbate the problems facing school districts with large poor and minority populations.

SUMMARY AND DISCUSSION

The results from this study underscore a paradox framed as two simple questions:

1. Are those who hold the most favorable attitudes about choice—namely lower-income, minority families—likely to realize meaningful choices among schools?
2. If choice were available to inner-city children, who would most benefit?

Many of the low-income and minority families who reside in urban school districts in the area, particularly those characterized by severe educational difficulties, favor choice and appear to see it as a vehicle for accessing better schools. Recall that Detroit residents rank the importance of particular school qualities in the same way as suburbanites. This suggests that, at least in theory, choice might serve to reduce social stratification in education.

However, a fundamental feature of most choice schemes is that they are voluntary. This means that even if such schemes were available to everyone, only some families would choose to send their children to schools other than those in their residential areas. Here the results of our research and that of others are discouraging. The departure of relatively more advantaged children from their home schools and districts can have an adverse effect on the schools and families left behind (Elmore, 1988; Witte, 1993). When children from poor districts opt for richer districts, the result can be financially detrimental to poor districts, without any realistic opportunity to react constructively and improve school services (Carnegie Foundation, 1992). Indeed, the messages sent to inner-city administrators and the families that remain in local schools may be distorted and regrettable, particularly if families judge the quality of schools primarily by location and social status. This is a case of "the rich getting richer, while the poor get poorer"—the essence of social stratification.

Another fundamental feature of choice is that the benefits depend on the range of options available. The willingness to act does not guarantee access. Not all residents in the Detroit metropolitan area favor choice; a substantial proportion oppose it, and these opponents include residents of high-resource school districts. If these school districts refuse to provide access to their schools, as they have in the past, the options available to inner-city families will be severely restricted. Even if access is provided, school districts may not be willing to adjust their programs to the educational backgrounds of poor and minority children. As Wells (Chapter 2, this volume) notes in St. Louis, and Witte (1993) observes in Milwaukee, the transition from inner-city public schools to suburban public schools or private schools can be extremely difficult for disadvantaged students. Even under optimal conditions, many students opt to return to the inner-city schools that they left.

Despite the appealing nature of arguments for the voluntary contracts between families and schools that undergird choice, we are pessimistic about the ability of choice to reduce the stratification of educational opportunities that characterize metropolitan areas such as Detroit. While disadvantaged families see choice as a means to acquire a better education for their children, and while the exercise of choice would undoubtedly benefit some children, we believe that the overall effect of choice would be to increase rather than decrease discrepancies in educational quality.

For those with a strong commitment to equity, any social policy that increases social stratification in education (intended or not) should be seriously questioned, even if it has positive results for some people. We admit that this notion flies in the face of a basic tenet of modern liberal thought: belief in the freedom of *individuals*, particularly meritorious individuals, to make choices based on their own interests. Clearly, the American political consensus supports this view and praises social policies that promote it (Glazer, 1987). Nonetheless, we would argue that social policies need to balance private interests with public interests, particularly in the area of education.

We call attention to Patricia Albjerg Graham's recent essay (1993) on the expectations Americans place on their public schools. Graham describes Zakia, a 9-year-old resident of a Boston welfare hotel. Rising at 5:30 A.M., Zakia's mother, toddler sibling in tow, takes two buses to guide Zakia to her public school of choice—away from the inner city—to be there in time for the free breakfast. It would be difficult to argue that Zakia's mother, willing to act on her clear belief in the value of education, should be denied the right to send her daughter to such a school, especially given the effort she is willing to expend. Nonetheless, the removal of more than a few Zakias (and their mothers) from inner-city schools would have a noticeably negative effect on schools that enroll large proportions of disadvantaged children.

How did the many Detroits of our nation develop the disastrous environments that they currently offer families? One by one, families left the cities when they were able to do so. They left for a myriad of noble and ignoble motives: to seek safer environments, to avoid sending their children to integrated schools, to settle in homogeneous communities that shared their values. But other residents were unable to leave, whether for economic reasons, lack of motivation, or the hostility they faced in neighborhoods elsewhere. A nation that mainly values the free will of individuals to seek a better life encourages voluntary choices among individuals, regardless of the long-term impact. Nonetheless, choice bears an unsettling resemblance to the very social, economic, and political processes that created the problems of urban education (Kantor & Brenzel, 1992).

We urge policy-makers, educators, and families to consider the potential effects of such social policies on *all* poor and minority families, even if those policies seem to offer some benefit to individual families willing to take advantage of them. The common good is a worthy consideration in public conversations about school choice.

NOTES

Acknowledgments. We gratefully acknowledge the support of the Spencer Foundation for this research, as well as the Office of the Vice President for Research at the University of Michigan. We also appreciate assistance from the 1991 Detroit Area Study Committee and its director, Charlotte Steeh, for data collection and retrieval, and from Mary Antony for residential and school district matching.

1. Farley (1991) computed an index of dissimilarity: "The numerical value of the index indicates the percentage of either group [black or white] who would have to move from one census tract to another to eliminate segregation. . . . Were a system of apartheid so thorough that all Blacks lived in exclusively Black neighborhoods and all Whites in all-White neighborhoods, the index would be 100" (pp. 276–278). In the 1980 census, the Detroit metropolitan area rated 89 on this index, similar to Chicago, Cleveland, and Gary, Indiana. Analysis of the 1990 census indicates that Detroit remains one of the most segregated metropolitan areas in the nation (Farley & Frey, 1994).

REFERENCES

Boaz, D. (1991). *Liberating schools: Education in the inner city*. Washington, DC: Cato Institute.

Bryk, A. S., Lee, V. E., & Holland, P. B. (1993). *Catholic schools and the common good*. Cambridge, MA: Harvard University Press.

Bryk, A. S., & Raudenbush, S. W. (1992). *Hierarchical linear models: Applications and data analysis methods*. Newbury Park, CA: Sage.

Carnegie Foundation for the Advancement of Teaching. (1992). *School choice: A special report.* Princeton, NJ: Author.

Children's Defense Fund. (1992). *City child poverty data from 1990 census.* Washington, DC: Author.

Christoff, C. (1994, March 17). Schools' battle far from over. *Detroit News,* pp. 1b, 8b.

Coons, J. E., & Sugarman, S. (1978). *Education by choice: The case for family control.* Berkeley: University of California Press.

Darling-Hammond, L., & Kirby, S. N. (1985). *Tuition tax deductions and parent school choice: A case study of Minnesota.* Santa Monica, CA: Rand Corporation.

Darling-Hammond, L., & Kirby, S. N. (1988). Public policy and private choice: The case of Minnesota. In T. James & H. M. Levin (Eds.), *Comparing public and private schools: Vol. 1. Institutions and organizations* (pp. 243–269). New York: Falmer.

Detroit Strategic Planning Project. (1987). *Race relations task force final report.* Detroit, MI: Author.

Elmore, R. F. (1988). Choice in public education. In W. L. Boyd & C. T. Kerchner (Eds.), *The politics of excellence and choice in education* (pp. 79–98). New York: Falmer.

Elmore, R. F. (1990). Choice as an instrument of public policy: Evidence from education and health care. In W. H. Clune & J. F. Witte (Eds.), *Choice and control in American education* (pp. 285–318). New York: Falmer.

Farley, R. (1991). Residential segregation of social and economic groups among blacks, 1970–1980. In C. Jencks & P. E. Peterson (Eds.), *The urban underclass* (pp. 274–298). Washington, DC: Brookings Institution.

Farley, R., & Frey, W. H. (1994). Changes in segregation of whites from blacks. *American Sociological Review, 59*(1), 23–45.

Fine, M. (1991). *Framing dropouts. Notes on the politics of an urban high school.* Albany, NY: State University New York Press.

Glazer, N. (1987). Equity and excellence in education: A comment. *Educational Review, 57*(2), 196–199.

Graham, P. A. (1993). What America has expected of its schools over the past century. *American Journal of Education, 101*(2), 83–98.

The house vs. choice. (1991, May 31). *Detroit News,* p. 8a.

Kantor, H., & Brenzel, B. (1992). Urban education and the "truly disadvantaged": The historical roots of the contemporary crisis, 1945–1990. *Teachers College Record, 94*(2), 278–314.

Kozol, J. (1991). *Savage inequalities. Children in America's schools.* New York: Crown.

Michigan House Bill No. 5121. (1993, October 12).

Milliken v. Bradley I, 418 U.S. 717 (1974).

Milliken v. Bradley II, 433 U.S. 267 (1977).

Moore, D., & Davenport, S. (1989). *School choice: The new, improved sorting machine.* Chicago: Designs for Change.

Plank, S., Schiller, K. S., Schneider, B., & Coleman, J. S. (1993). Effect of choice in education. In E. Rasell & R. Rothstein (Eds.), *School choice: Examining the evidence* (pp. 111–134). Washington, DC: Economic Policy Institute.

Rosenthal, R., & Rosnow, R. L. (1984). *Essentials of behavioral research: Methods and data analysis*. New York: McGraw-Hill.

Schmidt, P. (1994, February 2). Magnets' efficiency as desegregation tool questioned. *Education Week*, pp. 16–17.

Strate, J. M., & Wilson, C. A. (1991). *Schools of choice in the Detroit metropolitan area*. Detroit, MI: Center for Urban Studies/College of Urban, Labor and Metropolitan Affairs, Wayne State University.

Wells, A. S. (1993). The sociology of school choice: Why some win and others lose in the educational marketplace. In E. Rasell & R. Rothstein (Eds.), *School choice: Examining the evidence* (pp. 29–48). Washington, DC: Economic Policy Institute.

Wells, A. S., & Crain, R. L. (1992). Do parents choose school quality or school status? A sociological theory of free market education. In P. W. Cookson (Ed.), *The choice controversy* (pp. 65–82). Newbury Park, CA: Corwin.

Willms, J. D,. & Echols, F. H. (1993). The Scottish experience of parental school choice. In E. Rasell & R. Rothstein (Eds.), *School choice: Examining the evidence* (pp. 49–68). Washington, DC: Economic Policy Institute.

Witte, J. F. (1993). The Milwaukee parental choice program. In E. Rasell & R. Rothstein (Eds.), *School choice: Examining the evidence* (pp. 69–110). Washington, DC: Economic Policy Institute.

PART II

The Political and Institutional Definition of Choice

How do civic leaders and public educators respond to popular demand for wider and higher-quality school options? How do political forces and institutional habits limit the range of new schools created under choice programs? These are the fundamental questions addressed in Part II. Five quite different institutional settings are studied, illustrating how the form and character of choice programs can differ dramatically. This yields a variety of ways to structure school choice experiments.

Chapter 5 takes us to Montgomery County, Maryland, just north of Washington, D.C. Jeffrey Henig has studied the long history of school choice, stemming originally from efforts to desegregate the public schools. Educators began to create magnet schools in the 1970s to raise quality and to encourage cross-neighborhood transfers and greater racial integration. But relatively few parents have come to exercise their newfound right of school choice within the public sector. Many schools designated as magnets have arrived at, again, hazy identities. Parents know surprisingly little about specialized programs available in most magnet schools, with some notable exceptions. Even basic knowledge of the available options is inequitably distributed: Almost twice the proportion of white parents are aware of magnet schools, relative to Hispanic parents. A certain political rationality has overcome this choice program. School authorities have granted the program only tepid moral and financial support, and very little public visibility. This minimizes the risk of political opposition, especially resistance potentially fanned among parents in affluent areas of the county. Yet two or three particular magnet schools attract strong cross-ethnic support each year. Henig usefully examines these success stories.

Chapter 6 explores the case of Milwaukee, the most renowned publicly funded voucher program. John Witte has evaluated the workings and effects of this program for three years. He reports on whether parental satisfaction and student achievement improve over time among the participating families. The Milwaukee program is also fascinating in terms of the institutional response: Thanks to the voucher program, a handful of vibrant ethnocentric schools have blossomed within inner-city neighborhoods—be they Hispanic, black, or Anglo. Many low-income parents enthusiastically support the program and eagerly apply for their vouchers. As observed in San Antonio (Chapter 3, this volume), those working-class and impoverished parents who are better educated and already involved in their children's education are more likely to actively choose. Most recently the Wisconsin legislature voted to expand the program, allowing parents to redeem their public vouchers in parochial schools. This initiative remains snagged in the courts.

Chapter 7 demonstrates how school choices available to families are more extensive in many countries outside the United States. Marlaine Lockheed and Emmanuel Jimenez, looking across several nations, ask why and how private schools raise achievement more effectively than public schools. This question brings us back to which families actively choose nonpublic schools and how this selection process may interact with the differing qualities of public and private education. Lockheed and Jimenez usefully take us out of the institutional conditions characterizing North American educational structures. They also advance our conceptual understanding of what specific features of school organizations determine the greater effectiveness of private schools, observed in particular settings.

Chapter 8 reports recent evidence on the nationwide magnet school movement. These choice programs, now serving millions of children, stem from an earlier political commitment to desegregation *and* more recent interest in broadening school options for all families. But who specifically benefits from the creation of magnet schools? Do these seemingly innovative organizations provide truly new forms of teaching and learning? Do magnet schools prove more effective in boosting children's achievement? These are the questions that Rolf Blank and colleagues begin to address.

Chapter 9 reports on the most costly voucher initiative ever attempted in America: the Pell Grant program for postsecondary students. Thomas Kane takes us to this distinct institutional setting to ask whether, over the past two decades, Pell Grants have substantially changed the choices of students and the equity with which low-income students pursue a college education. His evidence is somewhat encouraging: Low-income and working-class youths have shown a higher propensity to enter two-year college programs, attributable in part to Pell Grants. But access to four-year colleges and top universities remains unchanged and unequal. Kane argues that three factors shape their "realistic choices" and apparent options: deeply entrenched institutional factors, lack of information, and the cultural patterns of low-income families.

CHAPTER 5

The Local Dynamics of Choice

Ethnic Preferences and Institutional Responses

JEFFREY R. HENIG

The concept of school choice has been long associated with the ideas of economic theorists. But not until the 1980s did this linkage grow tighter and more explicit. Detached from earlier connections with divisive racial politics, the new model of school choice draws on the market metaphor and the language of economics to support the claim that individual choice does not have to weaken the social commitment to integration. Increasing choice, proponents argue, has the potential to both improve the quality of education and support the goal of racial integration. My study of the magnet school program in Montgomery County, Maryland, indeed suggests that school choice has the potential to complement the pursuit of integration, but only when public officials have the capacity and support to act decisively. If we accept the market metaphor uncritically, we will neglect the importance of the institutional and political forces that maintain, or erode, the public interest in the pursuit of individualistic choice. This chapter examines whether parents make "choices" as idealized market actors, or whether institutional conditions guide and constrain where parents send their children to school.

THE MARKET METAPHOR

Milton Friedman's *Capitalism and Freedom* (1962) provided the most important early application of the market metaphor to school choice. His call for vouchers found a receptive audience among some scholars and policy activists. One observer concluded in the early 1970s that "on the intellectual circuit . . . vouchers are the hottest thing going" (La Noue, 1972, p. 138). But before the 1980s the political momentum for choice did not come from abstract economic ideas. The practice of educational choice, expressed in the operation of thousands of school districts around the United States, was shaped by pragmatic adjustment to legal and political currents rather than by fully articulated theoretical models.

As reviewed in Chapter 1, the evolution of choice-in-practice in American education was interwoven most intimately with the thread of racial politics from the 1950s through the 1970s. In the wake of the *Brown* decision, many southern school systems used "freedom-of-choice" to undermine the desegregation process. During the late 1960s and the 1970s, choice continued to be associated with racial issues, but when linked to the establishment of magnet schools, it came to be viewed as a tool for supporting rather than impeding integration. And the original association with magnet schools linked choice to notions seemingly inhospitable to free market visions: judicial intervention, federal encroachment on local control, and affirmative action.

It was not until the 1980s that the association between school choice and free market theorists grew tighter and more explicit. In *Rethinking School Choice: Limits of the Market Metaphor* (Henig, 1994), I trace the reemergence and reformulation of the pro-choice argument during the Reagan and Bush years. Among the factors that account for the reemergence of school choice on the public policy agenda were the Reagan administration's strategic retreat from the insistence that choice include private and parochial schools, the growth of a body of literature purporting to empirically demonstrate the feasibility and effectiveness of choice, and the linkage of choice to the broader themes of privatization and the New Federalism.

Also important—and more directly relevant to the analysis presented in this chapter—was the unhinging of school choice from its historical association with controversial racial issues. Choice advocates aggressively recast the debate to focus on improving the quality of schools rather than on working to make schools racially integrated. They insisted that allowing individuals greater freedom to pursue personal values need not undermine the social commitment to racial integration. Pointing to the apparent success of some magnet schools in bringing about voluntary integration, they argued that there is no necessary tension between individual choice and integration (e.g., Clinchy, 1985; Glazer, 1987). A renewed emphasis on the market metaphor and the language of economics helped make this portrayal of school choice quite convincing.

The market metaphor breaks the school choice equation into its demand and supply sides. Focusing on the desires, knowledge, and behavior of families, the demand side of the market model assumes that the quality of education is the chief consideration in a family's decision about schools, that the family has or can readily obtain accurate information regarding school programs and performance, and that the family will exercise the "exit option" from their neighborhood school (Hirschman, 1970) whenever it becomes feasible to obtain better educational value at equal or lesser cost.

The supply side focuses on the schools and how they are likely to respond to the desires of education consumers. Applied to the contemporary choice debate, the market metaphor carries a critique of current supply-side arrangements and a promise that choice can stimulate reform. The bureaucracy in which schools are enmeshed restricts their ability to be innovative and responsive. Buffered from parental pressure, educational professionals are free to substitute their own comfort and perquisites for those of their students. Increasing choice, it is argued, will displace the stultifying weight of government with the entrepreneurial spirit of the marketplace, setting the stage for greater diversity, efficiency, and educational effectiveness (Chubb & Moe, 1990).

This chapter empirically assesses these claims by analyzing the exercise of school choice in one locale: the magnet school program in Montgomery County, Maryland. The principal focus is on the demand side, with special attention to whether patterns of racial separation are likely to be mitigated or exacerbated by giving freer reign to parental desires (operating on institutionally limited information). I analyzed over 450 parental requests to transfer into Montgomery County elementary-level magnet schools submitted for the 1985 school year (Henig, 1990).[1] Whereas public choice analysts rely on theoretical models of how families *might* behave if granted greater options, this approach lets us assess how families actually *do* behave. Following the review of transfer data, I analyze the results of a survey of over 1,000 parents of children in both magnet and nonmagnet schools undertaken by the school system in 1985; this gives additional insight into how informed families are and what values they hold. These interrelated questions are addressed:

- Given the opportunity to choose among schools, how many families actually do so?
- Are white families more likely to transfer than minority families?
- What characteristics of a school and its students make it more likely to attract transfer requests?

- Are white families and minority families attracted by similar or different factors?
- Do racial preferences and antipathies influence transfer requests more or less than program characteristics and school resources?

In short, the survey data reveal that loosening the reins on individual choice does not preclude racial integration; neither does it necessarily advance integration. Rather, it is in large measure the institutional framework—the specific design of the choice program and the will and capacity of the educational bureaucracy to implement its provisions—that determines whether choice will complement or confound the pursuit of racial integration. My interpretation of the transfer and parent survey data thus leads me back to the supply side of the school choice equation. Critics applying the market metaphor have portrayed public officials—especially those within the professional education community—as driven by self-interest to undermine choice experiments. Yet in Montgomery County the education community helped initiate choice and has kept individual choice from eroding other collective values, such as racial integration. Uncritical acceptance of the market metaphor can distract us from the institutional framework that determines the consequences of expanded individual choice and from the key role of collective deliberation, democratic procedures, and governmental authority. Indeed, the school's political rationality pushes to maintain institutional stability and common commitments. Choice challenges prior conceptions of the public interest and which agencies hold authority to articulate collective social commitments.

FROM PERSONAL CHOICE TO SOCIAL GOALS: THREE PERSPECTIVES

Those who suggest that aggressive expansion of parents' right to choose their public schools will not undermine the nation's commitment to racial desegregation generally rely on assumptions about the criteria that families use in making their decisions or about the range of incentives that public officials can devise and maintain. Three perspectives, or arguments, can be distinguished.

The *racial neutrality* perspective assumes that preferences and needs for different types of schools are distributed among the population in a racially neutral pattern. In its simplest version, this thesis assumes that such preferences and needs are distributed more or less randomly, or according to idiosyncratic principles that elude generalization. Allowing school enrollment to be dictated by choice—rather than by the racially segregated pattern of where people live—thus will result in "natural" integration. Critical to this formulation is the presumption that direct preferences regarding the racial composition of schools are of minor importance. Once schools offer educationally meaningful diversity, the influence of racial criteria will diminish.

The *separation-not-segregation* thesis accepts that preferences for different types of schools may vary across ethnic groups and that individuals might strongly prefer to associate with those of the same race or cultural group. This view often is associated with a distrust of public officials' ability to gauge such preferences or to create incentives that will channel individual behavior into preferred patterns. Introducing individual choice may not boost interracial social interaction, according to this formulation, but racial separation that results from free choices is not legally objectionable and does not violate the public interest in racial equality as most Americans understand it.

The *managed choice* thesis assumes that preferences and needs for different types of schools vary across ethnic groups and that officials can take advantage of this variation to structure incentives that will increase racial integration. In this vision, public officials strategically distribute school resources and programs to attract whites to minority neighborhoods and minorities to white neighborhoods. The more responsive families are to variations in program offerings, the easier it will be for officials to channel them in the desired directions.

Like most of the nation's first generation of magnet programs, the Montgomery County magnet program was initiated as a managed choice program (Henig, 1989); its roots lay in a vision of pro-active governance, not benign laissez faire. Yet advocates of a market-oriented choice system are averse to managed choice, because it presupposes regulation and intervention by perceptive and efficacious officials. Separation-not-segregation is not seen as a politically viable alternative, since the public seems unwilling to rally behind a plan that explicitly gives up on the vision of a harmoniously integrated society. Accordingly, most advocates of a market-based choice system have adopted the racial neutrality thesis. But they have not hesitated to appropriate the experience of programs like that in Montgomery County to buttress their argument that choice and integration can be complementary.

Evidence from such districts suggests that white parents *can* be enticed into predominantly minority schools and neighborhoods—*when* programs are carefully designed, when unusual resources are made available, when admission procedures and quotas are backed by court orders, and when the threat of more massive, mandatory desegregation procedures looms as a likely alternative (Blank, Dentler, Baltzell, & Chabotar, 1983). But generalization from such contexts to the broader choice options envisioned by advocates can be misleading. The will and capacity of local public officials to make and maintain such commitments, absent external pressure from courts or the Justice Department, is problematic in the face of competing political and bureaucratic demands (Henig, 1994; Metz, 1986; Monti, 1985).

THE MONTGOMERY COUNTY MAGNET PROGRAM

The magnet program in the Montgomery County public schools (MCPS) offers an opportunity to observe the dynamics of choice in practice. MCPS is a large district comprising 495 square miles and approximately 103,000 students. The county, which rests on the northern border of the District of Columbia, has a population of relatively high socioeconomic status. The 1983 median household income was $39,154, compared with a nationwide figure of $20,885 (Montgomery County Planning Board, 1986; U.S. Bureau of the Census, 1984). The average years of school completed in 1984, for those 25 years of age or older, was 14.9, about two years above the comparable national figure; 22.6% had completed graduate degrees.

Although its population is still predominantly white, the minority population in the school system has increased dramatically, both in total numbers and as a percentage of total enrollment. Between 1970 and 1990, while overall enrollments were decreasing, the number of minority children in MCPS elementary and secondary schools increased from 10,034 to 39,543. In 1990, minorities constituted more than 38% of all enrollments and a much higher proportion in the area of the county on which this study focuses.

In 1977, MCPS established seven elementary magnet schools in the lower section of the county. The program was expanded to a total of fourteen elementary schools, two intermediate schools, and one high school in 1983; two more elementary schools were added in 1987. Children are assigned to a home school based on their local attendance zone. Their parents, however, are encouraged to consider transferring their child to a magnet school. Transportation is provided at no charge to students whose transfers have been approved. The county's policy is to approve transfer requests unless they result in racial imbalance, overcrowding, or substantial underutilization of a school. For the 1984 and 1985 school years, 85% of all transfer requests were approved either initially or on appeal (Larson & Kirshstein, 1986).

The county's general affluence and tradition of progressive politics provide a setting that is more conducive to school reform than most communities. Schools are well funded, teachers are relatively well paid, and the culture is relatively receptive to educational innovation. Many other school systems around the nation have adopted magnet schools in an ad hoc and decidedly superficial effort to meet federal pressure to integrate; the evolution of magnet offerings in Montgomery County owed more to indigenous forces and reflected, from the first, a desire to balance racial integration with educational diversity and parental choice.

In spite of such advantages, Montgomery County is not a small and sheltered suburb whose experiences have little relevance for urban schools dealing with severe economic and racial tensions. The nineteen schools with magnet programs, alone, serve a student population of about 10,200, a clientele larger than 95% of the nation's school districts. Moreover, these magnet schools show much higher levels of racial diversity and special needs than does the county as a whole. Thirteen of the schools have more minority than white students, and nine are over 60% minority. In seven of the schools, more than one of every three students is poor enough to be eligible for the school lunch program, and in six schools more than one in ten students is in a program for non-English-speaking children. Reflecting in part its convenience as a receiving ground for minority families fleeing the District of Columbia, this section of the county is racially and economically as urban as it is suburban in character.

The Data

Fourteen elementary school magnets with special programs were in operation in 1985. Some of these magnets attracted a large number of applicants, while others attracted very few. Oak View, with its French immersion program, attracted 108 transfer requests; North Chevy Chase, only 11. Some schools attracted transfer requests from minority and white families in relatively equal numbers. Piney Branch, for example, received transfer requests from 11 minorities and 15 nonminorities, and Takoma Park received 25 requests from minorities and 19 from others. Other schools proved attractive primarily to one group or the other; there were about 4 requests from nonminorities to every 1 for minorities to enter Rosemary Hills, for example, while for New Hampshire Estates the ratio was almost exactly the reverse.

Our analysis relates the pattern of transfer requests to four broad sets of school characteristics or factors that appear to attract parents when they are given an opportunity to choose their child's school. The *racial and class composition* of a school includes the ethnic composition of the students, the racial characteristics of the staff, and the racial and economic profile of the area immediately surrounding the school. If white parents choose predominantly white schools, with predominantly white teachers, in predominantly white and wealthier neighborhoods— or minority parents do the opposite—the racial neutrality thesis will be challenged.

A school's *resources and demands* include total enrollment, student turnover, overcrowding, the ratio of students to professional staff, the ratio of students to classroom teachers, the ratio of classroom teachers to aides, and the percentage of teachers with 16 or more years of experience. Low student–teacher ratios, for example, were found to be important factors in attracting parents to a magnet school in a largely black neighborhood in St. Paul (Levine & Eubanks, 1980).

Schools also differ in their *program and organization*. Choice advocates believe that diversity in programs allows parents to select the school that best meets their child's particular needs. Unfortunately, the evidence to date does not provide a sharp picture as to what types of programs and themes consistently attract parents (Rossell, 1985). Two schools offer language immersion; five offer programs for the gifted and talented; and two offer special computer instruction, often linked to science and math. The five remaining schools offer a diverse range of other specialties, including back-to-basics, individualized instruction, communication arts, and interdisciplinary education. In some schools, magnet programs are available to the entire school, in others to just a select subset of students; this was taken into account in the analysis. (Schools were given a score of 1 if they have a particular feature— such as a foreign-language magnet, a gifted-and-talented focus, or a whole-school magnet—and a score of 0 for that feature if they do not.)

The indicators of grade-level organization used in the analysis were whether or not schools have a kindergarten and whether or not the kindergarten is a full-day program. Since parents may be most likely to transfer their children before they become accustomed to a particular school, schools that start at kindergarten level may attract more students. A more elaborate grade-level indicator that distinguished among six grade combinations represented among the fourteen schools failed to account for any more variance than this simple indicator of the presence or absence of a kindergarten. Many Montgomery County parents consider full-day kindergarten an additional magnet attraction, so a separate variable was included in the analysis for this feature.

Finally, the analysis related the pattern of transfer requests to indicators of *school performance*. Presumably, parents are interested in transferring their children into schools that perform well. The average score on the California Achievement Test (CAT) provides a standardized indicator of each school's performance in the basic skills of reading, language, and math. Scores on such tests reflect the skills students bring into the schools, of course, at least as much as they do the independent contribution of the schools. But to parents looking for objective indicators on which to base their choice, such scores are salient.

To the extent that parents gauge school performance by talking to other parents, the number of requests to transfer into a school presumably would correlate with parents' level of satisfaction. In a survey conducted by the school system's Department of Educational Accountability in the spring of 1985, a total of 575 parents of children attending the fourteen magnet schools were asked, "If you could give your school just one grade for everything, what grade would you give it?" Converting the letter grades awarded into a grade point average (GPA) provided this study's indicator of parental satisfaction.

Findings: The Exercise of Choice

For those who see magnet schools as a vehicle for promoting choice *and* integration, the number and distribution of transfer requests provide some good news and some bad news (see Figure 5.1). First, the good news. In spite of the fairly wide range in racial and economic characteristics among these schools, every magnet school was sufficiently attractive to entice some parents to request a transfer in. No school attracted only whites or only minorities, and the proportion of total transfer requests coming from minority parents is high (46.5%). Choice advocates might point to the extreme success of one school—Oak View—as an indicator of the potential of choice policies. Oak View, with a magnet program based on immersing students in French from the moment they walk into kindergarten, attracted more white applicants *and* more minority applicants than any other program.

Other aspects of Figure 5.1 are less reassuring. The average number of transfer requests to each school (33.2) was small in relation to the average school enrollment of over 350. And while many minorities participated, their rate of participation was not as great as that of whites; minorities comprised 46.5% of transfers but 57.7% of students in the 14 schools. This suggests that the range of diversity in academic emphases and teaching styles that has proven politically feasible in Montgomery County is insufficient to entice most families to transfer from their home schools, at least at the elementary level. It especially is insufficient to entice minority families to transfer.

Figure 5.1: Number of Minority and White Requests to Transfer in, by School, in Order of Percentage Minority in Current School Population, 1985

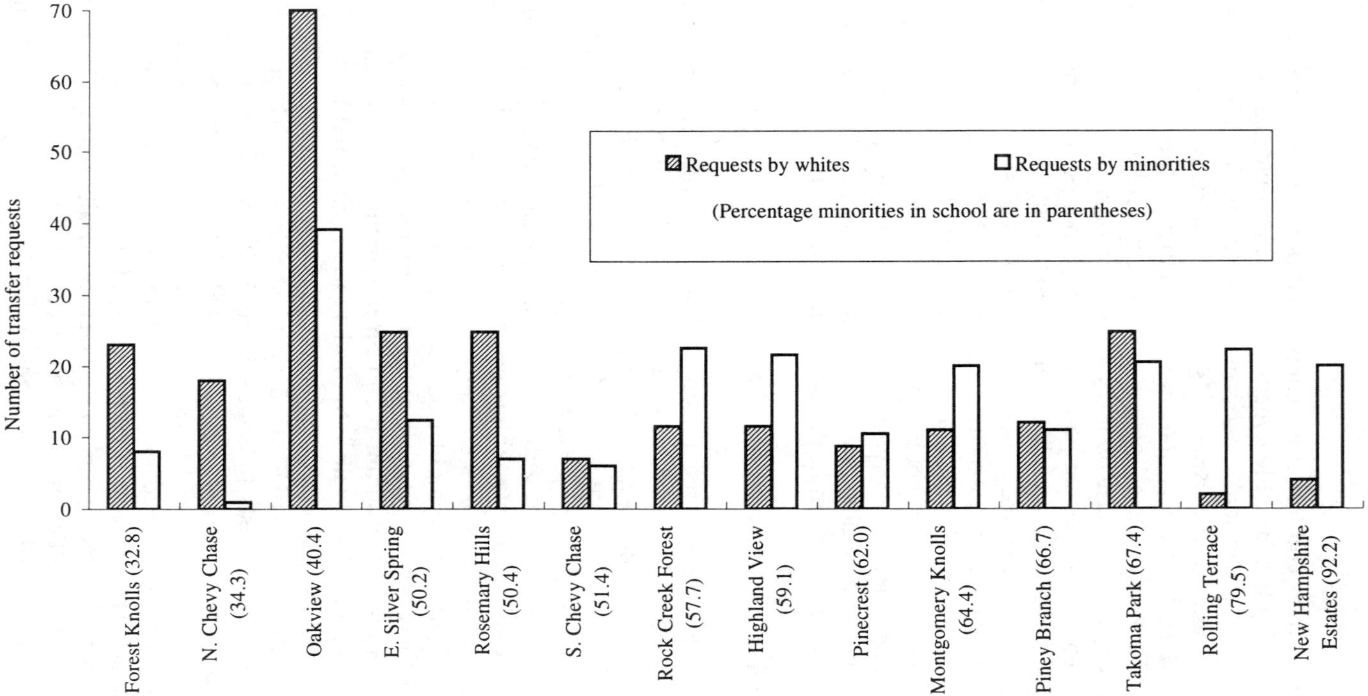
Number of transfer requests
70
60
50
40
30
20
10
0
Requests by whites
Requests by minorities
(Percentage minorities in school are in parentheses)
Forest Knolls (32.8)
N. Chevy Chase (34.3)
Oakview (40.4)
E. Silver Spring (50.2)
Rosemary Hills (50.4)
S. Chevy Chase (51.4)
Rock Creek Forest (57.7)
Highland View (59.1)
Pinecrest (62.0)
Montgomery Knolls (64.4)
Piney Branch (66.7)
Takoma Park (67.4)
Rolling Terrace (79.5)
New Hampshire Estates (92.2)

The low level of transfer requests makes it unlikely that individual choices will have more than an incremental effect on racial balance. Small shifts eventually can bring about substantial change (Schelling, 1978), but only if the changes are cumulative and consistently moving in a particular direction. More important are the indications that—unless aggressively regulated by authorities—choice may exacerbate, rather than ameliorate, racial segregation. As Figure 5.1 reveals, there are more requests from whites than minorities to transfer into schools that already have fewer minorities (those arrayed toward the left side of the figure), while the number of requests by minorities tends to be higher for schools with fewer nonminorities (those arrayed toward the right).

Table 5.1 reinforces the finding that parental choices are furthering segregation. Presented are simple statistical correlations between the number of requests to transfer into the 14 schools and various school characteristics. White families are most likely to seek transfers into schools with low proportions of minorities. This is the case whether we consider the minority population as a whole or break it down into its major constituent groups. Minorities who request transfers, on the other hand, are more likely to seek entry into schools with higher proportions of minorities. And there is a marked tendency for minority families to request transfers into schools in neighborhoods with lower incomes and more poverty.

On the other hand, when it comes to the school attributes that can be manipulated by school officials—programs and resources—the evidence suggests that white and minority parents may be applying similar criteria. Schools attracting the most transfer requests from both white and minority families include those with a lower percentage of older, experienced teachers, a higher ratio of students to professional staff, a higher ratio of teachers to aides, the presence of a kindergarten, and a foreign-language focus.

Some findings are surprising. The strong negative relationship with the proportion of teachers with more than 15 years of service could reflect parents' sense that younger teachers bring more enthusiasm and more contemporary techniques. Another possibility is that schools with a younger staff tend to be those with aggressive principals who have actively tried to reshape the faculty to fit the magnet program's special characteristics. The apparent tendency of white and minority parents to seek entry into schools with higher enrollment and student–staff ratios most likely reflects a reversed direction of causality: Schools that are popular become, over time, more overenrolled. Indicators of school performance do not show the strong and consistent relationship to transfer

Table 5.1: Bivariate Correlations: Requests to Transfer in, by Race

	Requests by Whites	Requests by Minorities	Ratio Requests: Whites/Minorities
Race and class			
Minority in school (by %)	-.57	.26	-.55
Black in school (by %)	-.31	.22	-.48
Hispanic in school (by %)	-.59	.13	-.27
Asian in school (by %)	-.43	.17	-.40
Professional staff minority (by %)	.14	.46	-.42
Minority in census tract (by %)	-.27	.35	-.45
Poor in tract (by %)	-.37	.29	-.35
Median income in tract	.05	-.53	.62
Resources and demands			
Total enrollment	.33	.14	-.08
Student turnover	-.11	-.13	-.15
Overcrowding	-.37	.11	-.44
Student/professional ratio	.34	.52	-.21
Student/teacher ratio	.02	.07	-.31
Teacher/aide ratio	.27	.60	-.22
% with 16+ years experience	-.65	-.58	.26
Age of school structure	.08	.22	.12
Program structure			
Grade level	-.12	-.37	.30
Kindergarten present	.24	.57	-.40
All day kindergarten	-.25	.08	-.25
Whole-school magnet	-.42	-.14	.11
Foreign language focus	.58	.64	-.12
Gifted and talented focus	-.05	-.45	.43
Math/science/computer focus	-.22	-.06	-.17
Performance			
Average CAT score	-.27	-.45	.45
Parent satisfaction (GPA)	-.19	.06	-.13
Parent satisfaction (white)	.15	.01	.33
Parent satisfaction (minority)	-.42	.06	-.55

requests that might be expected if parents were playing the role of educated consumer.

The results of a statistically more sophisticated analysis, which identifies the most important factors attracting parents when the effects of all the other school characteristics are taken into account, reinforce the basic pattern indicated by Table 5.1 and highlight some factors (Figure 5.2; see Appendix for regression results). The school characteristics that explained the most variance in *white* transfer requests were low proportions of teachers with more than 15 years of experience, low proportions of minorities in the current student body, and the presence of a foreign-language magnet program. Those that best explained re-

Figure 5.2: Factors with Independent Effects on Transfer Requests

Transfer requests by whites

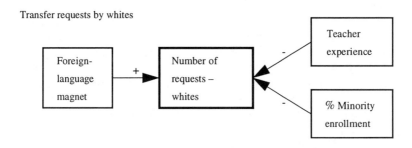

Transfer requests by minorities

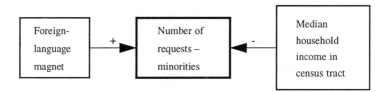

Ratio of transfer requests by whites to requests by minorities

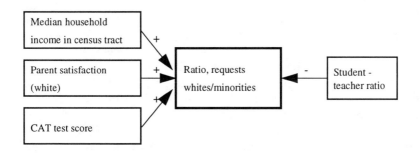

Note: These figures present only those factors found to have a substantial independent effect on transfers, as indicated in the regression analysis discussed in the Appendix. Boxes are sized in proportion to the standardized coefficients and represent the strength of the relationship.

quests by *minority* families were presence of a foreign-language program and location in a lower-income neighborhood. These parents are attracted to distinctive programs located in familiar settings.

That both white and minority families apparently are drawn to a magnet focus on intense foreign-language instruction would seem to challenge earlier studies. First, most other studies have tended to find gifted-and-talented programs, basic skills programs, or individualized instruction programs to be more popular than language instruction. Rossell and Clarke (1990) found foreign-language programs to be among the least popular for white parents. Second, much of the literature suggests that white and minority parents may prefer different types of programs, with white parents more responsive to selective academic programs and minorities responsive to traditional or career-oriented programs. The appeal of language immersion, however, primarily reflects one unusually strong program, the French immersion program at Oak View. (The other foreign-language magnet—Rock Creek Forest, offering Spanish immersion—has also attracted white and minority transfers.)

When Oak View is dropped from the analysis, however, the presence of a foreign-language program no longer retains significance in the regression analysis. For white transfers parental satisfaction displaced foreign-language focus as the third included variable. For minority transfers, the effect of dropping the Oak View case was more pronounced, and was suggestive of some criteria that minority families might be applying that differ from those of white parents. When the Oak View case was dropped, minority transfers were associated with higher proportions of minority students in the student body, the presence of a kindergarten, and a higher ratio of classroom teachers to aides.

Indeed, the failure of program features generally to stand out more emphatically may be the more significant finding. Parents may not be looking for particular instructional themes and styles so much as for the kind of energy, creativeness, and extra resources that *some* schools build around their magnet programs. This interpretation gets support from the tendency of parents to avoid schools with high proportions of very experienced teachers. In 1985, the longest-running magnet programs were eight years old, but some of the less popular schools had large numbers of teachers with 16 or more years experience. This discrepancy may indicate that some schools failed to reformulate their faculties to make the magnet programs deliver truly different teaching styles. Schools with blurry identities, not surprisingly, failed to attract new transfer students.

The racial and class patterns highlight the problematic nature of the racial neutrality thesis. Both whites and minorities seem to direct their choices toward schools in which their children will be less likely to be racially or socioeconomically isolated. Cultural familiarity is a strong point of attraction. Yet this criterion points them in different directions. Where white families were most likely to request transfers into schools with low proportions of minorities (which were those located in higher-income neighborhoods), minority families were more likely to opt for schools in low-income neighborhoods (which tended to be schools with higher proportions of minority students). The combined effect of these two flows can be seen in the last column of Table 5.1, which identifies factors independently related to the *ratio of white to minority requests* to transfer into each of the schools. Looking at this ratio tells us something about the types of schools that might become increasingly populated by white students if choice were allowed to operate unconstrained. Schools attracting more white than minority transfer requests were in higher-income neighborhoods and had higher test scores, lower student–teacher ratios, and higher levels of satisfaction among white parents.

Parental Information and Criteria for Choice

When program identity is strong—as in the case of the French immersion magnet at Oak View—the analysis of transfer requests suggests that both white and minority parents will respond. Except in that case, however, the impact of program differentiation appears to have been slight. And, lacking sharp program differentiation, the ethnic and class characteristics of the other students at the school may become a more salient feature.

This still leaves many questions unanswered, including some of indisputable policy relevance. The transfer analysis allowed us to look at the results of parental decisions, and in interpreting those patterns we can draw some inferences about the levels of information and the values being applied. But are parents making these choices based on ample or partial information? And does the racial tilt to the transfer process indicate that race is a key criterion to parents? Both the relatively low level of transfer requests and the weak influence of program characteristics, for example, may reflect inadequate dissemination of information rather than weaknesses in concept or implementation of the programs. Carver and Salganik (1991) have undertaken an analysis of the content, format, and distribution of information made available to parents in states and districts offering choice plans. While they "found a great deal of creativity and commitment of both energy and resources

being invested in providing information to families'' (p. 75), such attention was not universal, and some of the most valuable kinds of information were not generally available. Even if their decisions are informed,
the tendency of parents to request transfers to schools with proportion-
ally more of their own familiar ethnic group may reflect something other
than racial antipathy. Minority and nonminority parents may be applying somewhat different criteria in evaluating schools.

To get leverage on questions like these, it is helpful to look a bit
more directly at what is going on in the minds of parents as they confront the array of options before them. In 1985 a total of 1,083 parents
were interviewed by telephone; 575 from the 14 elementary school magnet schools and 505 from 13 nonmagnet schools selected from nearby
attendance zones. (See Larson & Allen, 1988, for more details on the
construction of the sample and an earlier analysis.)[2]

Many Montgomery County parents had never heard the terms *magnet school* or *magnet program*, and this lack of even the most basic information was more apparent among minorities, especially Hispanics (see
Figure 5.3). This lack of awareness is not simply because some magnets
had been in place only a couple of years at the time of the survey. In
fact, familiarity with the term was slightly higher among parents whose

Figure 5.3: Percentage of Parents Who Have Heard the Terms
Magnet Schools or *Magnet Program*

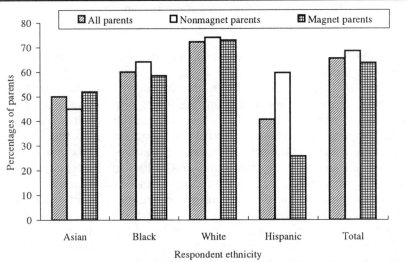

Figure 5.4: How Did You Hear About Magnet Schools?

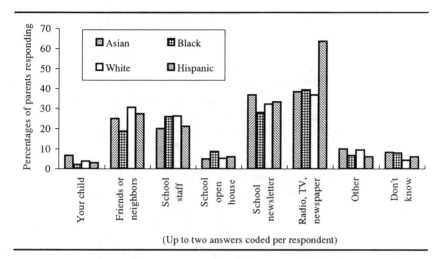

(Up to two answers coded per respondent)

children attended the schools with more recently inaugurated programs. That just over one-third (34.6%) of the parents in a county that has such high levels of education could be so uninformed emphasizes the challenge to public officials who want to make school choice meaningful. Clearly, the transfer patterns discussed earlier took place in an information-thin environment.

Among those who *had* heard about magnets, the sources of information are rather similar across racial and ethnic groups (see Figure 5.4). Respondents were permitted to select up to two sources, so summing percentages across the rows can total greater than 100 percent. The importance of the major media to all groups is notable. School newsletters also had a significant impact.

Better dissemination of information might lead to substantially higher levels of transfer activity, but it is not clear whether the direction of the activity would change. The answer depends in part on the parents' criteria for making transfer decisions. Parents were asked, for example, to indicate on a scale of 1 to 5 how important they considered six different dimensions of school performance:

- The teaching of *basic skills*
- The teaching of *critical thinking and problem-solving*
- A *safe and orderly environment*

- Attention to their *child as an individual*
- The *general student behavior*
- The provision of *special programs* for individual talents, abilities, or needs

Each group considered all of these dimensions highly important and gave basic skills the highest priority. The relative ranking of these six dimensions was identical for white and black parents; after basic skills, the order of apparent importance was critical thinking, safe and orderly environment, attention to child, special programs, and general student behavior. Asian and Hispanic parents were slightly more likely to express interest in general student behavior and slightly less interested in critical thinking than white and black respondents.

Although the aspects of schools parents consider important may not vary markedly across races, this does not guarantee that ethnic considerations will play only a minor role in school choice. The analysis of transfer patterns suggested that parental desires to avoid culturally isolating their child might send white and minority parents in different directions. The parent survey reinforces this conclusion. When parents were asked whether their child's school had "too many, too few, or about the right number of children of your ethnic group," about three-quarters of the respondents indicated that they felt the current racial mixture was about right, and this pattern held for every racial group.

Implications for the Supply Side

In spite of Montgomery County officials' proclaimed intent to structure incentives that would promote integration, white families tended to request transfers into schools with a lower proportion of minorities, and minority families tended to opt for schools in lower-income, high-minority neighborhoods. The school's ethnic and class composition had more influence than most other school characteristics considered in the analysis. The parental survey sheds some light on this pattern. While parents are interested in special educational programs, their dominant concern seems to be whether the school does a good job in fulfilling the traditional functions that we associate with education: teaching basic skills and problem-solving in a safe and orderly environment. This desire for a generic kind of "good school," shared for the most part across ethnic groups, challenges those who favor a managed choice approach to integration. Managed choice through magnet schools, after all, has emphasized using special programs to attract parents. Moreover, in order to overcome the hurdle posed by residential segregation, managed choice often has counted on racially selective appeals: placing programs presumed to appeal more to upper-income, predominantly white families (such as gifted-and-talented programs) in schools located in minority neighborhoods, and programs presumed to appeal more to minority families (such as those emphasizing discipline and back-to-basics approaches) in predominantly white neighborhoods. Such patterns cast doubt on the racial neutrality perspective, which holds that freely exercised individual choice will, more or less spontaneously, complement the socially defined goal of greater racial integration.

The expansion of choice *can* coexist with the continued commitment to important social goals, such as racial integration, but bringing about and sustaining such a complementary arrangement requires careful attention to institutional particulars: the strictness of the criteria limiting transfers that result in imbalance, the willingness of officials to deny transfers in the face of parental pressure, the capacity of officials to develop and sustain meaningful diversity among program options, and the extent of the effort to provide all segments of the community with the information needed to make wise choices. "The meaning of choice proposals," as Richard Elmore (1990) notes, "can only be understood in the context of specific alterations of institutional structures within specific constraints on organization, money, and information" (p. 297). Moreover, attending to such institutional particulars is not simply a matter of providing model designs to well-intentioned public officials. The difficulties that Montgomery County has encountered suggest that managing choice to promote integration is a problematic exercise, even when undertaken as a self-conscious effort by well-informed public officials in a relatively favorable cultural and fiscal milieu.

Given a pattern of requests that might have increased racial segregation, Montgomery County officials have relied primarily on the exercise of governmental authority to keep choice and integration goals in balance. This is most directly seen in the denial of transfer requests. By constraining the choice of some parents—rejecting about 15% of the requests for transfer on grounds that they would worsen racial imbalance—Montgomery County officials have been able to keep the magnet program from exacerbating segregation. In addition, county officials have resisted pressure to dramatically expand the number of magnets, as parents in other areas of the county have demanded to know why their schools should be denied the attention and resources of the magnets. The drawing power of magnets, and their utility as tools for managing integration, is likely to be diluted if magnet features are allowed to replicate, willy-nilly, throughout the system.

But the exercise of such authoritative action is politically dicey.

School officials are placed in an awkward position when they are forced to deny transfers at the same time they are publicly promoting the availability of choice. The tendency of black parents to shy away from schools in which their children might be racially isolated adds another complication. Because minority transfer requests were more likely to run counter to than support racial balance, school officials found themselves forced to deny a higher proportion of requests from minorities than from majorities. From 1983 through 1986, officials rejected 20.2% of minority requests to transfer into the 14 magnet schools, compared to 13.1% of majority requests (Larson & Kirshtein, 1986).

CONCLUSIONS

Parental choice and racial integration may not be incompatible, but neither are they spontaneously harmonious. Lacking sharper differentiation among programs, given imperfect and unevenly distributed information, and in light of the fact that matching children with programmatic specialties appears to be a lower priority for parents than pursuit of a generically good school, race and cultural familiarity continue to play a role in shaping parental choices among schools. This is true even in a district that is generally considered politically progressive, and where parents truly appear motivated less by a desire to avoid integrated schools than by a desire to avoid schools in which their child will be racially isolated.

Proponents of market-based choice systems might protest that the results presented here are particular to the Montgomery County program, and in one sense they are right. The particulars of the institutional framework in which choice operates *are* important in determining school-level results. There are many steps public officials could take to increase the participation of minority families, to provide incentives to parents to send their children to racially mixed environments, and to encourage schools to aggressively recruit students from outside their normal attendance zones. But it is not enough that a better design for choice can be envisioned. We also must consider whether such a design can be translated into policy, implemented, monitored, adjusted, and sustained over time—against sharp political challenges. Even if brilliantly conceived, any program for increasing school choice will necessarily be fluid in important respects. Circumstances change, and translating the idea of choice into practice involves making tough choices among competing values, each with its own shifting constituencies.

Faced with political pressures to protect neighborhood schools, extend successful magnet programs to other schools, keep per-pupil spending relatively equal, and provide a common core curriculum, while at the same time honoring parental choice and avoiding racial destabilization, Montgomery County officials have crafted a limited choice arrangement that fails to meet the hopes of marketeers. It is inaccurate to cast them in the role of obstacles to choice. Not only were school officials integral in bringing choice onto the policy agenda, they have also played an important role in protecting some key elements from erosion.

Public choice enthusiasts paint education bureaucrats as motivated solely by self-interest, which, they argue, is not compatible with consumers' interests. Yet in a contentious democracy, school bureaucrats are rightfully charged with advancing fairness, responsiveness, dedication to professional norms, and commitment to the public interest. The market metaphor has distracted the terms of debate through its evocation of the invisible hand. Because meeting social goals requires continual exertion, we must take special care that our short-term initiatives do not undermine the institutions that can most effectively maintain publicly shared values.

APPENDIX: REGRESSION ANALYSIS

Separate regressions were performed to identify significant factors influencing (1) requests by nonminority families to enter the school, (2) requests by minority families, and (3) the ratio of requests by nonminorities to those by minorities. A maximum of four independent variables was set for inclusion in the final regression results, in order to mitigate the degrees-of-freedom problem that arises due to the high ratio of variables to cases. In keeping with the exploratory nature of this study, the decision was made not to eliminate any of the independent variables *a priori*; instead intercorrelated variables were allowed to "compete" for inclusion. In the cases of independent variables that were highly correlated with one another ($r > .60$), two procedures were used. In these stepwise regressions, all were allowed to compete for inclusion, but once one was accepted, the others were eliminated. In backward stepwise regressions, many separate models were run using alternative combinations of the independent variables to identify those that provided the most complete and stable equations. The findings from these reduced regression models are reported in Table 5.2 (unstandardized coefficients are reported).

Table 5.2: Regression Analysis

Variable	Coefficient	Standard Error	Prob > t
Regression 1: Transfer requests by white families			
Teacher experience	-.891	.181	0.001
Minority in school (%)	-.526	.121	0.001
Foreign language	14.007	5.662	0.033
Constant	80.107	10.773	0.000
$F = 21.4$ Prob $> F = .0001$ Adj. $r^2 = .821$			
Regression 2: Transfer requests by minority families			
Foreign language	16.652	4.945	0.006
Income[a]	-.529	.1977	0.022
Constant	26.541	5.423	0.000
$F = 9.93$ Prob $> F = .0034$ Adj. $r^2 = .579$			
Regression 3: Ratio of requests by white families to requests by minority families			
Income in tract[a]	.2653	.0863	0.013
CAT score	.419	.140	0.015
Student/teacher ratio	-.957	.396	0.039
Parent satisfaction	9.658	3.888	0.035
Constant	-42.004	19.242	0.057
$F = 9.93$ Prob $> F = .0034$ Adj. $r^2 = .579$			

[a] Coefficient multiplied by 1,000.

NOTES

1. Much of this evidence first appeared in Henig (1990), and is used by permission of *Social Science Quarterly*.

2. My appreciation to Joy Frechtling and John Larson for their cooperation in providing me with these data.

REFERENCES

Blank, R. K., Dentler, R. A., Baltzell, D. C., & Chabotar, K. (1983). *Survey of magnet schools: Analyzing a model for quality integrated education* (Final Report of a National Study for the U.S. Department of Education). Washington, DC: James H. Lowry and Associates.

Carver, R. L., & Salganik, L. H. (1991). You can't have choice without information. *Equity and Choice, 7*(2 & 3), 71–75.

Chubb, J. E., & Moe, T. M. (1990). *Politics, markets, and American schools.* Washington, DC: Brookings Institution.

Clinchy, E. (1985, May). Let magnet schools guide the way to educational reform—and diversity. *The American School Board Journal*, p. 43.

Elmore, R. (1990). Choice as an instrument of public policy. In Clune, W. H., & Witte, J. F. (Eds.), *Choice and control in American education* (Vol. 1; pp. 285–317). New York: Falmer.

Friedman, M. (1962). *Capitalism and freedom*. Chicago: University of Chicago.

Glazer, S. (1987, May 15). Desegregation plans that use magnet schools arouse concern that they promote separate and unequal schooling for black children. *Editorial Research Reports, 1*(18), 226–238.

Henig, J. R. (1989). Choice, race and public schools: The adoption and implementation of a magnet program in Montgomery County, Maryland. *Journal of Urban Affairs, 11*(3), 243–259.

Henig, J. R. (1990). Choice in public schools: An analysis of transfer requests among magnet schools. *Social Science Quarterly, 71*(1), 69–82.

Henig, J. R. (1994). *Rethinking school choice: Limits of the market metaphor*. Princeton, NJ: Princeton University Press.

Hirschman, A. O. (1970). *Exit, voice, and loyalty: Responses to decline in firms, organizations, and states*. Cambridge, MA: Harvard University Press.

La Noue, G. (1972). The politics of education. In G. R. La Noue (Ed.), *Educational vouchers: Concepts and controversies* (pp. 128–145). New York: Teachers College Press.

Larson, J. C., & Allen, B. A. (1988). *A microscope on magnet schools, 1983 to 1986: Vol. 2. Pupil and parent outcomes*. Montgomery County, MD: Montgomery County Public Schools, Department of Educational Accountability.

Larson, J. C., & Kirshstein, R. J. (1986). *A microscope on magnet schools, 1983–1985: Implementation and racial balance*. Rockville, MD: Department of Educational Accountability.

Levine, D. U., & Eubanks, E. F. (1980). Attracting minority students to magnet schools in minority neighborhoods. *Integrated Education, 18*, 52–58.

Metz, M. H. (1986). *Different by design: The context and character of three magnet schools*. New York: Routledge & Kegan Paul.

Montgomery County Planning Board. (1986). *1984 census update survey: Planning area profiles*. Silver Spring, MD: Maryland National Park and Planning Commission.

Monti, D. J. (1985). *A semblance of justice: St. Louis school desegregation and order in urban America*. Columbia: University of Missouri Press.

Rossell, C. H. (1985). What is attractive about magnet schools? *Urban Education, 20*(1), 7–21.

Rossell, C. H., & Clarke, R. C. (1990). *The carrot or the stick for school desegregation policy: Magnet schools or forced busing*. Philadelphia: Temple University Press.

Schelling, T. C. (1978). *Micromotives and macrobehavior*. New York: Norton.

U. S. Bureau of the Census. (1984). *Statistical abstract of the U.S.* Washington, DC: U.S. Department of Commerce.

CHAPTER 6

Who Benefits from the Milwaukee Choice Program?

JOHN F. WITTE

Since Milton Friedman conceived of school vouchers in 1955, various theoretical plans have been put forward (Chubb & Moe, 1990; Coons & Sugarman, 1978). However, despite recent voucher initiatives in Colorado and California, only a few programs exist that provide substantial public funding to enable students to attend private schools. The Milwaukee choice program is one. Enacted in the spring of 1990, the program provides an opportunity for students meeting specific criteria to attend private, nonsectarian schools. I was appointed by the Wisconsin Department of Public Instruction as an independent evaluator of that program in September 1990.

In assessing the Milwaukee choice program one must consider who participates, who benefits, and who may be harmed. These fundamental empirical questions involve both the right of families to choose and the right of children to receive an adequate education. For proponents, choice is both a basic right and an instrument for improving all schools through increased parental participation and competition among schools. Opponents of choice, stressing that all students need quality education, fear that unrestrained choice would produce greater inequality than currently exists.

The Milwaukee program offers a long-term laboratory for empirically assessing these claims. A consistent set of findings from the first three years of the program—on the characteristics of participating parents, their attitudes toward education, and their experiences in their prior public schools—can help us determine which parents in low-income communities are more likely to pursue choice programs. I also report on how parents respond to their chosen schools, on how children perform, and on attrition from the schools.

Importantly, the Milwaukee program serves low-income and working-class families in the inner city. It offers a fascinating case for understanding how different ethnic communities respond to liberal choice conditions. Robust ethnic organizations have created new private schools in response to strong parental demand. The Milwaukee program was expanded in 1995, including a controversial attempt to make religious schools eligible. My evaluation research aims to identify how this popular program is working and how it can be improved over time.

THE PROGRAM

The spirit and the letter of the Milwaukee choice program are in stark contrast to public subsidy of elite or exclusive private education. The program was designed to avoid subsidizing students who already attend private schools or families that can afford private schools. Instead, its aim is to provide alternative educational opportunities for families that cannot easily exercise choice by residential selection or by purchasing private education.

Under the program, private schools receive public funds equivalent to the Milwaukee public school (MPS) per-member state aid ($2,987 in 1993-94) in lieu of tuition and fees from the student. Students must come from MPS district families with incomes not exceeding 1.75 times the national poverty line and must not have attended a private school in the prior year. The total number of choice students in any year until 1994 was limited to 1% of the MPS membership (968 in 1993-94).

From 1990 to 1993 private schools had to limit choice students to 49% of their total enrollment. Starting in the 1994-95 school year, the limit on choice students in any school was raised from 49% to 65%; the total number of students in the program can equal 1.5% of the MPS membership. Schools cannot discriminate on admission, and if a school is oversubscribed in a grade, pupils are selected on a random basis. In situations in which one child from a family is admitted to the program, a sibling is exempt from random selection. Table 6.1 reports basic data on numbers of participating schools and students over the 1990-94 period.

Enrollment in the choice program increased from 341 in September 1990 to 742 in September 1993. The number of applicants exceeded

Table 6.1: Participation in the Milwaukee Choice Program, 1990–94

	1990–91	1991–92	1992–93	1993–94
Students allowed in the choice program	931	946	950	968
Private nonsectarian schools in Milwaukee	22	22	23	23
Schools participating	7	6	11	12
Available seats	406	546	691	811
Applications	577	689	998	1049
Students participating during				
September	341	521	620	742
January	259	526	586	701
June	249	477	570	671
Graduating students	8	28	32	42
Returning choice students	—	178	323	405

the number of students enrolled in every year. The number of schools participating has increased from seven in 1990–91 to twelve in 1993–94. Our best estimate is that eleven more schools would be potentially eligible (assuming church schools remain ineligible). The biggest limitation on the program is the number of seats available in the participating schools. Although the per-school expansion from 49% to 65% of the students enrolled being eligible for choice vouchers may increase numbers slightly, unless new schools participate, the program will never enroll substantial numbers of students relative to MPS.

RESEARCH AND DATA

We mailed surveys in the fall of each year, 1990 through 1993, to all new parents who applied for enrollment in one of the choice schools, and in May and June of 1991 to a control group comprised of a random sample of 5,474 parents of students in the Milwaukee public schools. A follow-up survey of all choice parents, assessing attitudes relating to their year in private schools, was mailed in June of each year.

Although the response rates (given in Table 6.2) on some of the surveys were low compared to face-to-face interviews with national samples, they were higher than the approximately 20% response rates that MPS reports for typical surveys. There were independent measures of race and qualification for free lunches for both the random sample and the choice students. Thus it was possible to assess sampling bias and construct weights to offset that bias. [1]

Table 6.2: **Survey Sample Sizes and Response Rates**

	Surveys Mailed	Surveys Not Delivered	Surveys Returned	Response Rate
1990–91				
MPS parents 5/91	5474	224	1598	30.4%
Choice parents Wave 1, 10/90	349	31	149	46.9%
Choice parents Wave 2, 6/91	360	33	166	50.8%
1991–92				
Choice parents Wave 1, 10/91	453	29	207	48.8%
Choice parents Wave 2, 6/92	531	38	219	44.4%
1992–93				
Choice parents Wave 1, 10/92	318	17	132	43.9%
Choice parents Wave 2, 6/93	656	35	238	38.3%

The Milwaukee public schools supplied achievement and other student data for both choice students and the random sample of MPS students. The choice schools administered achievement tests for the choice students at the end of each school year. Case studies of all the participating choice schools were also carried out in 1991 and 1993 (see Witte, 1991; Witte, Bailey, & Thorn, 1993). Finally, beginning in the fall of 1992 and continuing in 1993, brief mail and phone surveys were completed with as many parents as could be found who chose not to have their children continue in the program. Approximately 46% of these parents were contacted.

Because the MPS random sample included higher-income families, a low-income subset of the sample was selected as a matched control group—the most appropriate comparison group to the choice families based on income measures. The low-income group, which included about two-thirds of Milwaukee students, was defined as qualifying for free or reduced-price lunches (below 1.35 or 1.85 of the poverty line, respectively). Most low-income students qualified for free lunches. For a comparison of the complete MPS sample and the choice sample, see Table 6.3.

WHO PARTICIPATES:
CHOICE FAMILIES AND STUDENTS

The choice program was targeted to provide an opportunity for relatively poor families to attend private schools. Over the first three years the program clearly accomplished this goal. The average income of

Table 6.3: **Ethnic and Income Composition of Samples**

| | Choice | | MPS | |
	New Participants 1990–92	Responded to Survey 1990–92	Total Sample 1991	Responded to Survey May 1991
Race				
African-American	76.3%	84.3%	55.3%	42.4%
Asian-American	0.0%	0.0%	3.8%	6.0%
Hispanic	17.9%	10.6%	9.7%	10.1%
Native American	0.6%	1.0%	0.9%	0.5%
White	4.3%	3.5%	29.3%	40.3%
Other	0.8%	0.6%	1.0%	0.8%
(*n*)	(625)	(311)	(5365)	(1541)
Income				
Low income	56.6%	54.3%	63.9%	59.5%
Non-low income	43.4%	45.7%	36.1%	40.5%
(*n*)	(622)	(311)	(5438)	(1541)

Note: Percentages may not add to 100% because of rounding.

choice families over the first three years was $11,625, with 59% reporting incomes below $10,000. This compares to a maximum allowable income for eligibility of approximately $22,000 for the average family of three, which was also the average in our MPS random sample. Low-income MPS parents—our matched control group—reported slightly higher family income than choice parents (an average of $12,100, with 53% below $10,000).

Over the first three years, 59% of the choice mothers reported being on AFDC or general assistance, compared with 39% of the MPS sample and 59% of the low-income control group. Employment rates for both full- and part-time employment were similar for choice and MPS parents. For the combined three years, 36% of choice mothers and 67% of the choice fathers were employed full time, compared to 33% of mothers and 59% of fathers among low-income comparison group members.

African-American students comprised 76.3% of those applying to choice schools; Hispanics, 17.9%. The MPS sample, in contrast, was 55.3% African-American and 9.7% Hispanic. The number of African-American applications was up slightly in 1992–93 from the previous two years, and the number of Hispanic applicants declined somewhat. Choice families were much more likely to be headed by a single parent (77%) than the average MPS family (49%) and somewhat more likely than the low-income MPS family (64%).

Choice families tend to have fewer children than low-income MPS families. The average number of children in choice families was 2.63, compared to 3.24 in low-income families. Again, the statistics on choice families were consistent in each of the three years. This may indicate that choice families, in attempting to concentrate the resources they have on a smaller number of children, make a greater educational investment per child.

Despite similar economic status, choice parents also reported higher education levels than low-income MPS parents. The biggest difference in education appeared in the category responding "some college." Over half the choice mothers reported some college education (53%), compared with 30% of the low-income MPS respondents.

Educational expectations were high for all groups, with choice parents having somewhat higher expectations than MPS and low-income MPS parents. Eighty-seven percent of choice parents in the first three years indicated that they expected their child to go to college or do postgraduate work. This compared with 76% of the MPS parents and 72% of the low-income MPS parents. These proportions are significantly different statistically.

Experience of Choice Parents in Prior Public Schools

To complete the picture of choice parents, the degree of their involvement in and satisfaction with their child's prior MPS schools was measured, as well as the amount of help they gave their children at home.

Based on three years of evidence, the one clear finding is that choice parents were significantly more involved in the education of their children before they entered the choice program than were MPS parents. Involvement was measured in terms of parents contacting schools, parental activity in school organizations and activities, and parents working with their children at home. The greatest differences were in the frequency with which parents contacted schools about their child's academic performance, classes, or behavior. For example, as shown in Table 6.4, 32% of choice parents reported contacting their schools about their child's academic performance five times or more, compared to only 19% of MPS parents. Consistent with the smaller family sizes reported above, choice parents were significantly more involved in their child's education at home—by helping with homework, reading with their child, and so forth.

On every dimension, choice parents were less satisfied with their child's public schools than the average MPS parent (see Table 6.5).

Table 6.4: Choice and MPS Parents' Frequency of Contacting Schools (Percentages)

	Times per Week			
Reason for Contact	0	1–2	3–4	5 or More
Choice parents, prior (public) school, 1990–92 data combined[a]				
Child's academic performance	13	26	28	32
Child's behavior	26	26	20	28
Doing volunteer work for the school	41	27	15	17
Participating in fund raising	27	41	19	13
MPS parents, 1991[b]				
Child's academic performance	24	33	25	19
Child's behavior	36	32	17	16
Doing volunteer work for the school	63	21	7	9
Participating in fund-raising	54	32	9	4

[a] $n = 409$. [b] $n = 1,577$.

Their greatest concerns were with the amount the child learned and with school discipline; parents were least dissatisfied with such factors, as school location, that have little to do with the operation of the school. When asked what grade they would give their child's prior public school, choice parents gave considerably lower grades than MPS parents. First-year choice parents gave their prior public schools a C, or 2.0, on average; second- and third-year choice parents gave their prior public schools a 2.5; MPS parents gave their schools a 2.8 on average.

Student Achievement in Prior Public Schools

Parents may have been dissatisfied with their children's prior public schools because their children were not doing well in those schools. Indeed, my research indicates that the choice students in this program entered very near the bottom in terms of academic achievement. To measure student achievement, the Iowa Test of Basic Skills (ITBS), which is given in grades 1–8, was used. Test scores were not available for all students in either group because tests are not given every year in MPS. Chapter 1 students, however, are tested every year. As an estimate of prior achievement, the spring or last test taken while the student was in MPS was used for just over half the choice students. This should yield as complete a picture as possible for a sizable portion of choice students. The most reliable statistic for achievement test scores is the mean normal curve equivalent (NCE), which estimates how

Table 6.5: Choice and MPS Parent Satisfaction with Prior (Public) School (Percentages)

School Dimension	Very Satisfied	Somewhat Satisfied	Somewhat Dissatisfied	Very Dissatisfied
Choice parents, 1990–92 data combined[a]				
Textbooks	27	57	12	4
Location of school	35	44	9	12
Opportunities for parent involvement	33	47	13	8
Teacher's performance	36	39	16	10
Program of instruction	30	43	20	7
Principal's performance	31	38	18	13
Amount child learned	33	29	20	17
Discipline in the school	27	34	26	13
MPS parents, 1991[b]				
Textbooks	29	63	6	1
Location of school	41	44	10	5
Opportunities for parent involvement	36	54	8	3
Teacher's performance	40	48	9	3
Program of instruction	33	56	9	5
Principal's performance	37	48	9	5
Amount child learned	36	47	13	4
Discipline in the school	27	48	17	8

[a] $n = 377$. [b] $n = 1,441$.

achievement scores would be distributed across students if a larger sample were available, approximating the bell-shaped normal distribution. Because a number of students may be bunched together, with small samples both prior test scores and change scores (discussed below) can be volatile.

In all three years, scores on the ITBS taken in prior public schools by students applying to the choice program were significantly below those for the average MPS student taking the same test, and significantly below those for the average low-income MPS student in the second year. Based on difference of means in the NCEs, however, the difference between choice and low-income MPS students was not significant at the .05 level in the first or third years, whereas it was in the second year. Difference-of-means tests indicate that all choice student scores were significantly lower (at the .001 level of significance) than those in the MPS sample. In comparison to the low-income MPS students, the 1990 test differences were not significant; the 1991 reading comparisons for both applying and accepted choice students were significant at the .05 level, while math differences were significant at .001.

The absolute level of the scores indicates the difficulty these students were having prior to entering the choice program. The median national percentile for choice students ranged from 26 to 31 over the three years; the national median is 50. The NCE, which is standardized to a national mean of 50, ranged from 37.5 to 39.8, which is about two-thirds of a standard deviation below the national average. It should be noted, however, that all MPS students in all years were also below the national average. The highest scores were for math, with NCE scores around 46. About 43% of the MPS students were above the median (50th percentile) on math, with only 35% to 36% above it on reading.

Who Participates: Conclusions

The overall portrait of choice students and families presents something of a paradox. The choice program was specifically designed to provide an opportunity for poor parents to send their children to alternative schools they could not otherwise afford. Three years of very consistent evidence indicates that in this it succeeds. In addition, there are numerous indications that these parents were frustrated and dissatisfied with the public schools their children had been attending and that their children were not doing well in these schools. Thus one could argue these are exactly the types of families that should have access to an alternative school setting. On the other hand, choice families tend to be better educated and more involved in their children's education than the average parent. One could reasonably argue that if these students and families remained in their prior schools, they could exercise important influence in attempting to improve these neighborhood schools.

WHO BENEFITS:
EFFECTS OF THE CHOICE PROGRAM

The impact of the choice program was measured through achievement test results, parent attitudes, parent involvement, and attrition.

Achievement Test Results

Figure 6.1 provides the aggregate test results for 1991–93 for choice students and for MPS students. ITBS tests were administered in April or May of each year. The choice students tested in 1991 did better than the MPS low-income group on reading but somewhat worse on mathematics (see Figure 6.1). Tests taken in the choice schools in the second year—spring 1992—showed lower scores than those of both the full MPS

Figure 6.1: Posttest Results, Iowa Test of Basic Skills — 1991, 1992, 1993

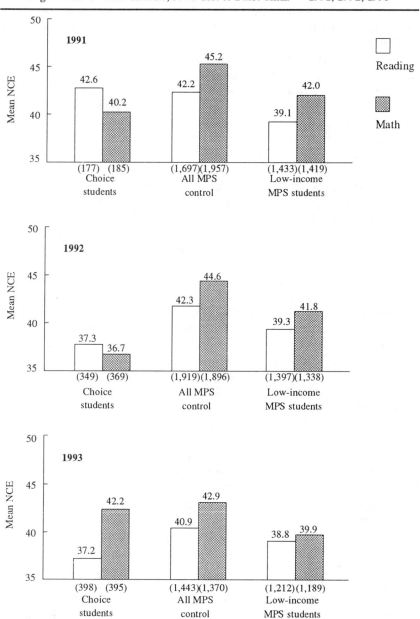

Note: *n*'s are given in parentheses.

sample and the low-income MPS students. Comparing the more relevant low-income MPS and choice students, the choice students' mean math NCE was more than 5 points lower; the reading score, which was higher in 1991, was 2 points lower.

The 1993 scores indicate another switch in the absolute yearly score differences, especially in mathematics. Reading scores for choice students were 3.7 points lower than those for the MPS sample and 1.6 points lower than those for the low-income MPS group. Math scores, however, switched from prior years. Choice students' math scores in 1993 were slightly lower than the total MPS sample, but choice students scored 2.3 points higher than those in the low-income sample.

Change Scores. Because the yearly scores do not report on the same students from year to year, the only way to accurately measure achievement gains and losses is to analyze those students for whom we have test scores in each of three years. We can then estimate how individual students changed relative to the national norms over each school year (see Figure 6.2).[2]

For the first year, the averages for all groups improved, except math among choice students. For the choice students, the gain in reading was considerable, although not statistically significant; math scores stayed essentially the same. The MPS numbers (a larger sample) indicate considerable and significant improvement in average math scores, with smaller gains in reading. Both low-income and all MPS students gained in math. Three of these gains were statistically significant, again due in part to the larger sample sizes available, compared to the smaller sample of choice students.

Quite different effects were observed in the second year. Change scores for choice students in math, and for MPS control students in both reading and math, were not appreciable. None of these differences approached standard levels of statistical significance. In contrast to the first year, however, reading scores dropped for choice students. The decline was 3.9 NCE points for all choice students between 1991 and 1992. Because NCE scores are based on a national norm, this means that choice students scored considerably below where they were relative to the national sample in the prior year. The decline was statistically significant at the .001 level.

The results shifted again in the third year. Choice students declined slightly in reading, which was not significant. On the other hand, for the first time, there was improvement in the math scores for the choice students. The mean math NCE went from 38.3 to 42.7 for a 4.4 NCE gain, which is statistically significant. MPS scores, on the other hand,

Figure 6.2: Changes in Scores on Iowa Test of Basic Skills in NCEs, 1990–91 to 1992–93

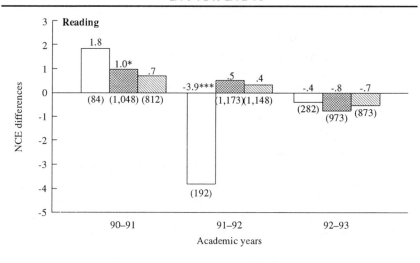

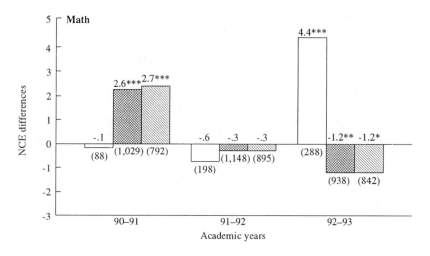

* *p* < .05,   ** *p* < .01,   *** *p* < .001

Note: *n*'s are given in parentheses.

declined for both tests and for both groups. The decline in math scores was significant and estimated to be 1.2 NCEs for both the total MPS control group and the low-income sample.

Other Factors Affecting Student Achievement. Variations in achievement could be based on a number of factors other than whether students were in MPS or choice schools. To provide an accurate and confirming picture of test achievement, one must therefore control statistically for these factors by using multivariate regression analysis. I estimated the second-year test score, controlling for prior achievement and student background characteristics, and then included a (dichotomous) variable to measure the effect of being in a choice or MPS school.

Table 6.6 reports on the discrete effect of participating in the choice program, distinguishing between reading and math achievement in 1991, 1992, and 1993. The unstandardized coefficients (b's) indicate the change in test score points associated with a unit change in the predictor. For example, a student scoring 1 point above the average pupil (in NCE units for reading in 1990) exhibited a .59 point advantage on the 1991 reading test. The other pupil-background factors are dichotomously scored (as a value of 1, if the characteristic is present). So, for example, in the first column we see that children from low-income families scored 4.14 points below the average student in reading in 1991.

The multivariate estimations of achievement for 1991 and 1992 in Table 6.6 clarify patterns observed earlier. For 1991, after controlling for the expected effects of student-background factors, we see that participating in a choice school was related to *higher* reading scores but *lower* math scores relative to the MPS control group. Neither effect, while significant in absolute terms, was estimated with sufficient accuracy to make it statistically significant. In 1992, again controlling for student differences and prior achievement (performance on a 1991 test), the only difference between choice and MPS children was on reading scores. These scores favored MPS students: The estimated effect of being in the choice program in 1992 was -3.35 NCEs, or approximately .25 standard deviation lower in reading achievement.

The 1993 results were indeterminate in reading but not in math. Change scores indicated that choice students had improved in math and MPS students had declined, and the multivariate models support that result. The estimated gain in math for choice students (3.86), controlling for a number of variables, was similar to the change score reported in Figure 6.2. As expected and consistent with 1991 and 1992, the previous year's test was an excellent predictor of current-year test results. For both models, being an African-American predicted significantly lower

Table 6.6: Regression Estimates of Student Achievement Effects of Family Ethnicity and Income, Child Gender, and Participation in Choice Program for 1991, 1992, and 1993

	1991 Test Scores		1992 Test Scores		1993 Test Scores	
	Reading	Math	Reading	Math	Reading	Math
Pretest scores						
Test score NCE, prior year	0.59***	0.64***	.60***	0.66***	0.61***	0.59***
Test grade percentile	-0.61**	-1.30***	-0.64***	-1.12***	0.47**	-1.10**
Child gender	.50	-0.24	1.72*	0.43	1.13	0.43
Low-income family [dichotomous, 1 = yes]	-4.14**	-4.02**	-2.61*	-1.93	-2.36	-3.04*
Ethnicity						
African-American	-3.73***	-3.43**	-6.31***	-4.87***	-4.74***	-5.27***
Hispanic	-3.44*	-4.07*	-1.42	-0.57	-2.73	-2.23
Other minority	-1.67	-0.53	-1.34	2.63	-4.93*	0.02
Participating in choice program	2.32	-2.07	-3.35**	-1.23	0.76	3.86***
Full equation						
Intercept	26.04***	29.37***	25.1***	24.5***	18.41***	28.3***
F statistic	98.72***	143.40***	126.3***	156.5***	129.00***	132.2***
Degrees of freedom	8,1096	8,1073	8,1305	8,1291	8,1243	8,1213
r^2	.42	.51	.43	.49	.45	.46
Mean test score	40.6	43.8	39.8	42.4	39.6	42.3

Note: Data are unstandardized coefficients.
* $p < .05$ ** $p < .01$ *** $p < .001$

test scores. Hispanics also did less well, although the difference only approached significance on the reading test. Being from a low-income family had the expected negative sign for both reading and math, but the effect was only significant for the math test.

Parental Involvement

Parental involvement and parental attitude measures for choice students were based on responses to the second wave of surveys conducted in June of each year. Those surveys were sent to all enrollees in the choice program. It is impossible to estimate the measurement error based on the attendant respondent bias. One can only speculate as to whether well-satisfied or unhappy respondents were more likely to respond.

Parental involvement is stressed in most of the choice schools and, in fact, is required in the contracts signed by parents in several of the schools. Parents can be involved in organized activities, such as working on committees or helping with teas and fund-raising events, and in educational activities, such as chaperoning field trips, helping out in the classroom, or assisting with special events. Choice parents' involvement, already high in their prior public school, increased when children were enrolled in choice schools in all areas but educational activities at home. These findings stem from annual surveys of choice parents. School contacts also increased after their children enrolled in the choice schools, with major increases for volunteer work and fund-raising activities. Parents also contacted their schools more often concerning their child's classes and academic performance, volunteering in the school, and participating in fund-raising. There were no significant increases in providing information, helping in the classroom, or contacts regarding their child's behavior. The latter may be a positive outcome, consistent with parents' approval of the disciplinary environment of the private schools (see Witte et al., 1993).

With respect to organized parent activity, every category of parental involvement was higher in the choice schools than in prior public schools, with the largest increase in attendance at parent meetings. Fifty-five percent of choice parents indicated they attended such a meeting at their prior public school, while 79% said they attended a meeting after enrolling in a private choice school.

Parental Attitudes

In all three years, choice parents were more satisfied with choice schools than they had been with their prior public schools and more satisfied than MPS parents with their schools (cross-sectional data appear in Table 6.7). Attitudes were more positive on every item, with "discipline in the school" showing the greatest increase in satisfaction over one year (18%). (This figure is based on the percentage of parents responding "very satisfied" or "somewhat satisfied.")

Choice parents gave their children's private schools higher marks than they gave their prior MPS schools. For the three-year period, the average grade parents gave their child's school rose from 2.4 for MPS schools to 2.9 for private schools, with the biggest increase (2.0 to 3.0) in the first year of involvement in the choice program.

What parents said they liked and disliked about the program was also consistent over the first three years. Approximately 70% of the positive open-ended responses mentioned qualities of the school, with

Table 6.7: Choice Parent Satisfaction with Choice Private School, 1991–93
(Percentages)

School Dimension	Very Satisfied	Somewhat Satisfied	Somewhat Dissatisfied	Very Dissatisfied
Textbooks	42	47	6	5
Location of school	46	37	10	6
Opportunities for parent involvement	52	39	4	4
Teacher's performance	54	35	6	5
Program of instruction	45	44	6	5
Principal's performance	48	38	7	6
Amount child learned	52	36	6	6
Discipline in the school	43	41	9	7

$n = 547$.

most referring to the education provided in the choice schools (better-quality education, class size, innovative programs).

Predictably, the negative comments shifted from first-year concerns, such as uncertainty over the program or a bad experience with the program (one school withdrew from the choice program), to second- and third-year concerns, such as school problems, fears about not qualifying for the program, transportation, and logistics.

Attrition

Perhaps the most troubling result of the first years of the choice program was the rate of attrition. Excluding students in the defunct Juanita Virgil Academy, first-year attrition (defined as the percentage of students who did not graduate and who could have returned to choice schools) was 40%, 35%, and 31% over the first three years. As indicated by the relatively modest drop from September to June (9.3% in 1991–92; 8.1% in 1992–93), most attrition took place after the school year ended. For the third year, if we exclude the two schools that serve at-risk high school students, the post-June average attrition rate dropped to 28% for the remaining schools. Although the overall trend was downward, approximately one-third of the students each year did not return to the choice schools.

Is this attrition higher or lower than in comparable public schools? This question is difficult to answer. Milwaukee data on transfers between schools from September until June are reliable: This mobility rate for comparable schools in MPS averages around 33%. This figure, however, includes both "in" and "out" transfers from schools between

September and June. Because the choice program attrition does not include in transfers, if we assume there were equal numbers of in and out transfers in MPS, the appropriate MPS rate to use for comparison would be 16.5%. Thus not counting Juanita Virgil, attrition during the year from the choice schools was *less* than in MPS in all three years and seems reasonable, given the residential mobility of inner-city families. However, overall attrition of choice students, including summer months, remains high.

Why are students not returning to the choice schools? In the first year of the program, attrition might have been explained by the uncertainty of the program due to the pending Wisconsin supreme court ruling, but that uncertainty would not explain the relatively high attrition rates in the second and third years. The data indicate that approximately half of the students leaving (49%) subsequently enrolled in MPS schools; 32%, in other private schools in the area (often religious schools); and the remaining 19%, in MPS contract schools, home schooling, or schools outside Milwaukee.

Of the reasons they gave for leaving, approximately 25% exited choice schools for family reasons, including moving. (Undoubtedly this category is underestimated, since some moving families could not be located.) Almost all of the remaining responses were critical of some aspect of the choice program or the private schools. The two leading problems with the program were the lack of religious training (10%), which has not been allowed by statute, and transportation (9%). Within-school problems most often cited were unhappiness with teachers (14%); dissatisfaction with the general quality of education (10%); and lack of specific programs in the schools (8%). A few parents expressed dissatisfaction with tight discipline and fund-raising responsibilities.

Attrition from the choice program remains a problem. Attrition also afflicts public schools, and its causes undoubtedly lie in part beyond school walls. But if students fail to remain in choice schools, it is impossible for these schools to live up to their potential.

CONCLUSIONS

The Milwaukee choice program is clearly successful in providing some families with an opportunity to attend alternative schools that they would be hard pressed to afford otherwise. The students come from poor and working-class families, and they have not done well in their prior public schools. To the extent that the purpose of the program is to create these opportunities, the program is succeeding.

In terms of benefits to students, results are less clear-cut. Test scores vary considerably, and it appears that choice students do no better than a randomly selected control group from MPS. Attrition from the program is also high, which means that few students are remaining in the schools over a period of years. On the other hand, parental involvement is higher in the choice schools, parents express considerably greater satisfaction with their private schools, and they overwhelmingly approve of the program.

This program should not be used as evidence, either pro or con, for evaluating more inclusive choice programs, including a recent proposed expansion of this program to include many more students and parochial schools. Programs proposed in other states, such as the voucher initiatives in Colorado or California, do not limit eligibility by income or require random school selection procedures as in the Milwaukee program. And families taking advantage of choice opportunities in these relatively unconstrained programs could well be different from those in the targeted Milwaukee program.

Legislation enacted in July 1995, which is being challenged in the courts, would expand the Milwaukee choice program to include religious schools and substantially increase the number of students allowed in the program. Other conditions of the program remain, except that private schools could now enroll prior private school students in grades K–3. Thus, if the families report qualifying low incomes, students currently in private schools would become "choice" students.

A parallel privately funded voucher program in Milwaukee, Partners for Advancing Values in Education (PAVE), has been offering scholarships to low-income students since 1992. However, that program includes religious private schools, and 95% of the students in the program attend those schools (Beales & Wahl, 1995, p. 6). Those students now would qualify for the publicly funded choice program. PAVE's own study indicated that their students are much more likely to be white (49%), come from two-parent families (43%), and have parents who graduated from high school (85% of mothers, 81% of fathers) than the low-income choice program parents (Beales & Wahl, 1995, Tables 5, 7, 8).

The point is that if the courts allow the new program to proceed, evaluation results from the prior program will clearly not apply. And, because the new legislation eliminated evaluations, nothing will be known about who participates in that program and with what effects.

This school choice experiment clearly has stimulated a vibrant response by parents and private schools alike to liberalized, yet constrained, market conditions. But wider choice and parental enthusiasm have not yet led to more effective schools. This missing link—and institutional constraints on school improvements—deserve much greater attention by those implementing choice programs. As for researchers, we need to examine this odd paradox whereby choice creates enormous enthusiasm among parents and private educators—but student achievement fails to rise.

NOTES

Acknowledgment. This research was supported by grants from Spencer Foundation and the Robert La Follette Institute of Public Affairs, University of Wisconsin–Madison.

1. Also analyzed were scales and demographic variables using three weights: a weight based on expected race; a weight based on expected low/ non-low income; and a weight combining both race and income. The combined race and income weight is the most accurate. Because for the MPS respondents the sampling bias for race was considerably larger than for income, the income-weighted analysis produced no significant differences except on the income variable itself. The race and income analysis produced only one marginally significant difference on the attitude scale means. These details are available elsewhere (Witte, Bailey, & Thorn, 1993).

2. Results are based on differences in NCEs, subtracting the first-year score from the second. NCEs are used because national percentile rankings (NPRs) are not interval-level data. One of the problems with the transformation from NPRs to NCEs is that the very lowest and highest ends of the distribution are compressed. This tends to inflate very low-end scores and deflate very high-end scores. The lower-end inflation may affect this population, which has quite a few test scores below the 10th National Percentile. NCEs are the national standard for reporting results across populations and grades for Chapter 1 and other programs.

REFERENCES

Beales, J., & Wahl, M. (1995). *Given the choice: A study of the PAVE Program and school choice in Milwaukee.* Los Angeles: Reason Foundation.

Chubb, J., & Moe, T. (1990). *Politics, markets, and American schools.* Washington, DC: Brookings Institution.

Coons, J., & Sugarman, S. (1978). *Education by choice: The case for family control.* Berkeley: University of California Press.

Friedman, M. (1955). The role of government in education. In R. A. Solo (Ed.), *Economics and the public interest* (pp. 123–144). New Brunswick, NJ: Rutgers University Press.

Witte, J. (1991). *First year report: The Milwaukee parental choice program.* Madison: Wisconsin Department of Public Instruction.

Witte, J., Bailey, A., & Thorn, C. (1993). *Third year report: The Milwaukee parental choice program.* Madison: Wisconsin Department of Public Instruction.

CHAPTER 7

Public and Private Schools Overseas

Contrasts in Organization and Effectiveness

MARLAINE LOCKHEED
EMMANUEL JIMENEZ

School choice advocates often claim that private schools possess effective attributes that differentiate them from public schools: greater flexibility in how they operate and in the way they are funded, direct accountability to those who use their services, and the ability of school-level managers and parents to make critical educational decisions (Coleman, Hoffer, & Kilgore, 1982). These organizational features, it is argued, enable private schools to provide education more effectively—to provide the type and quality of education students and their parents demand. And private schools may feel incentives to provide more effective education and at lower cost, compared to their public school counterparts.

Private schools serve as an organizational laboratory for alternative models of school-level management, which, if effective, could be adopted by public schools. Free of the bureaucratic constraints that encumber public schools, private schools can make more decisions at the school level. Public schools might not be able to employ the greater school-level autonomy of private schools because of differences in their sources of support and accountability.

But despite these claims about the organizational advantages of private schools, little empirical evidence has been available to inform them. Our research in five developing countries sheds light on the relative effectiveness and efficiency of public and private schools—within institutional settings that differ from conditions found in the United

States. This exercise usefully illustrates the variety of mixed markets for schooling that emerge under differing policy conditions. At the same time, the organizational features of private schools found overseas, which we show help to raise student achievement, may offer lessons for American educators.

We begin by reviewing the basic facts and figures on the public–private balance in schooling overseas. While the share of private enrollment in primary education is uniformly small across regions of the world, there is much more variability in secondary education, with some nations enrolling half of all students in private schools. Then we present recent research that compares the relative effectiveness and efficiency of private and public secondary schools in five diverse countries: Colombia, the Dominican Republic, the Philippines, Tanzania, and Thailand. These studies point to a robust private school advantage in terms of student achievement levels and unit costs, after carefully controlling for student background and selection.

We also peer into the black box of private and public school organizations to try to explain the observed differences in the five country case studies, focusing on differences in school resources and inputs as well as management practices. Although each of the country studies used data that were collected for local purposes, all contained similar core information. The data on Colombia and Tanzania were generated from a World Bank study of diversified education (see Psacharopoulos & Loxley, 1985). The Philippines data were collected by the Ministry of Education as part of its Household and School Matching Survey. The Thailand data were obtained from the Second International Mathematics Study conducted by the International Association for the Evaluation of Educational Achievement (IEA; Robitaille & Garden, 1989). The Dominican Republic data came from a survey modeled after the IEA (Luna & Gonzalez, 1986). Following the survey we present more detailed information from a small sample of public and private schools in order to identify private school practices that could boost performance in public schools.

THE PUBLIC VERSUS PRIVATE BALANCE IN EDUCATION

"The concept of free compulsory education," as Roth (1987) points out, "for which the state should be responsible, originated in Europe and North America but was not widely promoted until the nineteenth century. It is thus of comparatively recent origin. Private education has had a much longer history" (p. 16). Today, primary and secondary enrollment in most nations is predominantly in public schools. The share of public education, however, is substantially higher at the primary level than at the secondary. In Asia, for example, the average share of public enrollment was 16% higher in primary than secondary education in 1975.

Little evidence, however, has been systematically gathered on the financing of private schools (how much are private schools subsidized?), regulation (how strict is government control over the way the schools are run?), and ownership (are private schools sectarian, religious, or for profit?). The most comprehensive study is a review by James (1991) of the experiences of some 50 industrialized and developing countries. Her study indicates that in those countries where teacher salaries are paid by the state (mostly in Europe), private schools are subsidized at 80% or more of their costs. Some developing countries, such as Lesotho, Togo, and Chile, and some states in India, support their private schools to the same extent. Such heavily subsidized, privately managed systems are also the most heavily regulated. A wide variety of countries, such as Japan, the United States, the United Kingdom, Indonesia, Kenya, and several in Latin America, provide indirect subsidies to private schools through tax breaks or direct subsidies of up to 25% of costs. These governments have only slight control over individual schools. On the other hand, some countries that offer neither indirect nor partial support still attempt to regulate their private schools.

EFFECTIVENESS AND EFFICIENCY

What is the empirical evidence regarding the relative effectiveness and efficiency of private and public schools? In the United States, the provocative Coleman, Hoffer, and Kilgore (1982) report concluded that attending private schools improved the performance of students as measured by standardized tests of verbal and mathematical skills. Despite outstanding questions of selectivity bias and the modest magnitude of this effect (Murnane, Newstead & Olsen, 1985), the belief that the average student does better in private than in public schools is now widespread.

Evidence has been more scarce for developing countries. Our research project compared the relative effectiveness and efficiency of private and public secondary schools in five diverse countries, focusing on secondary schools, where private participation is most significant. Roth (1987) and James (1987) earlier studied the private sector's role in providing education in developing countries, although they did not compare costs or achievement in private and public schools. To carefully examine the relative effectiveness of private schools, we asked: Would a high school student, selected at random from the general student population, do better in a public or private school? In the absence of experimental data, our study compares students' performance on standardized tests in a cross-section of public and private schools, after taking into account student background, motivation, ability, and prior performance. Statistical techniques purge the influence of background factors from the achievement scores and ensure enough overlap in the distribution of student characteristics so that subsamples are truly comparable. Other statistical techniques are then used to control for possible selection bias.

Because it is difficult to measure many nonschool or family background effects (for instance, innate ability), we supplement the cross-sectional studies with studies using panel data that compare the differences in the achievement of public and private school students over two time periods. Nonschool effects that do not change over that time are netted out. In the studies of the Dominican Republic and Thailand, changes in achievement over two time periods are used rather than the level of achievement in a given time period. For the salient features of the case studies, see Table 7.1. As far as we know, this type of value-added analysis of private schools has only been conducted for one industrialized country (for U.S. high schools—Coleman et al., 1982; Hanushek, 1986; Lee & Bryk, 1989).

Table 7.1: Summary of Studies

Nation Studied	Year Data Collected	Number of Students	Number of Schools	Grade	Indicator of Achievement	Database
Colombia	1981	1,471	35	11	Average scores on math and verbal tests	Special survey
Dominican Republic	1982–83	2,472	76	8	Mathematics test	National school survey
Philippines	1983	446	—	7–10	Mathematics, English, and Filipino tests	National household survey
Tanzania	1981	446	—	11	Average scores on math and verbal tests	Special survey
Thailand	1981–82	4,030	99	8	Mathematics test	National school survey

Results: Relative Effectiveness

Because students' backgrounds influence their choice of schools, it would not be valid to infer differences among types of schools by simply comparing achievement scores on standardized tests. We must hold such background effects constant in our analysis. The private schools in these five countries charge tuition, while the public schools are almost free, so the most important factors in the choice of school are income (or income-related variables such as parents' education and occupations) and the relative cost of schooling. In Colombia and the Philippines, indices of family income for students in private schools are about twice as high as for students in public schools (see Table 7.2). In Tanzania, public schools attract a more comparable mix of students, relative to private schools. Public schools serve a sizable proportion of children in families where the father is employed in a white-collar job and the mother has some formal schooling. The range in income, however, is only slightly higher for private than for public school students in Colombia and lower in Tanzania and the Philippines, which suggests a substantial overlap in the income categories of the public and private student samples. Our analyses controlled for selection bias through statistical methods that are fully explained in Cox and Jimenez (1991). In both Thailand and the Dominican Republic, private school students come from families with more educated mothers and with fathers employed in white-collar occupations.

Table 7.2: Background Indicators for Private School Students as a Multiple for Public School Students

Indicators	Colombia	Dominican Republic[a]		Philippines	Tanzania	Thailand
		O-type	F-type			
Income (of head of household or father)	1.94	—	—	2.07	1.20	—
Coefficient of variation of income	1.24	—	—	0.72	0.83	—
Mother's education (% beyond primary)	1.87	1.62	2.21	1.23	1.27	1.61
Father's occupation (% white collar)	1.09	1.69	2.52	—	1.50	1.94
Percentage male	1.04	1.29	1.78	0.98	1.07	0.91

Note: The table shows the extent to which an indicator for private school students exceeds that for public school students. For example, in Colombia, the average household head income of students in private school is 1.94 (almost twice) that of students in public school. A figure close to one implies that an indicator for private schools is equal to that of public school sudents.

[a]   F-type schools are authorized to give Ministry of Education examinations. O-type schools are not so authorized.

Table 7.3: The Private School Advantage: Predicted Test Score in Private Schools as a Multiple of Predicted Test Score in Public Schools and in the Standard Deviation Units

Country	Indicator of Achievement	Relative Advantage	Effect Size
Colombia	Average math and verbal	1.13	0.55
Dominican Republic[a]	Mathematics (O-type)	1.31	0.89
	Mathematics (F-type)	1.47	2.16
Philippines	Mathematics	1.00	-0.09
	English language	1.18	0.33
	Filipino language	1.02	0.25
Tanzania	Average math and verbal	1.16	0.97
Thailand[a]	Mathematics	2.36	1.69

Note: The table shows proportional gain in the achievement score if randomly selected student, with the characteristics of the average public school student, attends a private school, holding constant that student's background.

[a] For the Dominican Republic and Thailand, the test score before the school year began was included as a regressor in the equation explaining achievement at the end of the year.

Given student background, students in private schools in all five countries generally outperform their public counterparts on standardized mathematics and language tests. Table 7.3 shows the ratio of a student's predicted score in a private school to his or her score in a public school. For example, in Colombia a student with the background of the average public school student would score 1.13 times (13%) better in a private school than in a public school. The predicted scores in each type of school are obtained from the regression equations relating background to achievement, as evaluated at the level of background characteristics of the average public school student. This holds the effects of prior background constant. The ratio varies considerably across countries but is consistently greater than 1 for all subsamples and achievement tests (with the possible exception of mathematics achievement in the Philippines, where the differences are insignificant). In terms of standard deviation units or effect size, the private school advantage is large and meaningful in almost all cases, ranging from .5 to 2 standard deviations. These differences in the effect size associated with private schools cannot be dismissed as trivial.

After we hold pupil background effects constant by measuring achievement at the average characteristics of public or private school students, we find that the advantage conferred by private schools is greater for the two countries with the best controls for student background: the Dominican Republic and Thailand (see Table 7.3). The data for these students contained test scores measured at the beginning and at the end of the school year, and the ratios measure change in the level of achievement over the course of one academic year (with controls for possible selection bias).

Do these results hold for students from different socioeconomic groups? Qualitatively, the answer is yes. The private school advantage persists even when the computations in Table 7.3 hold constant the background of the average private school student, whose status is higher than that of the average public school student. The Philippines study is the only one that looked at the sensitivity of the private–public differential to a wider range of socioeconomic indicators. Variations in socioeconomic status, within a reasonable range, did not reverse the private school effect. But the *magnitude* of the private school advantage substantially decreases for students with lower socioeconomic status. The more elite private schools in the Philippines tend to emphasize the development of English-language skills, and advantaged children have more exposure to English and better access to English materials.

We also sought to determine whether the academic background or social class of students in a school has an effect on the achievement of all students in that school. Average achievement levels for all pupils in each child's classroom were used to help estimate child-level achievement. In the Dominican Republic and Thailand, the only two countries for which data were available, the answer is yes: peer group effects are very important. However, these effects do not completely counteract the effects of school type.

Results: Relative Efficiency

Our calculations, based on each country's school expenditure data, indicate that unit costs for private schools are lower than those for public schools (see Table 7.4, column 1). Thus for the same unit cost, private schools provide as much as three times more learning as do public schools (column 2). Conversely, the same amount of learning in private schools can cost as little as 15% of its cost in public schools (column 3). These results indicate that private schools are more efficient than public schools, at least for secondary schools in these particular countries.

There is considerable variability within each school type, as seen among private schools in the Dominican Republic in Table 7.4. Philippine public schools (those that are locally funded) have lower unit costs than some types of private (elite) schools. Unfortunately, the survey

Table 7.4: Relative Average Cost and Efficiency of Public and Private Schools

	(1) Ratio of Private Cost to Public Cost	(2) Ratio of Relative Effectiveness to Cost[a]	(3) Ratio of Relative Cost to Effectiveness[b]
Colombia	0.69	1.64	0.61
Dominican Republic			
O-type	0.65	2.02	0.50
F-type	1.46	1.01	0.99
Philippines[c]			
Math	0.83	1.20	0.83
English	0.83	1.42	0.70
Filipino	0.83	1.22	0.81
Tanzania	0.69	1.68	0.59
Thailand	0.39	6.74	0.17

[a] Figures from Table 7.2 divided by column 1 of Table 7.4.
[b] Column 1 of Table 7.4 divided by figures from Table 7.2.
[c] Public cost estimates, weighted average of national and local costs. Costs are assumed to be the same for all three subjects and are based on World Bank estimates.

data do not distinguish between student achievement among types of public schools. It would be interesting to explore this comparison.

There are some important caveats. First, the orders of magnitude are rough. The cost estimates for Colombia and Tanzania are not precise because a number of private schools did not provide the necessary information. Second, in the Philippines, we used the average cost for a nationwide sample of schools, rather than the actual cost of the schools specifically included in the study. By comparison, in the Dominican Republic and Thailand, we had school-by-school cost data for the entire sample. Third, the cost figures generally do not include educational expenditures, such as books, supplies, and uniforms, borne by parents, not by government. We do not expect, however, that these data would change the results significantly.

LOOKING INTO THE BLACK BOX

Why are private schools in these nations more effective than public schools in boosting student achievement? Is it possible for public schools to reorganize themselves along lines developed by private schools? To inform these questions, we explored the effects of school-level resources and inputs, and went inside public and private schools to examine how they are organized and managed. In addition to looking at our case studies, we undertook a "minisurvey" of public and private schools in the five case study countries.

Observations from Case Studies

It is easy to assume that private schools may be more effective because they have more resources to bring to the classroom: better-educated teachers, more instructional materials, or a larger stock of institutional resources such as libraries, laboratories, or subject rooms. But we have seen that per-student expenditures in private schools are lower, not higher, than those in public schools, which suggests that the explanation for their greater effectiveness does not lie in the greater abundance of resources in general. Instead private schools may owe their greater effectiveness to their choice of resources. They may be more likely to select those resources that accelerate student learning, economizing on those that have little impact on student learning.

Indeed, the case studies show that in all countries, private schools tend to choose slightly higher student–teacher ratios and to use the savings to purchase other inputs. For example, in Thailand, private schools make more efficient use of teachers by recruiting candidates with slightly lower qualifications, giving them more in-service training, and promoting better teaching processes (homework, tests, and orderly classrooms). In the Dominican Republic, the most striking difference is that students in private schools have better access to textbooks (see Table 7.5).

Private schools may also be more efficient because of their internal management. Hannaway (1991) argues that schools and school systems organize themselves to satisfy those who fund them: parents, in the case of private schools, and local and national authorities, in the case of public schools. Private schools adopt a flexible organizational structure that can respond to the needs of individual students and the self-interests of personnel. By comparison, public schools adopt an organizational structure that promotes compliance with the objectives of not only individual parents and students but also the wider society. Hannaway argues that as long as public schools receive their financing directly from central sources, they will not be able to adopt the more flexible organization of private schools.

In an attempt to make public schools more responsive to local needs, efforts have been made to shift the responsibility for public school funding to local levels. This policy trend is observed in both industrialized and developing countries. However, in many cases, shift-

**Table 7.5: Average Private School Input and Management Characteristics
as a Multiple of Average Public School Characteristics**

Variable	Colombia	Dominican Republic		Tanzania	Thailand	Mini-
		O-type	F-type			Survey
Input mix						
Teacher salary	0.52	—	—	1.15	1.20	—
Student-teacher ratio/class size	0.85	1.00	1.00	1.07	1.05	1.10
Teacher's years of education	—	0.95	1.02	—	—	—
Minutes spent on maintaining class order	—	0.38	1.21	—	1.24	—
Proportion of students with textbooks	—	3.11	3.50	—	—	1.06
Proportion of teachers						
Qualified to teach math in student's school	—	—	—	—	0.17	0.87
With in-service training	—	—	—	—	2.29	—
Teaching enriched math class	—	—	—	—	1.54	—
Total resources	—	—	—	—	—	0.97
Total instructional materials	—	—	—	—	—	1.11
Management						
Total school-level autonomy	—	—	—	—	—	1.61
Instructional time	—	—	—	—	—	1.08

ing financial responsibility has been viewed as a means of relieving a burden on the central budget, rather than of providing stronger management for local schools. As a result, decentralization has neither supplied more material resources at the school level nor enhanced school-level autonomy over decision-making (Lockheed & Zhao, 1993).

Observations from the Minisurvey

Our minisurvey of schools in the five countries was undertaken from a distance. We invited a senior researcher in each country to gather systematic data about a variety of institutional practices in public and private schools, using a common survey instrument. In each country, the researcher was asked to identify three schools in *each* of the following categories: private elite, private nonelite, public elite, and public nonelite schools, for a total of 12 schools per country. The researcher or a representative visited all the schools, and interviewed the headmaster or principal teacher. Although 12 surveys were returned from each country, for a total of 60 schools, all types of schools were not represented equally. We received returns from 14 private elite schools, 17 private nonelite schools, 13 public elite schools, and 16 public nonelite schools.

The minisurvey confirmed many of our findings from examining the case studies. Although their students may have been more capable than those in the public schools, the private schools in this survey did not have more resources than the public schools. Instead, they are more able to manage themselves and to make school-level decisions.

Resources. In many respects, the public and private schools in the minisample were similar (see Table 7.6). The majority of both the private and the public schools were coeducational day schools (81% and 86%, respectively); only 20% had any type of boarding facility. Approximately the same proportion of public and private schools were classified as "elite" (45%): high-quality schools that cater to higher-income families. However, there were also significant differences between the public and private schools in our minisurvey. Public schools admitted more applicants (36%) than did private schools (23%) and were less likely than private schools to admit students on the basis of test performance (55% and 65%, respectively). A higher proportion of teachers in public schools were "fully qualified." Public schools were larger, enrolling more students and employing more full-time teachers; perhaps for this reason they were more likely to operate on two shifts. Public schools taught fewer different grades than private schools (5.8 and 8.5, respectively). While public schools differed from private schools in terms of numbers of students, teachers, and grades, they averaged only one more administrator.

Physically, the public and private schools in the minisurvey differed very little, and both sectors appeared to be relatively advantaged. In particular, the conditions for teaching did not differ significantly between public and private schools. Most students were accommodated in

Table 7.6: General Characteristics of Public and Private Schools in Minisample (Colombia, Dominican Republic, Philippines, Tanzania, and Thailand), 1990

Characteristics	Private	Public
Percentage of coeducational	80.6	86.2
Percentage of residential	19.3	20.7
Percentage of elite	45.2	44.8
Number of shifts	1.4	2.0
Number of students	1113.1	1917.0
Number of grades	8.5	5.8
Number of full-time teachers	43.5	85.1
Percentage of fully qualified teachers	89.7	94.0
Number of administrators	7.0	8.0

regular classrooms; most classrooms had seats and desks for both students and the teacher. Virtually all classrooms had chalkboards. Both public and private schools reported having an average of 11 of 13 important physical resources, such as telephone, typewriter, duplicating machine, school library, laboratory, and office for the school head. The only difference between public and private schools was that more private schools reported having a school library (93% and 79%, respectively), whereas more public schools reported having a copying machine (85% and 61%, respectively).

We also compared the availability of eight important instructional materials: chalk, writing implements, paper, instructional guides, illustrations, science kits, textbooks, and dictionaries. Public and private schools both made approximately five of the eight available to teachers. However, more private school teachers than public school teachers had a storage cupboard in which to store these supplies (66% versus 52%). Students in private schools also appeared to be slightly more advantaged than those in public schools. While most students in both public and private schools had writing implements and paper, private school students were more likely to have dictionaries (63%) and a complete set of textbooks (70%) than students in public schools (40% and 66%, respectively). The differences could reflect either the differences in student selectivity between public and private schools or investment choices by schools.

Official instructional time was relatively similar for public and private schools. Both types of schools reported having a school year of approximately 200 days, a school day of seven or eight periods, and periods lasting about 50 minutes. However, public schools were closed for nearly *four times* as many school days as private schools (15 versus 4).

The overall resources of public and private schools revealed in the minisurvey are remarkably similar. Such differences as emerge suggest a decision on the part of private schools to invest in resources more closely aligned with instructional goals: libraries, dictionaries, textbooks, classroom storage areas for instructional materials, and instructional time. By comparison, public schools tended to invest in personnel: teachers and building guards, and paying for higher teacher qualifications.

Management. Public and private schools differ significantly in terms of their management organization. In most developing countries, the central government finances public schools. Teachers are hired and deployed by a central agency, curriculum is set nationally, and admission to secondary school is controlled by national examinations with students placed in schools through central agencies. As a result, neither the local community nor the school principal exercises much control over key decisions. By contrast, private schools exercise managerial control over a wide range of decisions. For example, research has found that in U.S. Catholic private schools, principals, teachers, and parents have significantly greater control over decisions about the curriculum, instructional methods, allocating funds, hiring teachers, dismissing teachers, and discipline policies than do their counterparts in public schools (Hannaway, 1991). Similar differences in patterns of control have been found in the Philippines (Lockheed & Zhao, 1993).

In the minisurvey large differences between public and private schools emerge in two areas: (1) the degree of influence the principal exercises over school-level decision-making and (2) the importance placed on academic achievement. Private school principals reported more influence over school-level decisions and greater attention to matters of teaching and learning.

We listed 13 areas of school-level decisions, such as selecting, evaluating and dismissing staff; selecting teachers for in-service; evaluating teacher performance; adapting the curriculum; and establishing promotion and homework policies. We then asked principals to indicate which of five groups (head office or Ministry of Education, school board, headmaster or principal, teachers, parents or PTA) exercised the most influence over each area. Principals of private schools had influence over more areas of decision-making than principals of public schools (5.5 areas versus 3.4 areas, respectively); they also had influence over more areas than did any other group, including the head office. By comparison, principals of public schools influenced fewer of these school-level decisions than did the head office (3.4 areas and 3.9 areas, respectively). As a consequence, the head office or Ministry of Education influenced nearly four times as many decisions in public schools as they influence in private schools.

We also looked at each decision-making area. Principals were the most influential group in at least 40% of the private schools for *eight* areas: selecting teachers for in-service, purchasing equipment, evaluating teacher performance, selecting nonteaching staff, selecting students, dismissing school personnel, selecting teachers, and spending school fees. By comparison, public school principals were most influential over only *two* areas: evaluating teacher performance and selecting teachers for in-service. In addition, the private school principals spent more time selecting teachers for inservice training and improving pedagogy.

Another explanation for the higher achievement in Catholic private schools versus public schools in the United States is that they place greater emphasis on engagement in academic activities, including higher rates of enrollment in academic courses. This, in turn, translates into such differences in student behavior as spending more time on homework (Coleman et al., 1982). In developing countries, curricula are typically set nationally, and students have little choice over course selection. However, differences in the emphasis placed on academic achievement may vary between schools, and this may translate into differences between public and private schools in the level of student effort invested in academic activities.

In the minisurvey, we found that private school principals not only had significant influence over what occurred in their schools, they also established a school climate that promoted learning and rewarded those who contributed to its success. The minisurvey showed that private schools emphasized teaching and learning more than public schools and provided rewards for good performance. Private schools, for example, were more likely than public schools to use in-service training and regular staff meetings to strengthen teaching. Virtually all private schools offered monetary incentives for good teachers, compared to only about half the public schools.

Private school principals were more likely to be involved in teaching. On average, private school principals spent 7.2 hours a week teaching a regular class, compared with 4.8 hours per week for public school principals. Private school principals also spent significantly fewer hours on fund-raising, communicating with the head office, and performing general administrative duties than did public school principals (17 hours and 24 hours, respectively). Thus more of their time was available to attend to matters more directly related to teaching.

POLICY IMPLICATIONS

Looking outside the United States we see a variety of institutional conditions under which parents—from different social classes—can choose between public and private schools. In general we see that private schools often perform more effectively, compared to public schools. This finding is mitigated somewhat by the differing families served. Thinking internationally, what lessons can be distilled about the institutional arrangement of mixed school markets?

First, restrictive regulations on private schools may suppress an efficient way to provide education. In some cases, governments could encourage greater private sector participation in education. Policy-makers should keep in mind, however, that the relative efficiency of private schools depends on their operating within a particular institutional regime and incentive structure. Government subsidies, for example, may not be effective if they restrict the schools' ability to choose a suitable teaching staff and input mix to strive for greater efficiency.

Second, public schools could also emulate at least some of the organizational practices of their private counterparts. Government policies toward private schools are often based on the assumption that the quality of education private schools provide is not commensurate with what is being paid by the consumers. It is argued that parents are less able to correctly assess school quality than professional educators. The evidence, however, is that private schools, which are more autonomous and responsive to students and their parents, will deliver education in a cost-effective way.

The exact nature of reforms that lead to improved efficiency and equity in education is beyond the concern of the present book. They might involve contracting for educational services, as is now being done in the Philippines, or even some form of voucher system, as in Chile. Restrictive rules and regulations intended to protect consumers could be modified or tax exemptions could be granted for private schools. All such measures will have to be discussed in the larger context of the political economy of specific countries (James, 1987).

Although the rigorous methodology we have used in comparing public and private schools has allowed some clear advances in our knowledge, additional work is warranted. Databases are not strictly comparable across countries, making it impossible to advance cross-country generalizations. The scope of countries covered is limited. Better information, particularly regarding the social and private costs of different kinds of schools, needs to be gathered. It would be useful to compare results across the entire distribution of students rather than just for the average student. Finally, our studies covered only secondary schools.

These findings are preliminary and need to be tested with other data in other institutional settings. The achievement differences found may not persist if many students move from public to private school over time. Still, the studies offer initial empirical evidence on an issue that has been energized by bold claims and emotional debate. With additional evidence we can learn more about why many private schools outpace public schools—lessons that could spark improvements in both sectors.

REFERENCES

Coleman, J., Hoffer, T., & Kilgore, S. (1982). *High school achievement: Public, Catholic and private schools compared.* New York: Basic Books.

Cox, D., & Jimenez, E. (1991). The relative effectiveness of private and public schools: Evidence from two developing countries. *Journal of Development Economics, 34,* 99–121.

Hannaway, J. (1991). The organization and management of public and Catholic schools: Looking inside the "black box." *International Journal of Educational Research, 15*(5), 463–481.

Hanushek, E. A. (1986). The economics of schooling: Production and efficiency in the public schools. *Journal of Economic Literature, 25,* 1141–1177.

James, E. (1987). *Public policies toward private education* (Discussion Paper, Education and Training Series, Report No. EDT84). Washington, DC: World Bank.

James, E. (1991). Public policies toward private education. *International Journal of Educational Research, 15,* 359–376.

Lee, V. E., & Bryk, A. S. (1989). A multilevel model of the social distribution of high school achievement. *Sociology of Education, 61*(2), 78–94.

Lockheed, M. E., & Zhao, Q. (1993). The empty opportunity: Local control of secondary schools and student achievement in the Philippines. *International Journal of Education Development, 13*(1), 45–62.

Luna, E., & Gonzalez, S. (1986). *The underdevelopment of mathematics achievement: Comparison of public and private schools in the Dominican Republic.* Unpublished manuscript, Centro de Investigaciones UCMM, Dominican Republic.

Murnane, R. J., Newstead, S., & Olsen, R. (1985). Comparing public and private schools: The puzzling role of selectivity bias. *Journal of Business and Economic Statistics, 3*(1), 23–35.

Psacharopoulos, G., & Loxley, W. (1985). *Diversified secondary education and development: Evidence from Colombia and Tanzania.* New York: Oxford University Press.

Robitaille, D. F., & Garden, R. A. (1989). *The IEA study of mathematics II: Context and outcomes of school mathematics.* Oxford, UK: Pergamon.

Roth, G. (1987). *Private provision of public services in developing countries.* New York: Oxford University Press.

CHAPTER 8

After 15 Years

Magnet Schools in Urban Education

ROLF K. BLANK
ROGER E. LEVINE
LAURI STEEL

Magnet schools have become a significant factor in urban education. They offer a means for further desegregating schools, while at the same time enhancing the quality of education. Since magnet schools were initiated, however, there has been growing concern over whether they contribute to inequalities in American education. In this chapter, we examine the development, distribution, and unique characteristics of magnet schools, and discuss their impact on desegregation, school quality, and equity.

Our discussion draws largely on data collected in the 1991–92 school year as part of a national study of magnet schools.[1] This national survey reveals that the number of magnet schools has grown rapidly in large urban school systems since the later 1970s. Magnet schools and programs within schools have unique curricular emphases; a majority have flexibility in staff selection. Other significant findings concern student composition and enrollment. For example, the ethnic composition of magnet schools is the same as that of the districts in which the schools are located. Most magnet schools enroll students by lottery; one-third use some criteria for student selection.

Magnet schools now represent a fundamental shift in how public schools are organized. But the extent to which they offer real choice to parents and learning gains to children depends on magnets' institutional characteristics. For the first time we can now provide a detailed portrait of the magnet school movement and describe its organizational variability.

EVOLUTION OF MAGNET SCHOOLS

Magnet schools have their roots in districtwide specialty schools, such as the Bronx High School of Science, the Boston Latin School, Chicago's Lane Tech, and San Francisco's Lowell High School, some of which have been in existence since the turn of the century. Like their forebears, magnet schools offer special curricula, such as mathematics-science or performing arts programs, or special instructional approaches, such as individualized education, open classrooms, or team teaching.

During the 1970s, school districts began to use magnet schools both as an incentive for parents to remain in the public school system and as a means of desegregation. Often magnet school programs were placed in racially isolated schools or neighborhoods to encourage students of other ethnic groups to enroll. If sufficient numbers of white and minority students enrolled in schools outside their neighborhoods, districts could promote school desegregation without resorting to mandatory measures. At the same time, by introducing innovative curricula and instructional approaches, magnet schools could strengthen the educational program in those schools, contributing to overall improvements in educational quality.

With the 1975 court endorsement of magnet schools as a voluntary desegregation strategy, magnet schools expanded to encompass a broad range of programs. Some districts added such programs as humanities, languages, or career exploration to the more traditional program emphases. Other magnet programs provided distinctive instructional approaches, such as alternative education, individualized education, accelerated learning, Montessori, and open classrooms. Typically, student and parent input provided the basis for determining the specific programs provided in a community. Many districts carefully monitored interest and enrollment in the various magnet programs, adding, expanding, or dropping programs as necessary to remain consonant with student and parent interests.

Magnet schools have received federal support since 1976, primarily through two programs: the Emergency School Assistance Act (ESAA) and the Magnet Schools Assistance Program (MSAP). ESAA, a federal program designed to provide funds to school districts attempting to desegregate, was amended in 1976 to authorize grants to support the planning and implementing of magnet schools. Between 1976 and 1981, ESAA provided up to $30 million a year to magnet school programs (Blank, Dentler, Baltzell, & Chabotar, 1983, p. 8).

The climate of educational reform after the publication of *A Nation at Risk* (National Commission on Excellence in Education, 1983) further stimulated interest in magnet schools as a tool for reform. In particular, attention was directed to the programmatic aspects of magnet schools: What makes them distinctive? Are they more effective in enhancing student learning? In 1984, the federal government resumed support for magnet schools with the enactment of the Magnet Schools Assistance Program. The MSAP explicitly identified both program improvement and desegregation as objectives of magnet schools. Between 1985 and 1991, a total of 117 school districts received federal magnet school grants, totaling $739.5 million. Evidence strongly suggests that MSAP funding has been a significant factor in the development and operation of magnet programs. Districts currently receiving MSAP funds have proportionately more magnet programs than magnet districts that had not received MSAP support (Steel & Levine, 1994). When MSAP funding ended, however, a majority of districts were forced to modify their programs in some way, with one in five indicating they cut back the number of magnet schools and programs offered.

The school choice movement also contributed to a favorable climate for the growth of magnet schools. Magnet schools embody the principles of parental choice as well as competition, school-site autonomy, and deregulation. These same principles are central to the arguments supporting choice as an effective reform (Chubb & Moe, 1990; Raywid, 1989).

1991 NATIONAL MAGNET SCHOOL STUDY

The first national study of magnet schools in the early 1980s found that the number of districts offering magnet programs had increased dramatically since the courts accepted magnets as a strategy for desegregating schools in 1975: from 14 to 138 in five years (Blank et al., 1983). By 1983, over 1,000 individual magnet schools and programs within schools were being offered in these 138 districts.

As magnet schools have become more prevalent, debate over their merits has accelerated commensurately. Several studies have found that magnet schools contribute to school desegregation and to improving educational quality (cf. Archbald, 1988; Blank, 1990; Rossell, 1990; Witte & Walsh, 1990). At the same time, critics express concern over the potential for elitism and inequity that may result (Moore & Davenport, 1989).

In the 1991 study we assessed the status of magnet schools within public school systems by surveying a nationally representative sample of school districts. This survey was limited to multischool districts, that is, districts providing more than one school at one or more grade levels. A total of 600 such districts, representing 6,389 multischool districts nationwide, were randomly selected. Further studies were completed with magnet school administrators in all districts with magnet schools. We addressed three questions:

1. How many magnet schools and programs are there, and how are they distributed across local school systems?
2. What is unique or distinctive about magnet schools?
3. Do magnet schools offer equal opportunities for students to enroll?

These questions led us, in turn, to consider the significance of trends in magnet school distribution, the quality of the education offered in magnet schools, and the participation of ethnic minority and at-risk students in magnet schools and programs.

GROWTH AND DISTRIBUTION OF MAGNET SCHOOLS

The number of school districts offering magnet schools increased from 138 in 1982 to 230 in 1991. Although these 230 districts represent only 4% of the nation's multischool districts, they serve nearly a quarter of all students nationwide. The number of students enrolled in magnet schools has nearly tripled, from 441,000 to over 1.2 million; the number of individual schools offering such programs has more than doubled, from 1,019 to 2,433 (Blank et al., 1983; Steel & Levine, 1994). In 1991, there were 3,171 magnet schools or distinct programs situated within 2,433 schools.

The 1.2 million students in magnet schools represent nearly one-sixth of the public school population in districts offering magnet schools, indicating the growing popularity of these programs. As of 1991, substantially more students were enrolled in magnet programs than the 681,000 enrolled in nonsectarian private schools (National Center for Education Statistics [NCES], 1993). Further, the demand for magnet schools is much greater than the current supply. Over three-quarters of the districts with magnet schools cannot accommodate all students who want to enroll; more than 123,000 students are on waiting lists for specific magnet programs. (In the remainder of the chapter, the term *magnet program* will refer to magnet schools or programs within schools.)

Distribution Across School Systems

Because one objective of magnet programs is to promote desegregation, these programs are most likely to be found in districts in which racial imbalance and desegregation are important issues. As of fall 1991, 11% of multischool districts operated under a formal desegregation plan that assigned students to schools in order to attain a specified racial composition; these tended to be the larger districts, serving almost a third of the nation's students. While magnet programs are rarely the sole desegregation strategy chosen, by 1991, 29% of these districts offered magnet programs to nearly two-thirds of the more than 10 million students in all districts with current desegregation plans. Other strategies include rezoning, forced busing, controlled choice, and majority-to-minority transfer plans.

Desegregation plans and magnet programs are more commonly found in urban school districts than in rural or suburban areas (see Table 8.1). A majority of the large urban districts and a significant proportion of the smaller urban districts in the country were operating under desegregation plans in 1991–92, and almost the same proportion of these districts also offered magnet school programs.

In rural and small districts, where desegregation pressures are much lighter than in the large and urban districts, the relative prevalence of magnet schools is low. Only about 10% of suburban districts offer magnet school programs. As of 1991, over 8 of every 10 magnet

Table 8.1: **Percentage of Multischool Districts with Magnet Programs by District Size and Location (*n* = 6,389)**

District Enrollment/ Location (# Districts)	Percent with Desegregation Plans	Percent with Magnet Programs	Number with Magnet Programs
< 5,000 or rural (5105)	6.0	0.6	31
Suburb 5–10,000 (317)	17.0	4.7	15
Suburb > 10,000 (237)	21.5	8.9	21
Urban 5–10,000 (139)	42.4	21.6	30
Urban > 10,000 (230)	58.7	53.5	123
Not reported (301)	18.6	1.9	6

programs were located in large urban school districts; 7 of 10 programs, in districts with a predominance of minority students; and over half, in districts enrolling mostly low-income students.

Distribution of Magnets by District and Grade Level

Our survey showed that the number of magnet programs offered in a district varied widely, from 1 to 175, and the mean number of magnet programs per district was 14. However, half of the districts had 4 or fewer programs, and 20% had only a single magnet program. This number is somewhat dependent on the total number of schools within a district; small districts are clearly limited in the number of magnet programs they might offer. Of the remaining districts, 14% had between 11 and 20 magnet programs; 9% had between 21 and 50; 6% had more than 50; and only 1% had more than 100 magnet programs.

The proportion of a district's schools that had magnet programs also varied greatly (1% to 100%). In half the districts, at least 12% of the schools included magnet programs. Since many magnet schools operated as programs within a school, however, the proportions of students within magnet districts who were enrolled in magnet programs tended to be somewhat lower (1% to 80%).

Over half of magnet programs were located in elementary schools in 1991 (elementary schools comprise 60% of all U.S. public schools; NCES, 1993). One-fifth were at the high school level (compared to 19% of high schools among all public schools), and an additional 15% of magnet programs were at the middle level (middle level schools comprise 15% of all public schools).[2] The remaining 11% of magnet programs were found in nongraded or multilevel (e.g., K–12, K–8) schools.

Distribution and Growth Compared to Other Public School Choice Programs

As reviewed in Chapter 1, magnet schools largely originated with the desegregation movement in the 1970s. But they have become part of the broader debate around school choice. The 1991 national survey also solicited information on the prevalence and location of specialty schools other than magnet schools and on other programs offering voluntary choice. Among multischool districts nationwide, more than one in five offered either magnet or nonmagnet specialty schools, and one district in four offered some form of school choice, through either magnet programs or nonmagnet programs of choice (see Table 8.2). Unlike magnet programs, however, nonmagnet specialty schools and programs of choice

Table 8.2: Percentage of Multischool Districts with Magnet
Programs and Other Choice Programs (*n* = 6,389)

Type of Program Offered	Number of Districts with Program	Percentage of all Districts	Percentage of all Districts by Enrollment
Magnet schools/programs	230	4	24
Specialty schools (nonmagnet)	1,057	18	31
Programs of choice (nonmagnet)	1,189	23	26

were as likely to be found in small or rural districts as in large urban districts; they were also more likely to be found in districts with predominantly white student populations and less likely than magnet programs to be found in poorer districts.

While magnet districts comprised a relatively small portion of the districts offering choice in 1991, they tended to be those with much larger enrollments. The magnet programs were also considerably more extensive and diverse than nonmagnet specialty programs. The average number of magnet programs in a magnet district (mean = 14) was over twice the average number of specialty schools in a specialty school district, and the range of options offered by magnet schools was considerably broader. The total number of nonmagnet specialty schools in the nation was 2,217 (compared to 2,433 magnet schools); the curricular themes of nonmagnet specialty schools were predominantly in only three areas: career vocational (41%), instructional approach (33%), and gifted and talented (20%).

WHAT IS DISTINCTIVE ABOUT MAGNET
SCHOOLS AND PROGRAMS?

The educational designs developed in magnet schools have become a primary method of innovation and reorganization in urban education. The basic idea of a magnet school is to attract and enroll students based on their interest, not by assignment or ability level. To this end, magnet schools and programs focus on either an instructional approach or a particular academic subject or career path. In theory, all magnet schools and programs are distinctive because of this feature. Magnet schools are also structured differently from traditional schools; some exist as programs within schools, while others are whole schools. And magnets may differ from traditional public schools in class size, student–

teacher ratio, and selection of teaching staff. Our survey results provide useful data on the variability in how magnet programs are organized.

The data on magnet programs are based on self-administered questionnaires completed by magnet program directors. This initial phase of the study did not include independent observations, interviews, or analyses of school or program quality. The effects of magnet schools on student learning could not be analyzed with survey data. These critical questions comprise the primary aim of a planned second phase of the study.

Curricular Emphases

Across the nation, magnet programs provide a wide variety of distinctive curricula, including aerospace technology, travel and tourism, junior ROTC, biotechnology, mathematics, music, fine arts, science, drama, bilingual programs, cosmetology, and small animal care programs. In addition, they offer a variety of instructional approaches, including open classrooms, individualized education, Montessori, and basic skills.

Magnet programs have sometimes been thought to be primarily gifted-and-talented programs, but at the time of the survey, such programs comprised only one-eighth (12%) of the magnet programs nationwide. Most commonly, magnet programs had specific subject-matter emphases (38%) or provided a distinctive instructional approach (32%). Of the rest, 17% were career vocational and 15% centered on the arts. One-fifth of magnet programs combined different themes and approaches: self-paced instruction in programs together with a computer science or foreign-languages emphasis, for example, or a combination of vocational or subject-matter programs (such as technical training and science).

To attract students (and parents), school systems also design magnet program offerings that differ by grade level (Figure 8.1). Magnet programs emphasizing an instructional approach were more often found at the elementary level than at the high school or middle levels (one-third of elementary magnet programs versus only 12% of high school magnet programs). Recent innovations in primary education have coincided with the growth of magnet schools, and parents view magnet schools as an opportunity to take advantage of diversity offered in their districts.

The survey results reveal that subject-matter themes were found even more often at the elementary level (38% of programs) and the

Figure 8.1: Distribution of Magnet Curriculum Emphasis Across School Levels

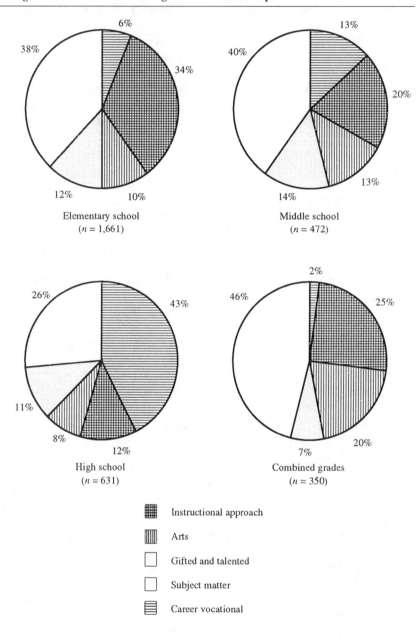

Elementary school
(*n* = 1,661)

Middle school
(*n* = 472)

High school
(*n* = 631)

Combined grades
(*n* = 350)

Instructional approach

Arts

Gifted and talented

Subject matter

Career vocational

middle level (40%) than were instructional approach magnets. However, only 26% of high school magnet schools had a subject-matter theme. At the high school level, 42% of magnet programs were career-oriented or vocational. Some career-oriented and vocational magnet programs existed prior to the development of magnet schools, adding the objective of racial desegregation as the magnet school concept grew in their districts.

Program Structures

Magnet programs can be differentiated by whether all students in the school are included in the magnet program (*whole-school magnets*) or only some of the students in the school participate in the magnet program (*program within school*, or *PWS*, *magnets*). Whole-school magnet schools can be further differentiated by how students enroll: (1) *dedicated* magnet schools, comprised only of students who apply and are accepted by the magnet program, and (2) *attendance-zone* magnet schools, comprised of students who apply and enroll from across a district, plus students from a school's regular attendance zone who are automatically enrolled in the magnet program.

In PWS magnet schools only a portion of students in the school participate in the magnet program. These programs are often semi-autonomous. Students may take some or all of their classes apart from the rest of the school. In the 1992 survey, a total of 38% of the nation's 3,171 magnet programs were classified as PWS magnet schools. However, since these programs, by definition, are smaller than schools, only about 20% of the population of magnet students were in such magnet schools. A significant proportion (about one-fourth) of PWS magnet schools housed more than one magnet program, with an average of 2.2 PWS magnet programs per school. PWS magnet schools can also be embedded within whole-school magnet schools. Approximately 200 PWS magnet schools, or 16% of the total, were embedded within attendance-zone or dedicated whole-school magnets.

The enrollments of PWS magnet schools are considerably smaller than regular schools at the same grade level. Whole-school magnets, on the other hand, are slightly larger than average at the middle and high school level, probably due to their predominant location in large urban districts. Whole-school magnets comprised about one-third (32%) of the nation's magnet programs. Unlike PWS magnet schools, all students in the school participate in the magnet program, and all must have explicitly chosen to participate. A problem some dedicated magnet schools face is attracting enough students to be filled to capacity (from 500 to

2,000 students). Dedicated magnet schools sometimes offer one or more PWS programs, open to subsets of the students in the school as an added incentive.

Attendance-zone magnet schools, which comprised more than one-quarter (26%) of all programs, emerged in response to parents' concerns about restricted access to the special programs provided by magnets. In PWS magnet schools, participation in the magnet program is governed by racial balance guidelines or goals, thus restricting access of students in the neighborhood. Attendance-zone magnet schools extend access to magnet programs to students in the surrounding neighborhoods, regardless of their ethnicity. In this way, they help alleviate concerns regarding the elitism of magnet programs. However, there are two potential drawbacks to attendance-zone magnet schools: Students enrolled in the magnet based on their residence may be less interested in the magnet's distinctive program or approach, and the desegregation impact of the magnet may be reduced.

Most elementary magnet schools are whole schools; most high school magnet schools are programs within schools (see Figure 8.2). In 1991, nearly three-quarters of the elementary-level magnet schools were schoolwide programs (36% attendance-zone and 31% dedicated magnet schools) and only 27% were programs within schools. At the high school level, 69% were structured as programs within schools.

Because elementary schools are generally smaller, it may be easier to implement a schoolwide program and to attract sufficient students interested in the magnet program's special focus or approach to fill the schools. PWS magnet schools, on the other hand, may be more amenable to the departmentalized structure characteristic of secondary schools. PWS magnet schools also allow the school to provide a number of distinctive programs, thus attracting a wider range of students. The greater prevalence of whole school–attendance zone magnet schools at the elementary level may also reflect parents' concerns about access to the special programs offered by magnet schools. Such concerns may be especially pronounced at the elementary level, where greater importance is typically attached to the concept of a "neighborhood school."

Class Size

A key component of any educational program is personnel. In our survey of magnet program directors, a substantial minority of magnet programs were reported to have lower *student–teacher ratios*. At the elementary level, 24% of the districts reported that smaller class sizes characterized their magnet schools; only 4% reported larger class sizes.

Figure 8.2: Magnet Program Structures by School and Grade Level

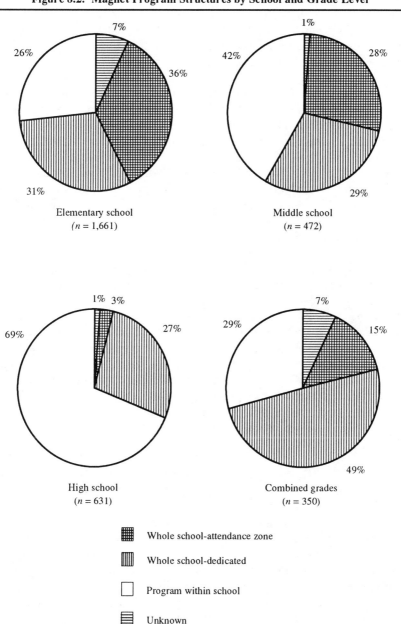

Similarly, for middle schools, 22% of the districts reported smaller class sizes, and for high schools, 36% of the districts reported smaller class sizes for magnet schools. Only 3% of the districts reported larger class sizes for middle school or high school magnet programs. PWS programs averaged four fewer students per class than the regular programs in their schools.

Smaller class size in a proportion of magnet programs reflects the fact that nearly three-fourths (73%) of the magnet programs had additional staff funding. These allowances often provide additional teachers, permitting instruction in specialty areas or lower student–teacher ratios. The potential implications of lower ratios for educational quality and costs are significant. Nearly 15% of the districts reported that additional staffing allowances were used for instructional and administrative aides, and another 15% reported supporting additional administrative staff.

Assigning Teachers

Teacher assignment policies and practices in magnet programs differed from those characterizing nonmagnet schools in a majority of the magnet school districts (58%). Principals in magnet schools were significantly more likely to be permitted to actively advertise for and recruit new teachers, possibly due to the special skills and knowledge needed for the magnet curricula themes. The process of assigning existing teachers within a district is generally more selective in magnet schools, with preference given to teachers with experience and commitment to the program's theme or approach. In some districts, seniority is not given the same consideration in magnet teacher assignment as in typical teacher assignment procedures.

DO MAGNET SCHOOLS OFFER EQUAL OPPORTUNITIES FOR STUDENTS TO ENROLL?

A common view about magnet schools is that they are oversubscribed and that methods of selecting students produce magnet schools dominated by higher-achieving students. Another view is that students (and parents) more familiar with magnet schools and the processes for applying have a major advantage in enrolling.

One way to assess opportunities for enrollment in magnet schools is to examine differences in participation by race and student background. The survey data also provide information on the degree of selectivity of magnet school programs, and we can examine the demand

and accessibility of magnet schools through data on waiting lists and transportation services to magnet schools.

Participation of Minority Versus White Students

From the 1991–92 survey of magnet schools, we estimate that approximately 1.2 million students were enrolled in magnet programs. Of the total magnet enrollment, 61% of all students were black, Hispanic, or other minority. This percentage is very close to the 62% of all students who were minorities in the districts with magnet programs. However, the enrollment rates differed by type of magnet program structure. In the 1,081 PWS magnet programs, 61% of the magnet students were minorities. However, in the 556 schools in which the programs were located, 71% of the students were minorities. Thus magnet programs within schools do appear to have attracted white students in order to reduce isolation and improve racial balance.

At the time of the survey, the ethnic composition of magnet programs varied widely depending on the ethnic composition of the district. In districts where black, Hispanic, or other minority students were the majority, the proportion of minority students enrolled in magnet programs was *lower* than the average proportion of minority students in the districts (68% versus 80%). In districts where a majority of students were white, the opposite was true: The proportion of minority students in magnet schools was *higher* than in the districts overall (46% versus 31%). It thus appears that magnet programs are more likely to attract and enroll students from the nondominant ethnic group.

Participation of At-Risk Students

One criticism frequently leveled at magnet programs is that they are elitist—the population of students served is an advantaged one. To examine this issue, the proportion of students enrolled in magnet programs who were eligible for free or reduced-price lunches, the proportion who were limited or non-English proficient (LEP or NEP), and the proportion who had individualized education plans (IEPs) were compared with overall district characteristics.

Students from low-income families comprised nearly half of magnet program enrollments but were still underrepresented in magnet programs relative to their prevalence in the district: Low-income students, on average, comprised 47% of magnet enrollments but 51% of all students in magnet districts. In majority white and more affluent districts, however, low-income students were somewhat overrepresented in magnet programs. Students who were limited or non-English proficient and special education students (i.e., students with IEPs) were less likely than other students to be enrolled in magnet programs. On average the proportions of LEP or NEP and special education students in magnet programs were only two-thirds of their overall prevalence in the districts.

Selection Criteria

In 1991–92, 24% of districts could accommodate all students who wanted to enroll in magnet programs. For the other 76% of school districts, one or more criteria were used to select students who applied.

Over half (58%) of districts with magnets that use selection procedures used a lottery system (i.e., random selection). Many districts also applied rules or guidelines for magnet student selection, including sibling enrollment, grade-level preference, time on waiting list, and attendance zone (for attendance-zone magnets).

More than one-third of the 3,171 magnet schools and programs reported using specific admission criteria in addition to the district procedures and rules. More than half of these programs used standardized test scores (17% of all programs) or teacher recommendations (16%). Grade point average and artistic or creative ability were used in a significant portion of programs. Other commonly used selection criteria were attendance or conduct requirements, specific course requirements, student interest in the focal area or approach, grades in specific courses, interviews, parental involvement, writing samples, recommendations (from other than teachers), and sibling attendance. Specific selection criteria were much more common among secondary-level magnet programs, where 54% had specific criteria compared to only 24% of elementary magnet programs.

Demand and Outreach

Not all students who want to attend magnet schools are able to do so. Thus, in addition to looking at levels of participation in magnet programs, it is also useful to look at unmet demand.

Waiting Lists. The popularity of magnet programs and the effectiveness of outreach strategies can be inferred from the large proportion of programs with waiting lists. One program (a K–12 arts program in a large city) reported a waiting list of more than 3,400 students; another program had a waiting list of 3,000. Overall, more than half (53%) the magnets reported that they maintained waiting lists, indicating a demand in excess of capacity for a majority of magnet programs. Among the different types of magnet programs, those most likely to have waiting lists were gifted-and-talented magnet programs (62%), followed by career or vocational programs (58%) and arts programs (56%). Overall, approximately 60% of the students on waiting lists were black, Hispanic, or from another minority group, which corresponds to the overall proportion of minority students in magnet districts (62%).

Outreach Strategies. At the time of this survey, the typical magnet district employed more than six different outreach strategies to attract students (see Table 8.3). This high level of outreach effort is a good indicator of the serious commitment that most districts have made to their programs. Without such outreach, the chances of magnet programs successfully attracting students from other neighborhoods are negligible.

Relatively few districts routinely sent information or application forms to all parents (39%) or provided transportation for those visiting magnet schools (32%). More than one-third (36%) of the districts employed other means to disseminate information about their services, including presentations at fairs, forums, and expositions; use of videotapes; parent and student outreach programs, such as telephoning to inform them about program opportunities; and full-time parent information centers or full-time staff to disseminate information.

Transportation. Transportation is an important factor in the accessibility of magnet programs to students throughout the district. Districts can facilitate enrollment at specific schools through the provision of transportation (or transportation subsidies). Conversely, the absence of transportation can strongly discourage out-of-neighborhood enrollment. Transportation subsidies were most widely available for elementary school magnet schools, with nearly five out of six districts providing full or partial subsidies to elementary magnet students. For middle and high

Table 8.3: Percentage of Districts Using Various Outreach Strategies (*n* = 230)

Information/applications to students	95
Printed brochures	92
Information/applications mailed by request	86
Visits and tours of programs	79
Presentations by magnet teachers or students at other schools	70
Advertising in local media	64

school magnets, however, more than one district in five did *not* provide transportation subsidies—presenting a significant barrier for students who might wish to enroll in magnet programs.

CONCLUSIONS

The 1991 national survey of magnet schools provides a general picture of magnet schools as a major strategy for voluntary choice and desegregation in large urban systems. In the past decade, the number of districts with magnet schools has almost doubled. The number of magnet schools has more than doubled, and the number of students has tripled. More than half the magnet districts and eight of every ten magnet schools and programs are located in urban districts with more than 10,000 students.

To meet their desegregation goals, magnet schools must vigorously compete for students. The main attractions for students and parents are the special curricular themes and instructional methodologies offered by these programs. In order to be attractive to students, a diversity of programs that reflect the demands and interests of the community must be offered. The curricular emphasis most frequently found in magnet schools at elementary and middle levels is "subject matter" (e.g., mathematics, science, or foreign language); at the high school level, the most common emphasis is career–vocational.

Magnet schools have often been viewed as havens for high-achieving students within urban school districts. The national survey results present a quite different picture. A majority of districts (58%) assign students to their magnet schools by lottery. Only one-third of magnet schools and programs reported using specific selection criteria— 23% use test scores, 22% use teacher recommendations, and 17% use grade point average. These statistics reveal that while a portion of magnet schools and programs do serve higher-achieving students, primarily the gifted-and-talented programs, most magnet programs serve a broad distribution of students in big city school systems.

There is evidence from the national data to suggest that magnet schools and programs may be contributing to desegregation goals. In minority-dominant districts, magnet programs enroll higher-than-average proportions of white students (relative to the overall proportion of white students in the district). In white-dominant districts, the reverse is true.

Magnet programs not only compete for students, they may also improve the quality of schools, recruiting skilled teachers with areas of expertise related to the special focus of the curriculum. Special staffing allowances also characterize magnet programs. As a result, more than one-fourth of magnet programs have smaller class sizes than regular schools at the same grade level.

To understand the effects of magnet schools on urban education, further studies and analyses need to examine the local decisions and context in which magnet schools operate, the extent to which magnet schools actually change the education process, and the extent to which student learning is improved. The second phase of the Magnet Schools Study will attempt to examine these critical questions.

NOTES

1. The Magnet Schools Study was commissioned by the U.S. Department of Education (contract No. LC90043001) and carried out by the American Institutes for Research. The views expressed here are those of the authors and do not necessarily represent those of the Department of Education.

2. Elementary school is defined as no grade higher than grade 6; middle level, as low grade 6-8, high grade 7-9; high school, as low grade 7-10, high grade 12; and combined as other grade combinations.

REFERENCES

Archbald, D. (1988). *Magnet schools, voluntary desegregation and public choice theory: Limits and possibilities in a big city school system.* Unpublished Ph.D. dissertation, University of Wisconsin–Madison.

Blank, R. (1990). Analyzing educational effects of magnet schools using local district data. *Sociological Practice Review, 1,* 40–51.

Blank, R., Dentler, R., Baltzell, C., & Chabotar, K. (1983). *Survey of magnet schools: Analyzing a model for quality integrated education.* Prepared by James H. Lowry and Associates and Abt Associates for U.S. Department of Education, Washington, DC.

Chubb, J., & Moe, T. (1990). *Politics, markets, and America's schools.* Washington, DC: Brookings Institution.

Moore, D. R., & Davenport, S. (1989). *The new improved sorting machine.* Madison, WI: National Center on Effective Secondary Schools.

National Center for Education Statistics (NCES). (1993). *Public and private elementary and secondary education statistics: School Year 1992–93* (NCES Report 93-332). Washington, DC: U.S. Department of Education.

National Commission on Excellence in Education. (1983). *A nation at risk: The imperative for educational reform.* Washington, DC: U.S. Department of Education.

Raywid, M. (1989). The mounting case for schools of choice. In J. Nathan (Ed.), *Public schools by choice: Expanding opportunities for parents, students, and teachers* (pp. 13–40). Bloomington, IN: Meyer-Stone.

Rossell, C. H. (1990). *The carrot or the stick for school desegregation policy: Magnet schools vs. forced busing*. Philadelphia: Temple University Press.

Steel, L., & Levine, R. (1994). *Educational innovation in multiracial contexts: The growth of magnet schools in American education* (Report No. 1 from the Magnet Schools Study). Prepared by American Institutes for Research for U.S. Department of Education, Washington, DC.

Witte, J., & Walsh, D. (1990, Summer). A systematic test of the effective schools model. *Educational Evaluation and Policy Analysis, 12*(2), 188–212.

CHAPTER 9

Lessons from the Largest
School Voucher Program

Two Decades of Experience with Pell Grants

Thomas J. Kane

Before Pell Grants were established in 1973, the postsecondary system looked in many respects like the K–12 system today: Students interested in attending college could choose between a private system and a heavily subsidized public one. With the introduction of Pell Grants, as with GI benefits decades before, the subsidy was attached to the student, who was given the choice to spend it at a public or private school. Between 1973 and 1994, the Pell Grant program disbursed $96.3 billion (1993 dollars) in grants to low-income students (College Board, 1994).

We thus have more than 20 years of experience with a federal means-tested school voucher program. Although we have built artificial boundaries in the policy community between those working on postsecondary issues and those working in the K–12 public school arena, we can see that implementing a school voucher program at either the postsecondary or the K–12 level raises many of the same nagging questions. Though the analogy clearly has limits, our postsecondary experience with Pell Grants is relevant to three important concerns in current school choice debates:

1. Does a targeted means-tested voucher program affect the enrollment decisions of disadvantaged youth?
2. To what extent will greater choice lead to segregation along racial or socioeconomic lines?

3. What implications does the postsecondary experience with proprietary vocational schools have for regulating small private
   schools in the K–12 sector?

This chapter draws on our experience with Pell Grants in order to
shed empirical light on these concerns. I focus empirically on the first
and third issues.

PELL GRANTS AND ACCESS TO
POSTSECONDARY EDUCATION

The Basic Educational Opportunity Grants program (renamed Pell
Grants in 1980) was established in 1973 to provide financial assistance to
full-time college freshmen. (For an excellent description of changes in
program rules over time, see Mortenson, 1988.) In 1975 the maximum
grant was $3,628 (in 1993 dollars). Half-time students were added in
1975; all undergraduates were made eligible in 1976. In the past
20 years, inflation has eaten away one-third of the value of the maximum grant, which for the 1995–96 school year is $2,340. The pro-
gram provides roughly $6 billion in aid each year to roughly 4 million
recipients.

Program eligibility is based on a number of factors, such as family
income, family size, number of siblings in college, and the student's
earnings and assets. Changes over the years in the Pell Grant formula
have opened the program to middle-income families. For instance, the
benefit reduction rate on parental income was reduced between 1979
and 1981. State taxes were added to the list of deductions from family
income beginning in 1988, and families with multiple students in college
had their grants raised in 1988.

While the maximum Pell Grant was not even rising as fast as inflation, the cost of attendance at a public four-year university was outpacing the rate of inflation by a wide margin. As portrayed in Figure 9.1,
tuition, room, and board at a public four-year university grew by 41%
between 1980 and 1993, even after accounting for inflation. Over the
same period, the maximum Pell Grant fell by 22%. [1]

A number of studies have attempted to measure the effect of college
costs on access (for a review, see Leslie & Brinkman, 1988). Most of this
research compares enrollment rates of low-income students in states
with lower public tuition to enrollment rates of low-income students in
states with higher tuition. Based on this "natural experiment" provided

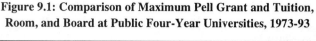

**Figure 9.1: Comparison of Maximum Pell Grant and Tuition,
Room, and Board at Public Four-Year Universities, 1973-93**

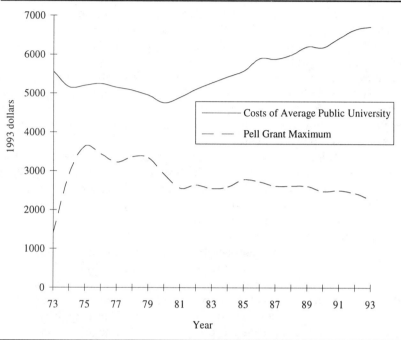

Source: The College Board, *Trends in Student Aid: 1984 to 1994*
(Washington: Washington Office of the College Board, 1994).

by differences in state policy, the evidence suggests that costs have a
strong impact on college access for low-income youth.

I analyzed the relationship between public tuition levels (by state)
and enrollment rates (by family income) for three independent data
sets. For each, similar specifications were used to generate cross-
sectional estimates of the effect of tuition on going to college. For the
first analysis, I drew samples of 18- and 19-year-olds from the October
Current Population Survey (CPS) from 1977 through 1991. The dependent variable is the proportion of youth who report being enrolled in
college (either two-year or four-year) or report having attended a year
of college. There were approximately 4,834 such students in each year
of the survey. To facilitate the use of family background measures, the

sample consists only of those 18- and 19-year-olds who were not heads of or spouses in their own households (approximately 85% to 90% of the original sample).

For the second analysis, I used the National Longitudinal Survey of Youth (NLSY), which contains data on college attendance, family background, standardized test scores, and place of residence for a sample of roughly 12,000 individuals, age 14 to 21 years old, in 1979. The data reported here contain members of the cross-section sample as well as the supplementary sample for disadvantaged youth. I categorized as enrolled all those who entered college at any point during the survey. Because family income is often not reported for those over 19, I limited the sample to those who were age 14 to 19 in 1979.

For the third analysis, I used the High School and Beyond (HSB) survey of the senior class of 1980, which reports data for roughly 12,000 high school seniors, tracking them over a six-year period.[2] I limited the sample to the 10,292 youth who participated in the first follow-up, who reported family background information, and who took the standardized test administered in the base year.

In studying the relationship between state differences in enrollment rates and public tuition levels, I focus on differences in resident tuition at public four-year comprehensive institutions. The results would be similar using tuition at two-year colleges, since states that charge high public tuition at two-year schools also tend to charge high tuition at four-year schools. Even though roughly 20% of college students enroll at private institutions, private college tuition is not likely to have a large impact on the proportion of a state's population attending college. Although private tuition levels may help determine where a student attends college, public college tuition is presumably the marginal price that affects whether a student attends college at all.

Findings: The Influence of Tuition and Pell Grants on Student Choices

In all three data sets, the evidence suggests that enrollment rates were lower in states with high public tuitions. For instance, using the October Current Population Survey data, a $1,000 difference in public four-year tuition was associated with a difference of 3 percentage points in enrollment rates among young adults, age 18 to 19 (see Table 9.1). A $1,000 difference in tuition was associated with a difference of 5 percentage points in enrollment in the NLSY sample. The estimated impact of tuition differences was even larger in the HSB data (a difference of 10 percentage points in enrollment per $1,000 difference in enrollment).

**Table 9.1: The Effect of Public Four-Year Tuition on
College Enrollment in Three Data Sets**

	October Current Population Survey[a]	National Longitudinal Survey of Youth[b]	High School and Beyond Senior Cohort[c]
Public 4-year tuition/1000	-.0539*	-.0696*	-.1218*
	(.0077)	(.0221)	(.0215)
	Income Quartile Interactions		Family SES Quartile Interactions
Tuition by quartile 2	.0270*	-.0141	.0019
	(.0042)	(.0306)	(.0114)
Tuition by quartile 3	.0371*	.0584	.0393*
	(.0050	(.0334)	(.0143)
Tuition by highest quartile	.0340*	.0777*	.0585*
	(.0072)	(.0343)	(.0195)
n	51,004	6729	10,292

* $p < .05$

[a] Population: Dependent 18–19-year olds, 1977–91
   Dependent variable: Enrollment at either a 2-year or 4-year college
   Note: Other variables included in the regression were race dummies (black, Latino, and other),
            a gender dummy, dummies for census divisions, dummies for individual year, dummies
            fro parental education, family income, family size, and a dummy for home ownership.

[b] Population: 14–19-year olds in 1979
   Dependent variable: Enrollment at either a 2-year or 4-year college
   Note: Other variables included in the regression were race dummies (black, Latino, and other),
            a gender dummy, dummies for census region, a standardized test score (standardized by
            age), age dummies, dummies for parental education, and dummies for family income
            quartile. Both the cross-sectional and supplemental samples were used.

[c] Population: High school seniors from 1980
   Dependent variable: College enrollment by 1982
   Note: Other variables included in the regression were race dummies (black, Latino, and other),
            a gender dummy, dummies for census divisions, a standardized test score, dummies for
            family SES quartile, and dummies for parental education. Because the family income data
            reported by youth is often not reliable, socioeconomic status measures were used, which
            take into account income as well as parental education and parental occupation.

Given that the average enrollment rates were between 45% and 55% in
these surveys, all of the estimated impacts were quite large. The evidence suggests that the average youth and his or her parents are quite
sensitive to tuition costs.

I also tested for differential effects of tuition across family income
levels. If tuition is driving the differences in enrollment rates across
states and not some other difference between high- and low-tuition
states, then we might expect enrollment rates to be particularly low for

low-income youths in high-tuition states. Again, all three data sets are consistent in suggesting a positive interaction between the effect of tuition and family income. In the HSB sample, a $1,000 difference in state tuition levels was associated with a 12 percentage point difference in enrollment rates at the lowest family socioeconomic status (SES) quartile, 6 percentage points higher than those in the highest quartile. Therefore, not only are enrollment rates lower in the high-tuition states, they are particularly depressed for low-income youth. All of this is consistent with the hypothesis that costs matter, particularly for low-income youths.

The Effect of Pell Grants

Despite the influence of state tuition levels on college enrollment rates, the evidence for the effect of Pell Grants on the enrollment choices by low-income youths is much less clear. In Table 9.2, the data from the October CPS are broken into two periods: 1970–72 (before the Pell Grant program) and 1973–77 (post program enactment). The growth in enrollment rates for those from families in the lowest income quartile (most of whom would have been eligible for Pell Grants) is then compared to the trend in enrollment rates for those from the top three quartiles. Changes in enrollment rates were studied for women only, to avoid contamination by the Vietnam draft. Three different dependent variables are used:

Table 9.2: **Changes in College Enrollment Rates of Dependent 18- to 19-Year-Old Females of Family Income Quartile: 1970–72 to 1973–77**

	Any College Enrollment		Private College Enrollment		Public Two-Year College Enrollment	
Black	-.027	.044	.000	.034	-.029	.000
	.023	.020	.013	.013	.014	.013
Post (1973–77)	.025	-.008	.022	-.003	-.009	-.010
	.010	.010	.006	.005	.007	.007
Black by post	.027	-.015	-.010	-.027	.005	.012
	.028	.025	.016	.015	.018	.017
Lowest income quartile by post	-.026	.005	-.028	-.002	.034	.024
	.023	.022	.013	.009	.015	.015
Family background included?	No	Yes	No	Yes	No	Yes

$n = 12,163$

Note: The above were estimated within a linear probability framework. Included in all equations were dummy variables for income quartiles, region, and a constant term. Family background measures included 10 dummy variables for the education of parents and home ownership.

total college enrollment rates, enrollment rates in private universities, and enrollment rates in public two-year institutions.

Total college enrollment rates grew 2.6 percentage points more *slowly* for the lowest income quartile, although this difference is not significantly different from zero (refer to Table 9.2, column 1). Further, private college enrollment grew by 2.8 percentage points less for low-income students over the period after the Pell Grants were established. Only public two-year college enrollment seemed to grow more quickly for low-income youth. However, it is important to keep in mind that total college enrollment rates did not increase more rapidly, suggesting that there may have been some relative shifts in enrollment among different types of colleges. When family background measures such as parental education and home ownership are added, none of the effects are statistically different from zero.

Not all time-series evidence is equally negative regarding the effect of Pell Grants on enrollment rates. For instance, McPherson and Schapiro (1991) report that enrollment rates of low-income white students declined during the early 1980s as tuition costs began rising. Similar results are reported in Kane (1994). Thus Pell Grants may have offset, for other low-income and working-class groups, the suppressing enrollment effects of rising tuitions. However, I am aware of no evidence that contradicts the troubling finding that there was no disproportionate *increase* in the college enrollment of low-income youth after the Pell Grant program was established.

Such evidence certainly presents a challenge to the college cost and access hypothesis.[3] We would have expected the Pell Grants to have had a significant effect. The size of the maximum grant, particularly after 1975, was quite large relative to the cross-state variation in tuition levels. Hansen (1983) has reported similar evidence to question the effect of student aid programs on the choices of low-income youths.

Why Do Pell Grants Fail to Influence College Choice?

The evidence, therefore, presents a quandary: Despite large differences in enrollment between high- and low-tuition states, the impact of Pell Grants on low-income enrollment rates seems to be small. The two facts may be reconciled if there are hidden obstacles to low-income students, such as low program visibility, complexity of financial aid forms, or intimidating audit procedures. Low-income families simply may not know about financial aid rules and programs. For instance, a 1975 New Jersey study suggested that a quarter of college students with family incomes below $15,200 (1991 dollars) had not applied for aid.

Virtually all of these students would have qualified for a Pell Grant (New Jersey Commission on Financing Postsecondary Education, 1975; Orfield, 1992).

The complexity of financial aid forms may also be a deterrent. An Educational Testing Service study in the late 1970s suggested that the financial aid form for the Pell Grant required a reading ability at the tenth-grade level, due to its use of technical terms describing alternative financial assets (Franz, 1980).

Similarly, the Department of Education's auditing procedures may disproportionately deter low-income students. Schools are required to verify applicants' information for applications chosen by the Department of Education. The applications of lower-income applicants are more likely to display zero reported income or assets and algebraic mistakes, which are predictors of fraudulent or mistaken applications. Faced with additional paperwork to verify reported financial status, many students may be discouraged.

The Pell Grant benefit formula provides greater benefits to lower-income students. One might be tempted to target a K–12 school voucher in a similar way. Unfortunately, such means-testing necessarily imposes bureaucratic barriers that the most disadvantaged youth may be unable to negotiate. (For discussion of the relative effectiveness of aid to high- and low-income families, see Manski & Wise, 1983.)

The College Board (1981) made a number of innovative suggestions for lowering these barriers. For instance, nearly all of those who qualify for other means-tested programs such as Food Stamps and Aid to Families with Dependent Children (AFDC) could be given presumptive eligibility for Pell Grants. Further, just as the IRS offers a short form for certain tax filers, Pell Grant application forms—or similar application forms for K–12 voucher programs—could be simplified for those with fewer financial assets.

PELL GRANTS AND REGULATING PRIVATE SCHOOLS

The most vexing problem in administering the Pell Grant program has been the task of regulating private for-profit institutions. These programs typically provide training in a specialized field, such as cosmetology, real estate, travel and tourism, or truck driving. These schools currently enroll roughly one-third of guaranteed student loan recipients and one-quarter of Pell Grant recipients. The average annual tuition at proprietary schools equals about $6,500, only slightly more than the average annual expenditures per pupil at public schools. (For descriptions of issues facing the proprietary sector, see Lyke, Gabe, & Aleman, 1991; Schenet, 1990.)

Roughly 80% of proprietary school students currently receive some form of federal means-tested aid, as compared with 30% of other undergraduates (Fraas, 1990). Further, loan default rates are roughly four times as high for these students as default rates for four-year college students and twice as high as those for community college students. The large number of students receiving federal financial aid plus their high loan default rates have been red flags in the debate over abuse in pro-choice student aid programs.

Beyond tampering with eligibility rules and loan limits, the federal government has little direct leverage in regulating the proprietary sector. Although there are federal dollars at stake, the direct regulatory function has been left to state agencies and private accrediting agencies. This allocation of responsibilities is not accidental. According to Schenet (1990), the weak federal role is rooted in the legislation that established the federal Department of Education. It is prohibited from "any direction, supervision or control over the curriculum, program of instruction, administration or personnel of any educational institution, school or school system, over any accrediting agency or association" (p. 7).

Along one dimension, the problem of regulating private K–12 schools receiving vouchers would be simpler than that faced by federal regulators in the Pell program. A local school board would not have the problem of relying on lower levels of government or accrediting institutions—with no financial stake, or in the case of accrediting institutions, a presumed incentive to look the other way—as proxies for overseeing program quality. Under the Pell Grant vouchers, local proprietary schools have increased in number, rationally responding to the program's economic incentives. In turn, accrediting organizations hold little interest in constraining school expansion.

However, regulating private K–12 schools would still be problematic judging from experience in the postsecondary sector. First, there are few outcome measures with which to evaluate educational programs. Loan default rates, the primary indicator available to federal regulators, do not measure postsecondary school effectiveness. Nor do most other measures one could collect, such as graduation rates or job placement rates. Given the low-income character of many students attending proprietary schools, we might expect these schools to do poorly on such measures, even if they are well worth the federal investment. According to Apling and Aleman (1990), the median family income for proprietary school students in 1986 was $12,000 less than for undergraduates overall and $8,000 less than for community college students. Proprietary school students are also much more likely to be black (21% versus 9% of community college students) and to be slightly younger than community college students. Measures that take into account the prior background of the students enrolled in an institution (often referred to as "value-added" measures) are difficult to come by either in the postsecondary or K–12 sector.

The second reason proprietary schools are difficult to regulate is their size. According to Apling and Aleman (1990), the median fall enrollment at a proprietary school in 1988 was 64. Only 25% had enrollments greater than 175. Such small numbers pose at least two separate problems. Obviously the cost of oversight rises with the number of institutions to be evaluated. More important, small schools greatly reduce the usefulness of any statistical assessment, given small sample sizes. It would be difficult to reject the hypothesis that any particular school's students had scored poorly on a standardized test for any reason other than chance. As a result, regulating a number of scattered sites is likely to be expensive, and it would be difficult to identify all but the most glaring instances of abuse. The problem is further complicated by the fear of shutting down good schools that provide services to the most disadvantaged youth.

Finally, we do not know why proprietary school programs enroll such a high proportion of minority, low-income youth. A public community college is typically much less expensive to attend than a proprietary school. Although this has been the subject of much speculation, the question deserves more careful attention. Location is one possible explanation. Entrepreneurs may be adept at setting their schools in areas that lack public community colleges and vocational institutes. Aggressive marketing techniques also may play a role.

The postsecondary sector's experience with a voucher program suggests that, for a variety of reasons, local school boards are likely to have a difficult time regulating private providers of education. If the postsecondary sector is any indication, the new schools are likely to be small and specialized (see Chapters 3 and 6, this volume). The more disadvantaged the clientele and the more specialized the training, the more difficult it will be to measure program effectiveness. In the K–12 sector, the dearth of measures of effectiveness may worsen the problem. Further, even if reliable value-added measures were available, the small size of these schools may render inferential evaluation methods useless. Regulators are likely to be left with measuring inputs, such as classroom size, curricula, and teacher qualifications. And, unfortunately, the legacy of the Coleman Report (Coleman et al., 1966) and the literature it spawned is that such input measures do not tell us much about the quality of education being provided.

CONCLUSION

My goal in this chapter was simply to explore some of the lessons to be learned from our experience with school vouchers in postsecondary education. First, we must not forget that targeting vouchers means much more than simply defining eligibility rules. I presented evidence in this chapter suggesting that the establishment of Pell Grants in the mid-1970s has had little impact on the enrollment rates of low-income youth. This is surprising, given other evidence suggesting that low-income youths are quite sensitive to differences in tuition levels. One explanation is that only those students who were planning to go to college anyway were able to negotiate the barriers of learning about the program and filling out complicated application forms. Any attempt to target vouchers should understand and lower these barriers.

Second, the U.S. Department of Education has faced a daunting challenge in regulating the quality of education provided by proprietary schools. Three factors complicate such efforts: First, proprietary schools tend to be small, limiting the ability of quality-control techniques to identify the "bad apples." Second, they tend to specialize, making it more difficult to hold them to some external curricular standard. Third, they often take the most disadvantaged students. Therefore, even if one has an outcome measure such as a loan default rate or a graduation rate, it is very difficult to distinguish schools with low "value-added" from schools whose students would have fared poorly no matter what they did. Any school board attempting to regulate the quality of small private schools in the K–12 sector will face many of the same difficulties faced in the postsecondary sector.

NOTES

Acknowledgments. I wish to acknowledge helpful comments from David Breneman, Anne Piehl, and the editors.

1. Most states also have means-tested grant programs. However, even after a decade of decline in the relative value of Pell Grants, the federal Pell Grant system distributed 2.7 times more than all the state means-tested programs combined in 1991.

2. Although state of residence is not reported in the HSB, it was inferred from the modal location of college attended by those graduating from the same high school.

3. I am currently evaluating the effect of recent increases in tuition levels within states to test this hypothesis. Preliminary results suggest that even within-state tuition increases led to declines in enrollment rates.

REFERENCES

Apling, R. N., & Aleman, S. R. (1990). *Proprietary schools: A description of institutions and students* (Congressional Research Service Report to Congress No. 90–428 EPW). Washington, DC: Library of Congress.

Coleman, J., Campbell, E. Q., Hobson, C. J., McPartland, J., Mood, A. M., Weinfeld, F. D., & York, R. L. (1966). *Equality of educational opportunity.* Washington, DC: U.S. Department of Health, Education, and Welfare.

College Board, Washington Office. (1981). *Student aid and the urban poor* (Ford Foundation Series on Higher Education in the Cities). New York: Ford Foundation.

College Board. (1994). *Trends in student aid: 1984 to 1994.* Washington, DC: Washington Office of the College Board.

Fraas, C. (1990). *Proprietary schools and student financial aid programs: Background and policy issues* (Congressional Research Service Report to Congress). Washington, DC: Library of Congress.

Franz, E. B. (1980). *Evaluation of the reading level required for comprehension of the financial aid form.* Princeton, NJ: Educational Testing Service.

Hansen, W. L. (1983). Impact of student financial aid on access. In J. Froomkin (Ed.), *The crisis in higher education* (pp. 84–96). New York: Academy of Political Science.

Kane, T. J. (1994). College entry by blacks since 1970: The role of college costs, family background and the returns to education. *Journal of Political Economy, 102*(5), 878–911.

Leslie, L., & Brinkman, P. (1988). *The economic value of higher education.* New York: Macmillan.

Lyke, R., Gabe, T., & Aleman, S. R. (1991). *Early labor market experiences of proprietary school students* (Congressional Research Service Report to Congress). Washington, DC: Library of Congress.

Manski, C. F., & Wise, D. (1983). *College choice in America.* Cambridge, MA: Harvard University Press.

McPherson, M., & Schapiro, M. (1991). *Keeping college affordable.* Washington, DC: Brookings Institution.

Mortenson, T. G. (1988). *Pell grant program changes and their effects on applicant eligibility 1973–74 to 1988–89* (ACT student financial aid research report series, 88-1). Princeton, NJ: American College Testing Service.

New Jersey Commission on Financing Postsecondary Education. (1975). *The needs and resources of undergraduate students in postsecondary education in the state of New Jersey*. Princeton, NJ: Author.

Orfield, G. (1992). Money, equity, and college access. *Harvard Educational Review, 72*(3), 337–372.

Schenet, M. A. (1990). *Proprietary schools: The regulatory structure* (Congressional Research Service Report to Congress). Washington, DC: Library of Congress.

CONCLUSION

Empirical Research
on Educational Choice
What Are the Implications for Policy-Makers?

RICHARD F. ELMORE
BRUCE FULLER

THE PERSISTENCE OF CHOICE AS A POLICY ISSUE

Choice is everywhere in American education. It is manifest in the residential choices made by families with school-age children; it is capitalized in the housing prices found in neighborhoods. Choice also occurs when parents decide how to care for their preschool-age child and in the consequences of those choices for their youngster's readiness for elementary school. It occurs when parents use their knowledge, skill, and social connections to get their children assigned to one teacher or another, to one program or another within a given school, or to one school or another within a given district. Choice is present when families, sometimes at great financial sacrifice, decide to send their children to private schools instead of public schools. And choice occurs when parents jockey for places in selective public high schools or when students are chosen by lottery for magnet schools with specialized academic programs. In these and many other ways parents and students make choices that influence their educational futures. And in all instances, these choices—and the options from which to choose—are strongly shaped by the wealth, ethnicity, and social status of parents and their neighborhoods.

Choice is everywhere, yet for some critics of American education there is not nearly enough, or not nearly enough of the right kind of choice for the right sort of people. These critics usually portray public schooling as a monolithic and unresponsive bureaucracy, driven more by the self-interest of politicians and bureaucrats than by the interests of parents and students. They see increased choice as driving a lethargic educational system toward greater responsiveness and effectiveness (for example, Chubb & Moe, 1990; Hannaway, 1991).

Other critics, however, see choice in American education as serving the interests of the already privileged and increasing the gaps between those who are already successful at manipulating the system and those who are not (for example, Moore & Davenport, 1990). They see choice as driving the privileged and less privileged further apart, exacerbating school inequalities. They believe that many people are denied choices when they lack information, money, or accessible options.

The issue for policy-makers, then, is not whether Americans do have educational choices. Many do. Nor is the question whether they should have educational choices. Virtually everyone in our democratic society—increasingly skeptical of institutional authority—agrees that parents should exercise some control over their educational choices. Rather, the issue confronting policy-makers is what kind of choices policy should promote, with what constraints, and for what purposes. As we demonstrated in Chapter 1, the emergence of choice as an educational policy issue can be traced, in part, to attempts by the modern state to accommodate its actions to increasing social diversity and to rising political pressure for more responsive public services. The emergence of choice can also be traced to more specific attempts by urban school systems, since the 1960s, to preserve the participation of the white middle class in public schools and to provide a positive vision of what public schooling can become in the face of increasingly strident criticism. These forces are unlikely to go away in the foreseeable future. While choice may wax and wane as a front-burner political issue, the pressures for attention to choice in American education are deeply rooted in the culture, social structure, and political fabric of this nation.

Political debates around educational choice involve more than the usual amount of ideological posturing and political polemics—far outpacing empirical investigation of the actual effects that diverse forms of choice have on individuals and institutions. This book brings together scholars who are doing serious empirical work on school choice in an attempt to begin to build a broader understanding of the institutional and educational effects of this policy. We believe that, since choice is a persistent motif of educational policy, it is important to encourage the creation of a cumulative body of research on the subject and to understand what that research might mean for policy-makers—local, state, or federal—who continue to confront the issue in its multitude of forms.

FOUR PROPOSITIONS ABOUT EDUCATIONAL CHOICE

In this concluding chapter, we focus on the policy implications of empirical research on educational choice, drawing mainly on the research reported in earlier chapters. We have distilled these conclusions into four main propositions. As with all propositions drawn from empirical research, these are tentative and subject to local conditions, but we think it is important to state them succinctly.

Proposition 1: *Increasing educational choice is likely to increase separation of students by race, social class, and cultural background.*

Enhanced educational choice is often justified by its advocates as a strategy for improving educational opportunity. In the abstract, this seems a plausible argument: Low-income, minority parents and their children are seen, in this view, as being trapped by circumstances beyond their control in inferior schools. Providing choice to these parents—in the form of open access to other public schools or vouchers redeemable in private schools—is seen as providing a way for these parents and their children to break free of the constraints of poor schools. Low-income, minority parents, the argument continues, probably have the same aspirations for their children as any other parents. Therefore, the argument concludes, providing choices to these parents will lead the children to better schools and all schools will improve as a result.

As plausible as this argument sounds, it does not seem to be borne out in the actual effects of choice programs. What does seem to be the case is that both low-income parents and white middle-class parents seem to be favorably disposed toward increased educational choice, and that support for choice is higher among parents who view their children's schools negatively (see Chapters 4 and 6). But this generally optimistic picture of the effects of choice quickly disappears as we examine the more specific details of parental attitudes and responses to choice programs.

Choice appears to have a stratifying effect, by social class and ethnicity, even when it is explicitly designed to remedy inequality. Lee, Croninger, and Smith (Chapter 4) find, for example, that while many parents express strong preferences for increased choice, nearly one-third of the parents they surveyed in the Detroit metropolitan area expressed no opinion about choice and these parents had significantly less education and family income than those who favored choice. They also find that parents who express a preference for high educational standards are less inclined to support choice and that there is considerably less support for cross-district choice plans that would bring together students from different social backgrounds than for within-district choice plans that would provide constrained choice for students of similar backgrounds.

Likewise, Wells (Chapter 2) finds that in the St. Louis metropolitan desegregation plan—aimed at moving poor and working-class students from the inner city to the suburbs—youths who chose to leave the inner city and persisted in that choice differ markedly from those who left and returned or those who stayed behind. The highly committed choosers stand out in the degree of parental support for their decisions, in their attitudes toward educational achievement, and in their racial attitudes. Witte (Chapter 6) finds that even in a program heavily targeted toward low-income parents, those who choose the option of publicly financed enrollment in private schools are better educated and more likely to be involved in their children's schooling, both before and after their decision, than parents who did not choose. In their study of magnet school programs, Martinez, Godwin, and Kemerer (Chapter 3) demonstrate that students and parents who choose magnet schools differ systematically from those who do not in parents' education, educational expectations, and involvement. And Henig's study (Chapter 5) reveals quite different preferences between minority and white parents as represented by the characteristics of the magnet schools they choose.

These findings reinforce an emerging pattern of evidence from other sources (see, e.g., Wells, 1991; Willms & Echols, 1993) showing that, regardless of the design of choice programs, they tend markedly to differentiate choosers from nonchoosers in ways that increase the social stratification of schools rather than reducing inequality. For this reason, authors in this volume urge caution and skepticism about the claims of advocates that choice will equalize educational opportunity. Certainly, minority and low-income parents need better schools, and simple equity would suggest that they ought at least to have the same choices as everyone else, but existing approaches do not yet provide these benefits.

These findings on the effects of choice should be seen in the context of other research showing that (1) family background is a stronger predictor of children's success in school than school qualities and (2) over the past 15 years there has been an increase in the racial, ethnic, and economic isolation of students in American public schools (Fuller & Clarke, 1994; Hanushek, 1994; Orfield, 1993). If the propensity to choose and children's performance in school are heavily influenced by parents' social class and educational background, then it seems plausible to expect that, other things being equal, increasing parental choice will accelerate both the social stratification of schools and the gap in student performance between schools enrolling high concentrations of poor and working-class students versus those with predominantly white, middle-class students.

These findings should give policy-makers pause. It seems likely, for example, that interdistrict or metropolitan choice plans would provide enhanced opportunities for inner-city parents and students who have a strong achievement orientation but would further isolate parents and students whose expectations are less well formed and whose knowledge of how to take advantage of complex choice options is limited. It also seems likely that within-district choice programs focused on inner-city schools would further separate parents and students based on their educational background, their prior involvement in school, and their knowledge of how to engage complicated choice schemes. Hence, even choice programs that are designed to increase educational opportunity could have the effect of further stratifying parents and students within groups that are already at a disadvantage in the existing structure.

This sort of conclusion should come as no surprise to those who are knowledgeable about the operation of markets, even the constrained markets represented by the programs described in this book. Markets create product differentiation and segmentation of consumers by providing for the free play of preferences around alternatives. Among the distinctions that markets make are those based simply on consumers' propensity or ability to choose. It should hardly be surprising, then, that some parents are at a relative disadvantage in understanding whether they have choices, or what those choices might be if they should choose to exercise them. As Henig reveals in Chapter 5, even simple awareness of the term *magnet school* differed systematically based on parents' ethnicity and social class.

Nor should it be surprising that sometimes choices are conditioned on the family's economic resources, such as the ability to provide transportation to another school or to miss work and wait in line to sign up for a popular choice. This feature of markets becomes problematic only if there is some overriding public interest in helping people to make ''good'' choices, as there is when educational choice programs progressively separate certain parents and students from access to higher-quality educational programs or to other parents who value such programs.

This connection between educational choice and social stratification poses a serious challenge to policy-makers. Policies that intentionally create or aggravate social stratification based on income, race, and social class should provoke special scrutiny. It is unclear at this point whether the stratifying effects of choice programs are a consequence of the design of the programs or simply the inevitable collective result of the individualistic exercise of choice. Some things are relatively clear, however. One is that the current design of choice programs, even those designed to enhance equal opportunity, is not adequate to deal with the stratification issue. Another is that if public funds are used in ways that foreseeably increase racial segregation and inequality, they may violate the Constitution. Rectifying the tendency of choice programs to increase social stratification will likely require *more* governmental intervention rather than less. Insofar as choice advocates see enhanced choice as a way of taking the government out of private educational decisions, attention to the stratifying effects of choice will likely provoke political conflict.

The evidence also suggests that the designers of choice programs should look hard at the problem of nonchoosing parents. A large part of the stratification problem seems to result from parents and students who simply do not choose, rather than from differing preferences among those who do choose. That is, once parents and students make the decision to choose and actively exploit the opportunities that decision presents, they seem to have preferences that are remarkably similar across race and social class (see Chapter 5). This finding suggests that the design of choice programs should focus more on getting large proportions of families to make choices, rather than simply catering to the preferences of active choosers. The stratification problem probably requires a careful rethinking of both demand-side and supply-side features of choice programs:

- Would more carefully designed parent information programs yield a higher proportion of active choosers?
- Would requiring all parents to choose, rather than passively making choices available only to active choosers, result in a decrease of social stratification in parent choices?
- Would a gradual introduction of the idea of choice to parents and students, by stressing initial choices of teachers and alternative instructional approaches within schools, for example, yield a

higher proportion of active choosers when parents are presented with larger choices, such as the opportunity to choose a school outside their attendance area?

These questions cannot be answered in the context of existing choice programs. They would require more carefully designed programs than presently exist. Nor are they questions that are amenable to simple, ideologically determined answers. They would require considerable attention to details in the design of choice programs (see proposition 3, below). In the meantime, our advice to policy-makers is to treat with considerable skepticism the claim that educational choice enhances equality of opportunity.

Proposition 2: *Greater choice in public education is unlikely, by itself, to increase either the variety of programs available to students or the overall performance of schools. Coupled with strong educational improvement measures, however, choice may increase variety and performance.*

Another common argument for enhancing school choice is that it will increase the quality and diversity of educational offerings and, consequently, boost student achievement. One version of this argument is that choice increases competition among schools, leading to a better fit between the preferences of parents and educators, a greater focus on learning in new school organizations, and hence more learning on the part of students. Another version of the argument is that bureaucratic administration distracts teachers and principals from their central mission and shifts their energy to the narrow demands of political constituencies. Substituting market incentives for bureaucratic controls reduces the role and costs of urban school bureaucracy, and refocuses the energy of educators on classroom innovation and student learning.

The evidence on this argument is mixed. Lockheed and Jimenez (Chapter 7) find in their cross-national study that achievement differences between public and private schools, after carefully controlling for the social background of students, favor private schools. They also find that while public and private schools are similar in resource levels, they differ both in the locus of management control—private schools focus more decisions at the school site—and in their degree of attention to academic learning—private schools focus more time on academic subjects. This evidence is consistent with the findings of Coleman, Hoffer, and Kilgore (1982), Chubb and Moe (1990), and Hannaway (1991), who highlight differences in achievement results and organizational characteristics between public and private schools.

Other analysts have suggested, however, that aggregate achievement differences between public and private schools are relatively small, that they may be explained by unmeasured motivational and other background differences, and that the variation among schools *within* the public and private sectors in both achievement results and organizational characteristics is wider than that found between the two sectors (e.g., Willms & Echols, 1993). This suggests that it is more important to understand the organizational characteristics of effective schools, whether public or private, than to focus on public–private differences (Murnane, 1985).

Witte's study (Chapter 6) of Milwaukee's public voucher program for poor parents choosing private schools suggests that achievement effects are weak and variable and favor neither public nor private schools. He also finds a relatively high turnover rate—about one-third—among students whose parents have chosen private schools; this suggests that, at least in the early stages of the program, many parents see little advantage of private over public schools once they have experienced private schools.

The evidence from public school choice programs is equally ambiguous. Henig (Chapter 5) finds, in his study of Montgomery County magnet schools, that the curricular themes of magnet programs seem to have less influence on parental choice than other characteristics, such as the school's ethnic composition and characteristics of teachers. Henig concludes, "parents may not be looking for particular instructional themes and styles so much as for the kind of energy, creativeness, and extra resources that *some* schools build around their magnet programs." The major premise of magnet school programs is that parents of all races, income levels, and social backgrounds can be drawn to schools by developing schools around distinctive curricular and instructional themes. Henig's study suggests that active choosers may be basing their decisions on other grounds and that attempts by public school systems to engineer choices by creating alternatives may not work under permissive conditions like those found in Montgomery County. It is also possible that, despite the differences in labels among magnet schools, there may be very little difference in the actual curriculum and instruction within the schools. Hence, parents may be making reasonable choices by focusing on characteristics other than curricular themes. One of the earliest studies of public school choice, in the Alum Rock voucher experiment, found little evidence of systematic variation in instruction among schools that had nominally different themes; it also found that parents tended to choose schools based on characteristics, such as location, that had little to do with schools' curricular themes (Bridge & Blackman, 1978; Elmore, 1990).

These ambiguous findings about the relationship among choice, school innovation, and student performance lead us to the conclusion that introducing choice will not, by itself, result in large changes in educational programs or student performance. It does make sense, however, to think about choice policies operating in tandem with other educational improvement initiatives to foster variation in educational programs and to focus school leaders on student performance. Knowledgeable designers of public school choice programs have, for a long time, argued that choice plans need to be combined with policies that reinforce high expectations that all students will achieve and that promote the systematic development of alternative instructional strategies, rather than simply relabeling existing strategies (Fliegel, 1990). The evidence on differences between the bureaucratic environments of public and private schools also suggests that dramatically streamlining and focusing central school bureaucracies on supporting high-quality instruction in schools could result in more attention to student learning.

Proposition 3: *Details matter in the design and implementation of choice policies.*

School choice is often portrayed in policy debates as an either–or issue: Either parents and students will have choices or their choices will be subject to bureaucratic control. Choice advocates often argue—incorrectly—that present public school systems do not permit choice and that providing choice requires eliminating public controls on enrollment decisions and providing money directly to parents and students. Opponents of choice often argue—also incorrectly, we have found—that most choice plans have the same invidious effects, *regardless of how they are designed.*

The world of school choice portrayed in this book is rather different from this either–or picture. It is a world in which specific decisions in the design and implementation of choice programs have consequences for parents and students that are sometimes consistent and sometimes inconsistent with the intentions of policy-makers. *Design details matter,* and we are only beginning to understand how and why they matter.

One major design issue that we previously mentioned is the degree to which choice programs are designed simply to provide an option for those who wish to choose—what might be called "option-demand" programs—or to require active choice of all parents and students—what might be called "universal-demand" programs. All of the programs studied in this volume are option-demand programs, and we have seen that such programs create, by their design, a large category of non-choosers who are disproportionately poor and minority and who tend to engage their children's schools less actively. So the design of the program itself disadvantages certain parents, by enhancing opportunities for parents who are already active choosers and disregarding those who are less inclined to be active choosers. While option-demand programs may seem reasonable to school administrators and policy-makers, because they appease vocal and active clients and they create highly popular schools, they accentuate differences in opportunity between choosers and nonchoosers. Hence choice programs should include not only strategies that offer opportunities for already active choosers but also strategies that attempt to increase the proportion of active choosers and decrease the proportion of nonchoosers.

Another design issue has to do with the educational content of the options made available to parents in choice programs. From the studies reported in this volume it appears that the designers of choice programs fail to think either very systematically or very deeply about the class-room-level content of the options they are offering parents and students. In the metropolitan St. Louis case described by Wells (Chapter 2), the parties settling the desegregation case assumed that, by definition, suburban schools would be preferable to inner-city schools for urban minority youth. In fact, judging from the reports of students, these schools seemed neither well prepared to accept students from the inner city nor particularly aware of the additional responsibility that the arrival of these students entailed. There was, in other words, no fully developed educational logic to the program, only a kind of logistical logic that entailed the movement of large numbers of students from one place to another.

The studies by Henig (Chapter 5) and Martinez, Godwin, and Kemerer (Chapter 3) suggest another dimension of the educational content issue. There is evidence in both studies that when educators deliberately design programs around coherent educational approaches, parents are attracted to these novel and distinct options, and these programs seem to have positive educational effects. Henig, for example, notes the appeal of foreign-language immersion at Oak View School in Montgomery County to both white and minority parents, while parents chose along racial lines when it came to schools with blurry identities. The Martinez team's study shows that when school administrators develop options that fit cultural and educational preferences of parents, families choose them and they may experience positive effects on their children's learning, notwithstanding increased stratification by family social class and prior school involvement. This latter effect stems from school authorities' insistence that opportunity to enter a multicultural school depends upon the child's prior academic performance.

For the most part, though, there is little evidence that educators focus very systematically on the supply side of educational choice. The studies by Henig (Chapter 5) and Blank, Levine, and Steel (Chapter 8) suggest that while magnet school programs carry different labels, there is not much evidence that would lead one to predict how they would differ in their curriculum, teaching, and achievement outcomes. In the absence of such genuine differences, it seems highly unlikely that parents would base their choices on program characteristics that hold direct achievement benefits for their children.

The studies in this volume suggest that the design and implementation of choice programs is a fertile area for future empirical work and an area on which policy-makers should focus their scrutiny. The notion that introducing demand-side choice will lead more or less automatically to the creation of distinctive supply-side educational alternatives seems implausible. Parents on the whole choose programs based more on their social composition and convenience than their educational content, except where educators have invested great care in developing distinctive school options. Furthermore, since parents and students with the least social capital seem also to be the ones who are least likely to engage in active choice, there are few demand-side incentives in choice programs for educators to engage in the deliberate design of programs that appeal to, and work well for, the most disadvantaged students. So it seems unlikely that choice, by itself, will stimulate creativity and improvement in the development of new, more effective educational programs. The problem seems to lie in the fact that the designers of choice programs have focused most of their attention, in all but a few cases, on demand-side issues, such as who gets to choose and how choices will be coordinated, rather than on crucial supply-side details, such as how schools and classrooms actually differ.

Proposition 4: *Context matters in the design and implementation of school choice policies.*

The local cultural and institutional context of choice has an important impact on its consequences for different groups of parents and students. Market theories, for the most part, assume that consumers' preferences can be described and aggregated in relatively simple ways and that all consumers are more or less engaged in the same process of rational search for value-maximizing choices, operating with similar information and few practical constraints. The studies in this volume cast considerable doubt on this simplistic view. Different groups of educational clients seem not only to have very different predispositions to choose, they also seem to bring very different cultural and social assumptions to the choices they are expected to make.

Wells (Chapter 2) finds distinctive differences among individuals in the same group in the cultural capital they bring to educational choices. For example, minority parents and students who did not take advantage of the St. Louis metropolitan transfer option were more inclined to be distrustful and fearful of whites, less inclined to regard whites as their superiors, and less inclined to accept the view that schooling is the road to upward mobility. These attitudes are formed from a lifetime of experiences with individuals and institutions, and they are not likely to be easily changed by one novel intervention like school choice. Nonchoosers might, in other words, be actively expressing cultural values, rather than simply failing to express a preference for something we would like them to choose. This applies to suburban whites—seeking to preserve culturally familiar school settings—as much as to working-class Hispanics who seek culturally consonant (nonmainstream) school settings. Kane's evidence on Pell Grants (Chapter 9) suggests that despite billions of dollars spent on "college vouchers," the constrained expectations and habitual pathways of low-income high school graduates have proven stronger than economic incentives.

Lee, Croninger, and Smith (Chapter 4) show how the social and demographic context of choice exerts considerable influence on the way people understand their options. The Detroit metropolitan area is a largely black inner city surrounded by largely white and considerably more affluent suburbs. Racial isolation by political jurisdiction is extreme due to the nation's most segregated housing market. In this context, their data suggest that choice comes to be construed as a possible route of escape from the inner city by some minority parents and as a possible threat to homogeneity and predictability by white parents. There is, for example, a *negative* relationship in their survey data between a desire for high academic standards and support for choice. One would predict the opposite relationship if parents saw educational choice as a way of expressing a preference for high-quality education. This finding only makes sense if one associates choice with a movement away from homogeneous, racially identifiable "high-quality" schools. Whether choice is perceived as a device for improving education, or as a threat to established cultural and social boundaries, depends on the specific social context in which the issue arises.

While it appears that context matters a great deal in the design and implementation of choice policies, it is also clear that we know very little about the interaction between context and policy in this area. The studies in this volume have only scratched the surface of this interaction. It is unlikely that we will be able to reliably predict the effects of choice programs on different local populations in the absence of evidence and deeper understanding of these contextual forces.

SCHOOL CHOICE AND EDUCATIONAL IMPROVEMENT

The advocates of choice, like all reformers, are optimists regarding their own proposals and pessimists about competing reform proposals. Hence debates around choice tend to be couched in simplistic terms. Choice is alleged to remedy the defects of excessive bureaucracy and to make schools more responsive and effective, without incurring any significant social costs. We think the evidence suggests a more cautious and skeptical view of choice as an instrument of educational reform. Enhanced choice does seem to activate certain parents and students; it does not, however, activate certain others. It may produce useful innovations in previously unresponsive systems. And, other things being equal, it seems to increase the social disparities between those who choose and those who do not. There is strikingly little evidence that enhanced choice triggers the kind of educational improvement on the supply side that its advocates predict and little evidence that active choosers are looking for distinctive educational programs when they make their choices. There is some suggestive evidence that cultural and political contexts have an impact on the effects of choice programs, and we currently understand little about these effects.

What do these overall findings suggest about the role that enhanced educational choice might play in the long-term improvement of American education? As we noted in the beginning, the issue presented to policy-makers is not whether there should be educational choice but *what kind* of choices public policy should promote, *within what constraints*, and *for what purposes*. In democratic societies the role of policy-makers is less one of deciding whether or not to grant choice than of how to guide, orchestrate, and augment the choices that are available to parents and students.

We have suggested that using choice as an instrument of improvement requires considerably more governmental action and involvement than the rhetoric of choice advocates leads one to believe. If, for example, we want choice to produce more equitable access to better education for all students, then it is clear that we have to design policies that do a more effective job of engaging the large proportion of parents and students who currently appear to be nonchoosers. In the absence of serious progress on this front, it is unlikely that enhanced choice will produce anything resembling more equitable access. If, for example, we want choice to result in the improvement of school and classroom programs, then it seems clear that we have to dedicate much more effort than we have in the past to designing and implementing distinctive educational alternatives. In the absence of serious progress on this front, it is unlikely that choice will do anything other than simply move high achievers around from one school to another, mistaking the effect of concentrating strong and motivated students for an effect of the school or the choice system. If, for example, we want to develop choice systems that are sensitive to the cultural and social differences among groups of parents and students, then it seems clear that we have to understand a good deal more than we presently do about how individuals understand and construct their choices from their cultural backgrounds. In the absence of progress on this front, it seems likely that we will continue to produce choice systems that will work well for people who already have choices but will fail to engage those who do not.

Using choice to improve education, then, is a serious and complex task that is not easily amenable to guidance by simple ideological principles. We have suggested that the idea that choice will produce better results with less public authority or bureaucracy is highly problematic. Policy-makers should take seriously both the distributional impacts of choice and the achievement effects for specific groups of students. Policy-makers are accountable not only for the beneficial effects of choice policies on those who choose, but also for the detrimental effects on those who, for whatever reason, fail to choose. And policy-makers are accountable not just for the enhanced consumer satisfaction of people who are already active choosers, but also for the overall improvement of opportunity and performance for all students. These democratic responsibilities—and the public interest in both fairness and school effectiveness—require policy-makers to be skeptical and deliberate in their use of choice as an instrument of reform. They should ask tough questions about the effects of choice policies and develop hard evidence on which children benefit and which do not.

REFERENCES

Bridge, R. J., & Blackman, J. (1978). *A study of alternatives in American education: Vol. 4. Family choice in education*. Santa Monica, CA: Rand Corporation.

Chubb, J., & Moe, T. (1990). *Politics, markets and America's schools.* Washington, DC: Brookings Institution.

Coleman, J., Hoffer, T., & Kilgore, S. (1982). *High school achievement: Public, Catholic, and private schools compared.* New York: Basic Books.

Elmore, R. (1990). Choice as an instrument of public policy: Evidence from education and health care. In W. Clune & J. Witte (Eds.), *Choice and control in American education: Vol. 1. The theory of choice and control in American education* (pp. 285–318). New York: Falmer.

Fliegel, S. (1990). Creative non-compliance. In W. Clune & J. Witte (Eds.), *Choice and control in American education: Vol. 2. The practice of choice, decentralization, and school restructuring* (pp. 199–216). New York: Falmer.

Fuller, B., & Clarke, P. (1994). Raising school effects while ignoring culture? *Review of Educational Research, 64*(1), 119–157.

Hannaway, J. (1991). The organization and management of public and Catholic schools: Looking inside the black box. *International Journal of Educational Research, 15,* 463–481.

Hanushek, E. A. (1994). *Making schools work: Improving performance and controlling costs.* Washington, DC: Brookings Institution.

Moore, D., & Davenport, S. (1990). School choice: The new and improved sorting machine. In W. Boyd & H. Walberg (Eds.), *Choice in education: Potential and problems* (pp. 187–223). Berkeley, CA: McCutchan.

Murnane, R. (1985). Comparisons of private and public schools: Lessons from the uproar. *Journal of Human Resources, 20,* 263–267.

Orfield, G. (1993). *The growth of segregation in American schools: Changing patterns of separation and poverty since 1968.* Alexandria, VA: National School Boards Association, Council of Urban Boards of Education.

Wells, A. S. (1991). Choice in education: Examining the evidence on equity. *Teachers College Record, 93,* 156–173.

Willms, D., & Echols, F. (1993). The Scottish experience of parental choice in schools. In E. Rasell & R. Rothstein (Eds.), *School choice: Examining the evidence* (pp. 49–68). Washington, DC: Economic Policy Institute.

About the Editors and the Authors

Richard F. Elmore is professor of education and chair, programs in administration, planning, and social policy, at Harvard University's School of Education. His research focuses on state–local relations in education policy and the organization of schooling. Mr. Elmore is a senior research fellow of the Consortium for Policy Research in Education.

Bruce Fuller is associate professor of comparative policy and education at Harvard. He has worked in policy and program development positions for the California legislature and the World Bank. Mr. Fuller's research focuses on how government attempts to alter the school and family and how these local institutions vary across ethnic communities and cultural settings.

Gary Orfield is professor of education and political science at Harvard. His work looks at problems related to urban poverty and the racial resegregation of schools. Mr. Orfield has helped design and implement choice and magnet school programs aimed at equalizing educational quality for inner-city children.

Rolf K. Blank is director of education indicators programs at the Council of Chief State School Officers in Washington, D.C. He has conducted research on magnet schools over the past 15 years. Mr. Blank also conducts research on state curricular standards and the condition of public education across the states.

Robert G. Croninger is associate director of the University of Michigan's educational opportunity program and a doctoral student in educational studies. His research focuses on organizational change and the social context of learning, including the advancement of democratic values and community.

Kenneth Godwin is professor of political science, University of North Texas. Trained at the University of North Carolina, Mr. Godwin has taught at the University of Washington and Oregon State University. His work currently focuses on the evaluation of educational programs.

Jeffrey R. Henig is professor of political science and director of the

Center for Washington Area Studies, George Washington University. In addition to his work on educational politics, he also does research on neighborhood organizing and anti-crime efforts. Mr. Henig's complete study of the Montgomery County schools appears in *Rethinking School Choice: Limits of the Market Metaphor*.

Emmanuel Jimenez is an economist and chief of human resource research at the World Bank, Policy Research Department. In addition to his research on public and private schooling, Mr. Jimenez has published widely on development economics, social service financing, and urban development. He served on the faculty of economics at University of Western Ontario.

Thomas J. Kane is assistant professor of public policy at Harvard's Kennedy School of Government. His research focuses on issues of poverty and the evaluation of policies and programs aimed at equalizing access to higher education. Mr. Kane also has written on how welfare recipients view antipoverty programs.

Frank R. Kemerer is regents professor of education law and administration at the University of North Texas. He directs the Center for the Study of Education Reform and focuses on constitutional issues in the education arena. Mr. Kemerer is currently examining the constitutional issues surrounding school voucher programs.

Valerie E. Lee is associate professor of education, University of Michigan. She teaches sociology of education, research methods, and evaluation. Ms. Lee's research centers on how the organization of schooling influences equity and stratification. Her most recent book (with Anthony Bryk and Peter Holland) is *Catholic Schools and the Common Good* (Harvard University Press).

Roger E. Levine is a senior researcher at the American Institutes for Research. He directs data collection for the national magnet schools study. Mr. Levine also conducts research on teacher attrition and organizational change within public schools, and investigates how low-income youths are counseled in school about their available choices.

Marlaine Lockheed is a principal education specialist within the World Bank's Human Development Department. She currently directs research on the effects of school decentralization programs in developing countries. Ms. Lockheed also has focused considerable attention on gender-equity issues. Her most recent book (with Adriaan Verspoor) is *Improving Primary Education in Developing Countries* (Oxford University Press).

Valerie Martinez is assistant professor of political science at the University of North Texas. Her work centers on evaluating the local effects of public policies. In addition to her long-term evaluation of two San

Antonio choice programs, she assesses social welfare programs for youths and older adults.

Julia B. Smith is assistant professor of educational administration at the School of Education, University of Rochester. In addition to her work on the effects of public school choice, she currently studies how organizational and pedagogical reforms help to equalize children's achievement in mathematics and basic literacy.

Lauri Steel is principal research scientist at the American Institutes of Research. As associate director of Project Talent, she studied gender differences in school achievement and long-term consequences. Ms. Steel also evaluates the effects of youth training programs on positive work and social outcomes.

Amy Stuart Wells is assistant professor of educational policy at UCLA's School of Education and Information Studies. Her work focuses on the politics of school desegregation, choice, and efforts to reduce student tracking. Ms. Wells's latest book (with Robert Crain) is *Stepping Over the Color Line: African-American Students in White Suburban Schools* (Yale University Press).

John F. Witte holds a joint professorship at the University of Wisconsin, where he is a professor of political science, and the La Follette Institute of Public Affairs. His work has focused on educational reform, tax policy, and the political processes underlying each. In 1990 Mr. Witte was appointed as the state evaluator of the Milwaukee choice program, a study funded in part by the Spencer Foundation.

Index